INDIANA
High School Basketball's

Most Dominant
PLAYERS

Dave Krider

ROOFTOP
publishing

Rooftop Publishing™
1663 Liberty Drive, Suite 200
Bloomington, IN 47403
Phone: 1-800-839-8640

First published by Rooftop Publishing 5/3/2007

Publisher: Kevin King
Senior Editor: Lesley Bolton
Cover Design: April Mostek
Book Design: Andrew Craig
Production Manager: Brad Collins

ISBN: 978-1-60008-028-9 (sc)

Library of Congress Control Number: 2007927889

Printed in the United States of America
Bloomington, Indiana

This book is printed on acid-free paper.

DEDICATION

I would like to dedicate this book to my beautiful wife, Lois. She has supported me faithfully throughout our nineteen-year marriage and quietly accepted all the many, many hours that my writing has taken up. She is my soulmate and most precious gift from God.

AUTHOR'S NOTE

To even be considered, the players featured inside had to either be named Indiana's Mr. Basketball or win at least one state championship. The word "dominant" is very meaningful to this book, because each player dominated his era. Those who were chosen either won or shared a staggering twenty-eight state championships and fourteen Mr. Basketball titles. Though I know there were other worthy players over the years, I am quite satisfied that I have covered the careers of twenty great ones.

During my career covering high school sports, I was able to see fifteen of these players either in person or on television. My first major inspiration was watching Milan's Bobby Plump, Ray Craft, and company stun mighty Muncie Central on our tiny black-and-white television set as a junior high freshman.

The next year (1955), my hometown, Elkhart, opened the largest high school gym in the world (8,200 seats), and I was hooked on Hoosier Hysteria forever. Throw in Oscar Robertson and the great Indianapolis Crispus Attucks teams during my sophomore and junior years of high school, and I grew up during what I still believe was the Golden Era of Indiana high school basketball.

This book was a great joy to put together, and it was a real treat to interview many of my heroes from years past. It would not have been possible without the help of many, many people, most of all Kevin King of Rooftop Publishing, who had the faith in me and turned me loose.

Special thanks goes to Jason Wille of the Indiana High School Athletic Association and Roger Dickinson and his staff at the Indiana Basketball Hall of Fame. The sports information departments at Indiana, Purdue, Butler, Cincinnati, Iowa, and Michigan State provided key statistical material.

A very special thanks goes to Indiana Governor Mitch Daniels for writing a superb foreword for this book. A true Hoosier basketball fan, he hit the nail on the head in every way. Governor Daniels, if you ever need a second income, you have a bright future as a sportswriter!

Others who made important contributions included Bob King, Garry Donna, Joe Wolfla, Ronnie Rogers, Dick Stodghill, Chuck Landis, Jackie Smith, Bob Whalen, Bill Green, Jim Brunner, Ann Turner, Nancy Wooden, Earl Mishler, Elizabeth Swift, Ruth Dorel, Linda Talley, and Larry Underwood. There are many others who are quoted in the individual chapters.

Invaluable book sources were: *The Franklin Wonder Five*; *Bobby Plump: Last of The Small Town Heroes*; *But They Can't Beat Us: Oscar Robertson and the Crispus Attucks Tigers*; *Hoosiers: The Fabulous Basketball Life of Indiana*; and *The Big O: My Life, My Times, My Game*.

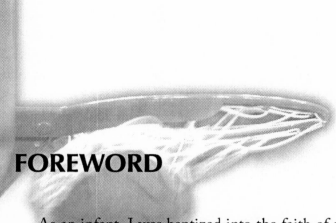

FOREWORD

As an infant, I was baptized into the faith of my fathers. At the age of ten, I was baptized into Indiana's second religion, the sport of basketball.

The Daniels family arrived in Indiana from the American South in the summertime, which to me meant baseball. To be sure, you could find a baseball game in our new neighborhood, but even on the hottest day, you could hear the sound of a roundball on asphalt.

I found our two faiths co-located; the church we joined had a gym. To this day, its basketball program remains the biggest youth recreation program in Indianapolis. We learned about God's love and the pick-and-roll on the same hardwood floor.

In Indiana, we are prepared to accept that James Naismith may have put up the first peach basket, but we are convinced that no one ever successfully shot a ball through one until the first Hoosier hung one above his barn door. When we hear "Friday Night Lights," we assume you're talking about the incandescent, indoor variety.

Our lifelong devotion has its downsides. Every Hoosier is a basketball expert, or thinks he is. At twenty-one, I thoughtlessly accepted a friend's offer to make a few spare bucks refereeing fifth and sixth graders at the YMCA. It was the worst job I ever had; every spectator could see every play much better than I could—I was too close to the action, apparently—and no one's kid ever, ever committed a foul.

If refereeing in a state of experts is tough, coaching ball in Indiana at any level must be torture. Robert E. Lee once said that it seemed that all the best generals were writing for newspapers, and that's how Hoosier coaches must often feel, as they are required to ply their trade in front of the most knowledgeable fans anywhere. It must be like singing "Amazing Grace" in front of the Mormon Tabernacle Choir.

In recent years, I've added more perspective about the depth to which basketball is woven into our state's character. Traveling constantly to the small towns of Indiana as very few people do these days, I've become familiar with the dozens of weather-beaten signs that remind a visitor of a long-ago sectional or regional championship team. The old team photos in diners all over our state are as precious to our sense of who we are as summer tractor shows or the monuments on our courthouse lawns.

The Milan '54 story, at its fifty-year anniversary, took on a very special significance for me, a first-time candidate for public office in that year. I came to realize that its hold on us involved more than basketball or even the all-American love for the underdog; it told us that, in Indiana, a kid from anywhere who works hard and plays for the sake of the team can go to the top. God willing, we'll always be that kind of state.

Hoosier kids, and their parents for that matter, might struggle to name the American presidents (as for governors of Indiana, forget it!), but EVERYONE knows Oscar and Rick and Bobby and Damon and Big George. We talk about them as though they were our neighbors and, as well as we feel we know them, they might as well have been.

And what a great neighborhood it has been. All those backyard games and youth league nights pay off; per capita, no state in America has produced more basketball greatness than Indiana, or comes close.

Dave Krider hasn't written the first book to take us back through our fabulous basketball past, but he's given us another very important set of memories about our most exceptional Boys of Winter. Read and reminisce.

—Governor Mitch Daniels

CONTENTS

1. STEVE ALFORD 1

2. DAMON BAILEY 15

3. RON BONHAM 33

4. DAVE COLESCOTT 43

5. MIKE CONLEY 57

6. JAY EDWARDS 65

7. LYNDON JONES 75

8. GEORGE McGINNIS 87

9. RICK MOUNT 103

10. STRETCH MURPHY 125

11. GREG ODEN 133

12. BOBBY PLUMP 143

13. JIMMY RAYL 161

14. OSCAR ROBERTSON 171

15. GLENN ROBINSON 185

16. BILLY SHEPHERD 195

17. SCOTT SKILES 209

18. HOMER STONEBRAKER 227

19. FUZZY VANDIVIER 233

20. JOHN WOODEN...243

STEVE ALFORD:

A Gym Was His Classroom

Just after Steve Alford's second birthday, his parents, Sam and Sharan Alford, sent out Christmas cards proudly proclaiming—quite prophetically—that their firstborn eventually would be crowned Indiana's Mr. Basketball. Already looking the part, he was pictured on the front of the card holding a basketball.

By age three, Alford already was sitting on the bench while his dad coached the Monroe City High School basketball team. He would dress neatly in a jacket and tie and carry a piece of paper to write down numbers. He learned how to add by watching numbers change on the scoreboard, and he learned how to read and spell by looking at game programs and mostly last names on the backs of players' uniforms.

Alford got his first taste of organized basketball at the tender age of five, in a Vincennes YMCA league, while his dad was coaching at nearby South Knox. Of course, he continued week after week to sit on the varsity bench and absorb everything that went on. He was so immersed in the sport that during his early elementary school years, he would go into a closet and "broadcast" games. As he grew older, he kept records in his own scorebook.

1

The great attraction to young Alford was "having a dad who was a coach," he explained. "I just grew up in the state of Indiana. It was church on Sunday, the *Bob Knight Show* at noon, and then (in February) pairings of the state tournament. It was a ritual you just waited on. Basketball always was a priority."

Alford was so dedicated to his father that he only missed two of his games until he left for college. One miss was due to the chicken pox and the other to competing in the Elks Hoop Shoot regional free-throw contest in Warren, Ohio. He placed fourth in the nation that year, at the age of ten.

If he couldn't get into a gym, he would shovel off his driveway and play with gloves on. "I never let the snow stay on our driveway," he said with a touch of pride. "I'd play in all kinds of weather—rain, when it was in the nineties."

He became a fanatical trainer as he desperately attempted to put muscle on his slim frame. He would jump rope and do fingertip pushups every night before he went to bed, even in elementary school. He honed his dribbling by weaving around a series of brooms and chairs. He developed his early shooting touch by firing ping-pong balls at Pringles cans. He always had some type of ball in his hands. And he wrote down every single detail as he began keeping journals.

"He squeezed tennis balls every night," Sam Alford related. "We knew when he fell asleep because we could hear the balls falling on the floor."

Young Alford loved living in Martinsville, where his dad was head coach for four years, and where he came to idolize local basketball star Jerry Sichting. It was just fifteen miles from Indiana University and its great program under another of his idols, Bob Knight. He definitely was not a happy camper when his dad took the head job at New Castle, which had a population of 18,000.

He was only in the fifth grade, but still had to be convinced—even though the New Castle Trojans played in the world's largest high school gymnasium/fieldhouse. It was a huge palace, which seated 9,325, with a capacity of 10,000 for big games. He readily confessed,

"I was awed when I walked in and got my first view of it." From that moment on, he said, "I always had tremendous respect for it. Every time I walked in there, I needed to give it everything I had."

As a seventh grader, Alford began working out with New Castle varsity players, which greatly enhanced his progress.

As an eighth grader, he faced the first crisis of his budding basketball career. He was requested to visit his counselor and talk about his long-term goals. In no uncertain terms, he told her he was going to be a professional basketball player. "She said she couldn't put that down," he recalled. "I guess she was looking for businessman, doctor, or lawyer. I said, 'Leave it blank, then.' I don't know if I went home and cried or not."

He'll never forget his first varsity appearance as a freshman. "Dad put me in a game and everybody booed," he said. Fans are fickle, of course, and Alford added with a touch of irony, "My senior year, he took me out and they booed." Some fans obviously just can't be pleased!

Whatever Alford got on the court, however, he earned through fanatical devotion to workouts during the off season. Each summer, he would practice up to five hours a day. He estimates that he used to wear out seven or eight nets every summer. Even on vacations, his first objective was to find a basketball court. He never got enough of it. Basketball was life itself to Steve Alford.

Did Sam Alford ever fear burnout in his oldest son? "I worried about it a little bit," he admitted. "But he wouldn't talk about it. He wouldn't listen."

Due basically to lack of strength, Alford shot the ball across his body, from left to right, instead of straightening his elbow and having a good follow through. "He had a horrible shot," Sam Alford confessed. But he did have good hand-eye coordination. To develop good form, he was told to practice the correct form without a ball. Next, he started shooting jump shots from ten feet—but aiming only at the backboard. Then he moved to the foul line and shot free throws. The final phase was to shoot jump shots from the foul line.

"Dad did a really good job changing my shot," Steve praised. "I got thrown to the wolves as a freshman. For three weeks, I didn't take a shot. It was muscle memory. I had to learn to get the ball on the right side of my head. By my junior year, my shot was just the way I wanted it. I loved to shoot the basketball. There are natural shot-takers and shot-makers. As I evolved, I was more of a shot-maker."

Alford used to shoot with his dad, who was a national free-throw champion at Franklin College. The game was "shoot until you miss," with the coach going first. Well, Sam would make fifty or sixty in a row, and Steve would have to rebound. "I learned the importance of being a shot-maker, because I got tired of rebounding," he affirmed.

In addition to countless hours of practice, Alford credits added physical strength as a major key to his improved shooting. "The real problem was because of my build," he analyzed. "When I got my first driver's license, I was five-ten and 125 pounds." By his senior year at New Castle, he was six-two and had "bulked up" to 155 pounds. In college, he eventually reached 185.

Though he scored just thirty points in nineteen varsity appearances as a freshman, Alford followed with an excellent sophomore year. He averaged 18.1 points, with a high game of 30, shot .780 from the free-throw line and .580 from the field as the Trojans compiled a 13-9 record.

Alford used to grab his dad's gym keys and run more than a mile over hilly terrain whenever he wanted to shoot in the gym. Once he got his driver's license, his first request was the keys to the family car. "I lived in the gym, just because my family had the biggest playground in the country," he said. Being able to drive brought another bonus, because then he also could attend opponents' games and bring back scouting reports.

Early in his junior year, Alford embraced something much more important than his beloved basketball—he went to the altar at New Castle United Methodist Church and became a Christian by accepting Jesus Christ as his Lord and Savior. He also served as president of the New Castle Fellowship of Christian Athletes huddle. "I began praying before and after games in elementary school," Alford noted. "I always was taught to be thankful and grateful. My faith has been everything to me in high school, college, my pro career, and now in business and coaching," he said. "It is the one stable thing I can always go to."

He improved greatly on the court as a junior, averaging 27.3 points, with a high game of 44. He shot .596 from the field and a sizzling .905 (133-147) from the free-throw line. He made 49 straight free throws during one stretch. He also had 121 rebounds and 121 assists, as the Trojans finished with a 12-10 record.

Alford's free-throw shooting was a source of immense pride and became somewhat legendary around New Castle. He would shoot between 100 and 300 per day, and always charted them. For every one he missed, he had to do ten fingertip pushups or wind sprints, according to what "game" he was playing on that particular day. Any misses among the last ten attempts would draw double punishment. By his senior year, his self-punishment eased considerably because he regularly was making 97 or 98 of every 100.

He developed a free-throw shooting routine as a sophomore and followed it religiously throughout his career. Fans would chant, "Socks, shoes, 1-2-3, swish!" The chant became so famous that it wound up emblazoned on T-shirts and buttons in later years while he was starring at Indiana University.

Alford's workouts were incredible. He would do a full workout, play pickup games, then finish with another full workout. During his workouts, he said, "I'd go as hard as I could for as long as I could, then shoot ten free throws. It was quality more than minutes."

As he honed his jumper, Alford created another tradition. He explained, "I would hang the net [tangle it on the rim] on my last shot, in respect for the workout and the gym. I would end the workout by shooting the perfect shot. It was for a job well done. I shot until it happened. It was always fun to come to school the next morning and the custodian would say, 'Hey, I see you were in here last night.'"

He was totally driven because he loved the game so deeply and because he often was viewed by outsiders as a small, slow, white kid who was just overachieving. "I always had to get by all that stuff," Alford conceded. "I used that as motivation."

If Alford was going to fulfill his parents' predictions of being Mr. Basketball, he would have to beat out Marion superstar James Blackmon. One night, he came home around 11:00 and told his dad, "That was one of the best workouts I ever had."

Sam knew which buttons to push, so he told his son, "I just got off the phone with Bill Green [the Marion coach] and he told me Blackmon is still in the gym shooting."

"I was naive enough to believe him," Steve confessed. "I immediately turned around and went back to the gym for another hour."

Perhaps he had once read about ageless baseball pitcher Leroy (Satchel) Paige, who always said, "And don't look back—something might be gaining on you."

Blackmon and Alford did go head-to-head every year in a big North Central Conference match-up. In their senior year, Alford outscored Blackmon, 48-41, and completed a rare triple-double with 10 assists and 10 rebounds as New Castle posted a 103-79 victory. If anyone ever earned Mr. Basketball honors for a single-game match-up, Alford did that night.

Alford's final year in the world's largest high school gym was magical, indeed. On back-to-back nights against Marion and Indianapolis Cathedral, New Castle played to crowds of 10,000. The Trojans' star, who played before twelve such crowds during his prep career, noted, "That really prepared me for life in college, the pros, and beyond. That's why I feel so blessed. Very few [high school players] can look back and say they played before 20,000 persons on one weekend. Most kids can't say that about their whole career."

His phenomenal free-throw shooting came up big that last year, as he put together a string of sixty-four in a row, which ended at Shelbyville. He also made his last eighty in the friendly confines of his home court. During practice, he established a personal record of 217 in a row. "Just messing around" in later years as a Manchester College coach, he established a new personal record by sinking 218 in a row.

Of course, not even Steve Alford was perfect. He actually missed two crucial free throws near the end of a game against Anderson. "I went back to the fieldhouse and shot free throws for an hour or an hour and one half," he related. "I made it a goal never to miss a two-shot foul again. I never did until my next-to-last game at IU against UNLV."

In the closing minutes of his last regular-season home game, Alford experienced a special moment, when he assisted his brother, Sean, a reserve who was two years younger, on a basket. "That was really cool—just a lot of fun," he said.

The New Castle superstar really shifted into high gear during his final shot at winning a state championship for his dad. He sparked the Trojans to sectional and regional titles, reaching the Sweet 16 at famed Hinkle Fieldhouse in Indianapolis. On his final day wearing a New Castle uniform, he went out in a blaze of glory.

In the first round, he exploded for a career-high 57 points— which still is tied for number one in state-tourney history—as the Trojans defeated Indianapolis Broad Ripple, 79-64. Dog-tired, he still pumped in 38 that night, but the Trojans fell to eventual state champion Connersville, 70-57.

The New Castle sharpshooter never will forget his unerring free-throw accuracy as he made an incredible eighty-two of eighty-three foul shots through seven state tourney games. He swished thirty-one of thirty-two in the sectional, sinking his last eleven. He then drilled all fifteen attempts in the regional.

In the semi-state, he made a phenomenal twenty-five of twenty-five against Broad Ripple. It reminded him of his younger days when he competed in the Elks Hoop Shoot national free-throw contest. "We always shot twenty-five," he noted. "I thought how great that would be to shoot twenty-five in a game. To do it in Hinkle and in the semi-state ... Seven or eight different people tried to guard me. That was my most memorable game." Making his final eleven against Connersville, he closed his brilliant career with sixty-two in a row, which is believed to be an all-time state tournament record.

Alford's senior statistics were something to behold. It was one of the most dominating seasons ever put together by a Hoosier basketball player. He poured in 1,078 points—one point shy of the state record held by Carmel's Dave Shepherd—for a glossy 37.2 average. He shot a superb 60 percent from the field and a mind-boggling .944 (286-304) from the free-throw line. His free-throw percentage would have led the NCAA or the NBA that year. He also had 197 rebounds, 196 assists, and 145 steals to help the Trojans post a 23-6 record.

Even though he played without the three-point shot, Alford still ranks number 21 in Hoosier prep scoring, with 2,116 points. He was Mr. Consistency as he scored more than 20 points in 51 consecutive games and shot a superb .590 from the field during his career.

After realizing his dream of being crowned Indiana's 1983 Mr. Basketball, Alford was invited to Pittsburgh to play in the Dapper Dan Roundball Classic. He had to break his senior prom date with his girlfriend, Tanya Frost. Fortunately for him, she gave up the prom, too, and followed him to Pittsburgh, where he got little playing time and scored just four points. Yet, he insists, "The basketball game still was better [than attending the prom]."

The New Castle star admittedly gave up nearly all of his social life for basketball. But he stresses, "I don't really think I ever sacrificed, because of what was important to me. I probably couldn't tell you what those things [I missed] were, because I had such tunnel vision of where I wanted to go."

What about the things that Tanya was forced to miss? "She married me," was his quick reply.

They got engaged just before their senior year in college. She always rebounded for him, and one day late in the summer, she got out the stepladder to untangle the net—like she had often done in the past. However, this time she was staring at an engagement ring nestled comfortably on the back of the rim.

Despite his devotion to basketball, Steve Alford truly was an "All-American boy." He was handsome, a good student, a great role model, and very well spoken from having grown up in the glare of the media. "I was very fortunate," he agreed. "I had great parents and a great place to grow up. A lot of that credit goes to the people who helped mold me."

Looking back, Sam Alford said, "I was proud but not a boastful father. He always smiled, carried himself well, and interviewed well."

Before he headed off to Indiana University, Alford was named National Athlete of the Year by the Fellowship of Christian Athletes. "It was a great honor," he said. "Since eighth grade, I have had a great appreciation for that organization. That meant an awful lot to me." Today he serves proudly on FCA's national board of directors.

He also was named National Player of the Year by the National High School Athletic Coaches Association and played in the National Sports Festival.

So, he moved from "Camelot" to play for fiery IU coach Bob Knight. Or maybe it wasn't exactly Camelot at New Castle either. "My dad kicked me out of the gym seven or eight times," he revealed. "I was stubborn and very competitive. I knew I was [used as] an example, but that didn't make it any easier, because I didn't want to miss practice. And I had to walk home. I had a work ethic growing up—responsibilities that Mom and Dad gave me. I'd been around basketball all my life, been in umpteen locker rooms, practices, and watched a lot of film.

"I was a Bob Knight fan before I was an IU fan," he continued. "I had gone to the IU camp since third grade. I was living out a dream. I had my ups and downs, but, boy, I sure miss it! I'd go back and do it all again. I still talk to Coach Knight as much as I can. I see him in the fall and spring. He's helped me tremendously and is a great friend."

The mentally tough teenager definitely was well-armed to play for the demanding Knight, so well-armed that he led the Hoosiers in scoring (15.5), free-throw shooting (.913, which also led the nation), and was IU's first-ever freshman MVP.

In 1984, he was the youngest member of the U.S. Olympic team that brought home the gold medal. He averaged 10.3 points, was second in assists, and shot a brilliant .644 from the field. The U.S. team played an exhibition game against an NBA All-Star team, which drew an all-time record crowd of 67,596 to the Hoosier Dome. One of his high-profile teammates, Michael Jordan, bet him $100 he wouldn't last four years with Knight. Alford, indeed, did last four years, but Jordan still owes him. Get out that checkbook, Michael, and you should add a lot of interest!

Alford's gold medal had special significance because he later presented it to his dad during an emotional ceremony at New Castle High School. He explained, "One of my goals had been to win a state championship for my dad, but I was not able to do it." Thus, the gold medal was a worthy substitute.

As a sophomore, he again led the Hoosiers in scoring (18.1) and free-throw percentage (.921). He repeated the feat as a junior, too, averaging 22.5 points and shooting .871 from the foul line.

His junior year also included a brief—but very bizarre—suspension for allowing a local sorority to use his name and picture on a calendar to raise money for handicapped girls.

During his senior year, he served as team captain, and again paced the Hoosiers in scoring (22.0) and free-throw percentage (.889). He sparked the Hoosiers to a 30-4 record, and they won the NCAA championship with a 74-73 victory over Syracuse. He was absolutely superb in the title game, shooting seven-for-ten from three-point range, scoring twenty-three points, and assisting on the game-winning basket. He was named IU MVP for an unprecedented fourth consecutive year. He also was named Big Ten Conference MVP and first-team All-America.

Alford set IU career records with 2,438 points (19.5 average), 178 steals, and a sizzling free-throw percentage of .898 (535-596). His career free-throw percentage ranked number four in NCAA history. He also shot an excellent .532 from the field. His senior year was the first year the three-point shot was in effect, and he quickly added that to his arsenal, shooting an outstanding .530. The Hoosiers compiled a 92-35 record during his career.

The Hoosier great was the first pick in the second round of the 1987 NBA draft by Dallas, where he was a substitute for three years. He played one year for Golden State. During his short career, he scored 744 points, handed out 196 assists, and shot .870 from the free-throw line.

He attempted to play a fifth year, but was cut by Sacramento on Halloween. "Tanya was pregnant with our first child and I just wanted to get out," he explained. "Coaching was in my blood, so I decided to help my dad."

Not long afterward, however, he received a call from a small college in Indiana, Manchester, whose coach abruptly quit following a 0-8 start. He jumped at the job and became a head college coach in 1992 at the age of twenty-six. He turned the team around within a year and compiled a four-year record of 78-29—including a near-perfect 31-1 mark during his final season.

In 1995, he was named head coach at Division I Southwest Missouri State, and took his father with him as his chief assistant. Sam quipped, "I had to go if I wanted to see my grandchildren." Alford posted a 78-48 record there in four years. His final team defeated Wisconsin and Tennessee to reach the coveted Sweet 16.

In 1999, Alford came "home" to the Big Ten as head coach at the University of Iowa. He made a sensational debut, leading the Hawkeyes to a stunning 70-68 upset of defending NCAA champion Connecticut at Madison Square Garden. He has taken them to the NCAA tournament three times and to the NIT three times. His twenty-five victories in 2005-06 rank number two in

Iowa history. He compiled an eight-year record of 152-106 at Iowa before taking the head job at the University of New Mexico in the spring of 2007.

In regards to ever returning to his alma mater, Alford says, "The timing never has been right. It's either a crazy time or they haven't been interested."

In the off season, Alford runs five basketball camps in Iowa and one in Indiana. Sam Alford got him started on the camp circuit when he was a high school sophomore. "Dad would talk and I would demonstrate," Steve explained. "That was a way for me to get in five or six workouts a day. I always told Dad that my job was harder than his."

The Alfords have three children: Kory, an eighth grader; Bryce, a sixth grader; and Kayla, a third grader. Both boys, of course, play basketball. "They're getting there—they love it," Steve says. "But I don't want to be one of those crazy dads. I just want them to have fun playing."

If they ever return to New Castle, they can stay at the Steve Alford All-American Inn. Steve doesn't own it, but he is paid for the rights to his name.

Alford believes in giving back for all the things he has been blessed with during his career. For example, he has helped to raise over $100,000 for the Special Olympics of Henry County, which includes New Castle. He also has helped raise money for the Iowa City Ronald McDonald House for the past eight years.

At age forty-two, he hasn't yet lost his superb shooting touch. Sam Alford, now retired after nine years assisting his son, swears, "He can walk into a gym today and hit ninety-five of a hundred free throws, and he still can hit the three, too."

Despite having won every possible honor during his brilliant playing career, Alford insists, "It's never been about an honor. My biggest honor is just having had the opportunity to play the game. Honors are great, but I don't miss the honors. I do miss the game."

In Steve Alford's eyes, nothing ever will replace THE GAME. After all, it always has been life itself to him, and what could be more precious?

DAMON BAILEY:

Fairy-Tale Career

Damon Bailey was destined to have a fairy-tale basketball career, because as a very young boy, he developed an enormous work ethic and an unending love for the game, and was driven by a powerful competitive desire to win. His ability to lead and excel under pressure year after year was almost magical.

The six-three, 180-pound swingman solidified his already-legendary status as a senior by leading Bedford North Lawrence to the 1990 Indiana state championship before a national-record crowd of 41,046. He led the Stars—with no other Division I player—to the Final Four three times during his brilliant four-year career. Along the way, he broke the state's 29-year-old career scoring record with 3,134 points.

A little-known record—which may last longer than any of his other feats—is that he scored 787 points (28.1 average in 28 games) in state-tourney action from the opening sectional round through the Final Four.

He was not only named Indiana's Mr. Basketball, but was also crowned National Player of the Year by the likes of *USA Today*, Naismith, and Gatorade.

Not since Oscar (Robertson) had an Indiana basketball player been so well-known only by his first name.

The future superstar grew up in tiny Heltonville, population 500, the son of Wendell and Beverly Bailey. His father, who held many Heltonville High records, played a major, major role in Damon's basketball success because he laid all the groundwork. Wendell and other adults would play independent league games a couple times a week, and young Damon would tag along. At age four, Damon was shooting around during warm-ups, fell under the basket, and suffered a broken arm when he was stepped on by an adult. The injury, of course, failed to stifle his growing love for the game.

"Nobody was more instrumental than my parents," Bailey pointed out. "My dad definitely was very hard on me. He saw I wanted to be a very good player. That's great if the kid wants it. They were always there to push me and keep me focused on my goal. I appreciate all the time and effort they put in helping me become the player I did. I fell in love with the game at an early age. To me, it was not work.

"My dad was always on me about being an unselfish player. I was seven or eight years old, playing at the boys' club. I didn't pass to a boy who was wide open. I said, 'Dad, he can't catch it.' He said, 'That's not your problem.' All the post-game talks we had—some were heated. It was constantly a learning situation. Some games I only scored ten points, but it always was about other things—making players around you better."

Playing against his dad on their driveway also helped shape Damon's tremendous work ethic and competitive nature. "I don't know if I was born with it or it was taught," he conceded. "I never wanted to lose, whether it was cards or pool. Everything was a competition. I wanted to be the best out there. It wasn't going to be because of lack of effort on my part."

As a third grader, Bailey made the Heltonville fifth-grade team. During his elementary school days, he often played before crowds of 300 to 400 as word spread rapidly about this rising young phenom.

At age nine, Bailey came under the tutelage of Tom (Red) Taylor, whose Indianapolis Municipal Gardens age-group AAU teams dominated not only Indiana but the entire nation. His parents made great sacrifices, driving a 140-mile round trip for games and practices. Bailey was with Taylor all the way through high school, starring for five age-group national champions and being named national tourney MVP four times. Among his teammates were Eric Montross, Alan Henderson, and Brian Evans.

"I was so impressed with his anticipation," Taylor said. "He was shy, and I really had to push him into being a leader. He didn't really want to do that. He finally opened up when we won our second national championship [1980] at the University of Iowa. We cleared the floor so he could bring it down with about three or four seconds left. He went coast-to-coast going full speed, got around his man, and scored the winning basket on a lay-up at the gun.

"There were a lot of press there. They wanted to interview me, but I had said if we won, he was going to be our spokesman. He was twelve years old and scared to death, but I knew he was smart. He did a good job and he sounded like an adult. Of all those kids I had, Damon was probably the best I had at that time coming through. Nobody could dominate a game like Damon did at both ends."

Looking back, Bailey admitted, "I didn't want to do it. It was Red's way of throwing me—and knowing that at some point I was going to be facing this—to the media and telling the other kids on the team 'this is our guy.' There comes a certain amount of responsibility. Coach Taylor definitely was someone who gave me an opportunity to showcase my talents on a national stage. I was fortunate to play with a lot of great players. They were good kids. There was no jealousy, and the parents got along well."

Concerning the leadership role, Bailey said, "There is a certain degree you're born with, or you develop that personality somehow. I never screamed or got in someone's face, but I was going to work hard at being the best player I could be. Whatever I would say, they knew I cared about winning, and that was the most important thing to me. People appreciated that and allowed me to be an extension of a coach on the floor."

During Bailey's five national AAU championship years, Municipal Gardens compiled a phenomenal 73-1 record in state and national tourney competition. Its only loss was a one-pointer against a Georgia team during Bailey's junior year.

As a seventh grader at Shawswick Junior High, Bailey was placed on the eighth-grade team and sparked a group that had won just twice the year before to an undefeated season. The next year, he performed as a man among boys during another undefeated campaign. He amassed 22 points and 17 rebounds in one game, and 31 points and 16 rebounds on another occasion, as the gym seating capacity of 1,500 continually bulged at the seams.

Eighth grade was a huge breakout year, for at least three reasons. First of all, he received his initial college recruiting letter from Syracuse University. "It was a generic form letter," he conceded.

The second big happening was his first dunk. "As a kid, you always want to touch the net," Bailey said. "Then you want to touch the backboard, then the rim. I had always messed around in my driveway. I'd done it in practice, but never in a game (until eighth grade)."

The third—and most unexpected—event was the arrival of famed Indiana University coach Bob Knight to watch Bailey play for Shawswick Junior High. Among Knight's entourage was John Feinstein, who was writing a book, *A Season on the Brink*, which was published just before Bailey's freshman year at North Lawrence. In the book, Knight was quoted as telling his associates that Bailey already was better than any of his current guards, including gold-medal winner Steve Alford.

This statement—a typical Knight ploy to push his own players—created a national sensation, and Bailey's life was never the same again. "I didn't know I was going to be in the book until after the fact," Bailey said. "I was an IU fan, and to have Coach

Knight watch me play at such a young age was a great, great honor. I was fortunate to have parents who kept me in check to not get a big head. After playing for him, I realized that was just Coach Knight.

"I was fortunate to grow up in Indiana, a basketball-crazy state. Locally I had success, but it became more of a regional or national thing after being mentioned in the book. I kind of grew up with it [the media glare]. I grew up always being in the spotlight and adjusting to life accordingly. It was a sense of accomplishment."

North Lawrence High School coach Dan Bush had played with and against Wendell Bailey in independent basketball, and he watched Damon grow up. "We knew he was quite a player," Bush acknowledged. "He got everybody involved. He looked like he knew what he was doing—more so than most."

One day, Bush drove by the Bailey farm and saw his star of the future chopping wood. He stopped and told his dad, "Wendell, you shouldn't have him chopping wood. He might get hurt."

Wendell's quick reply was, "Well, do you want to chop?" End of discussion!

Concerning the book, Bush noted, "IU and Bob Knight had so many followers at that time. It put a lot of unfair pressure on Damon. I don't think it fazed him a bit. Most kids would have crumbled. Regardless of what people expected, he never seemed to let them down. He was mature beyond his years."

Bedford *Times-Mail* sports editor Bob Bridge also had to make some major adjustments after the book became a bestseller. "I had visitors from about every major publication in the country," he recalled. "My voicemail (home and office) was full from the time he started playing. There were newspapers, magazines, coaches, and people wanting tickets. It was amazing that he kept his cool through the whole thing."

Bridge had been impressed by Bailey even as a sixth grader, but he became a true believer during his freshman year. In his first varsity game—an 82-70 victory at Scottsburg—he showed absolutely no sign of jitters by drilling his first five shots. He scored 20 points on 5-of-6 shooting from the field and 10-of-12 from the free-throw line before fouling out with 3:29 left.

The statistics were excellent, but Bailey, who was playing with a senior-dominated team, really opened some eyes at the post-game press conference when he said, "Well, you know, my teammates made it so easy for me." It was obvious that his greatness on the basketball court would be working in perfect harmony with the intelligence of a seasoned politician.

The ballyhooed expectations became reality in Bridge's mind when the Stars met highly-ranked Bloomington South and its six-ten star, Chris Lawson, in Bailey's sixth varsity game. In his true coming-out party, the precocious freshman exploded for 37 points and grabbed 11 rebounds as the Stars rolled to an impressive 73-62 victory. He connected on fifteen of his eighteen shots from the field, including his last eleven. Damon truly *was* for real, and now everybody knew it.

Later in the season, Bailey pumped in a school-record 40 points and grabbed 13 rebounds in a 103-92 shootout victory over Jeffersonville.

The young phenom was so good as a rookie that he sparked the Stars to the coveted Final Four. Playing before a capacity crowd of 17,490, they bowed to eventual champion Marion, 70-61, in the state semifinals, although Bailey held his own with 20 points and 7 rebounds. They finished with a school-record twenty-three victories against four defeats.

The 6-2 Bailey led the Stars in scoring (23.6), rebounding (8.4), assists (3.8), steals (65), and field-goal percentage (.597). In addition, he shot .721 from the free-throw line and dished out 103 assists. He also was named first-team All-State, eventually becoming the first Hoosier ever to win that honor four consecutive years. *Sports Illustrated* added to the hype by naming him the number-one freshman in the U.S.

Bailey, who had run cross country (and won most of his races) as a seventh- and eighth grader, also played varsity baseball (outfield) as a freshman before concentrating on basketball. "He was a great athlete and could have played any sport," Bob Bridge said confidently.

By now, Dan Bush was a total believer in his young protégé. He noted, "After I'd been around him on a regular basis for a year, I knew the sky was the limit. I loved the way he worked in practice and picked things up." He admitted he was worried early on about Damon's publicity and relationships with his older teammates, "but that never was a problem. He was an easy kid to like."

Despite his unselfishness, Bailey surpassed his own school record five times during his sophomore year. He scored forty-two points against Terre Haute South and Floyd Central, forty-three against New Albany, forty-seven against Seymour, then topped it off with a fifty-one-point explosion in the regional against Jeffersonville.

Bailey's forty-two-point effort against Terre Haute South included the game-winning three-pointer from more than 30 feet, which produced a spectacular 77-74 overtime victory. His forty-two-point game against Floyd Central prompted losing coach Joe Hinton to tell the press, "He's not a kid. He has the mental maturity of a college player. He's so much smarter than the average high school player that it's unbelievable. Boy, he made some shots tonight."

The Stars, who set another school record with twenty-seven victories against just two defeats, repeated their march to the Final Four. This time they again were eliminated in the semifinals, 60-53, by another eventual state champion, Muncie Central, before another capacity crowd of 17,490. Damon finished with twenty-five points, nine rebounds, and four assists. For the year, he improved his averages to 31.1 points, 9.4 rebounds, a phenomenal .616 from the field, and .772 from the free-throw line.

On and off the basketball court, Damon Bailey was a teen idol. He took his responsibility as a role model quite seriously. "I grew up with it," he acknowledged. "There was a lot of good and bad with it. I knew I had kids looking up to me and I had to act in a certain way."

This "fishbowl" existence sometimes forced him to take long drives—just him and his country music playing on the radio—to grab two or three hours of solitude away from adoring fans and the media glare. He explained, "It was my way to get away, to be a normal kid, to clear my mind and have some sense of privacy. It [the constant attention] definitely wears on you. In my case, I just wanted to play basketball."

The media crush was so heavy that all interviews had to be conducted through Coach Bush, and only at the high school. The requests had to be measured as to their importance, and many were rejected. His parents never gave interviews or allowed media members to visit their home. "My dad told a lot of people that we were—and still are—simple people," Damon related. "It never was about the notoriety or being in books."

Damonmania probably reached its bizarre peak one late afternoon when a carload of girls grabbed some grass from his front yard and raced off like bandits with their spoil. Crusty Wendell Bailey was the lone witness, and he couldn't have been more mystified.

The Bedford North Lawrence fieldhouse seating capacity of 6,316 overflowed throughout Bailey's four-year career. A local pizza parlor was a hot spot because of its weekly ticket drawings. Season ticket sales were a great barometer of Bailey's drawing power. BNL sold 636 season tickets when Bailey was in eighth grade, 1,898 when he was a freshman, 5,053 when he was a sophomore, 5,350 when he was a junior, and 5,435 when he was a senior.

Naturally, opponents also wanted a piece of the action. They moved their home games to such sites as Market Square Arena (17,490), Hinkle Fieldhouse (15,000), Hulman Center (10,200), Southport (7,240), and Columbus North (7,042).

The Damon Bailey phenomenon was raking in thousands of dollars for opponents as well as the home team. In fact, seventeen years after Bailey's graduation, rumors still abound that "the athletic coffers at BNL are still pretty full."

The hordes of fans and media members constantly hounding Bailey gave him celebrity status, forcing the coaching staff to devise ways to ease the pressure. "Wherever we went, there were times we had to take him out the back door—just like Elvis," Dan Bush said. "We'd send him one way and the other kids another way."

He launched his junior year with a 50-point bomb as the Stars routed Salem, 80-55. They had an excellent 21-3 campaign, but it ended with a 76-72 overtime loss to Floyd Central in the regional opener. Bailey scored thirty-seven points despite being hampered by a broken finger on his non-shooting hand. That was to be the only year that he couldn't will his team to the Final Four.

Besides failing to reach the state finals, Bailey's junior year was noteworthy for an announcement that surprised absolutely no one: He planned to attend Indiana University, just twenty-five miles up the highway from Bedford. "I grew up being an Indiana fan," he affirmed. "They had tradition, and any kid growing up in Southern Indiana, it was his dream to be able to play at Indiana University. I tried to keep an open mind. I visited Purdue and I liked North Carolina."

He completed his junior campaign with slightly lower statistics. He averaged 27.2 points, 8.1 rebounds, and 5.0 assists. Still, he already held twenty school records, with his biggest year yet to come.

Because he was called a "man among boys" at every level, Damon, somewhere along the line, began calling his teammates "kids." He explained, "I had to mature at such an early age—a lot quicker than other kids. I've taken a lot of flack over that. I didn't mean any disrespect by it."

Well, his senior year, everything finally came together and he led his "kids" to their first-ever state championship. His most memorable regular-season game was against Madison, during which he drilled fourteen consecutive shots en route to a forty-one-point performance.

Early in his career, Bailey had faced every trick defense conceived by man: box-and-one, triangle-and-two, etc. Interestingly, though, many opponents began wising up and playing him straight-up man-to-man because he was satisfied to take a lesser scoring role. "I was content to set up the other guys," Bailey pointed out. "Those junk defenses really weren't going to work. We still were going to beat them by thirty."

Marching through the state tourney in 1990, the Stars were not going to be denied, no matter what defense they faced. They lost only twice—by a single point to Indianapolis Lawrence North and New Albany—during the regular season. Bailey scored thirty or more points in sixteen of the twenty-two games.

When they reached the coveted Final Four for the third time in four years, a national high school record crowd of 41,046 was eagerly waiting at the Hoosier Dome in Indianapolis. The ballyhooed event also had drawn an incredible turnout of 431 media members. This was Damon Bailey's last hurrah, and everyone in the country, it seemed, wanted to see how much magic he still had left in his bag of tricks.

The Stars couldn't have been blamed for seeing plenty of deja vu flash before their eyes when they trailed Southport 32-23 at halftime in the semifinal contest. After all, they never had gotten past that first round in two previous tries. This time, however, Bailey was not to be denied. He sparkled with 25 points, 10 rebounds, and 7 assists as the Stars eked out a 58-55 triumph. Now they were one game away from their first-ever state championship.

Elkhart Concord, which was unbeaten and ranked number one in the state, was the only obstacle still blocking their way to glory. This was it—what Damon and his mates had dreamed of and been working for all of their lives. They could almost reach out and taste it, but Concord was a formidable foe.

Looking back on that historic night, Bailey noted, "I didn't think about it [the crowd] before or after the game. I had a gift of being able to keep everything in check. You recognize and acknowledge it, but once the ball is tipped, it's pretty much like playing in an empty gym. Reflecting back now, it was simply amazing. We were just a bunch of country kids. I was the tallest. We were like a bunch of guys who were going to go out and get killed.

"We had seven county schools [which had consolidated into BNL] and we used to hate each other. We were not crazy about consolidation. It was really a time when all the communities came together. There were only one or two Bedford kids on our team. The country kids played a very big part, and our support was just unbelievable."

He didn't have to say it, but Damon Bailey was the leader—the catalyst—who drew everything together. He didn't have great talent surrounding him, but they knew their roles, and as longtime Purdue University assistant coach Bob King put it, "Those kids would follow him to hell and back."

The Stars gave it their best shot against Concord, but still trailed, 58-52, with 2:38 remaining. Dan Bush wasn't worried, because he knew Bailey always "had a knack to rise to the occasion. He never ran away from the responsibility of being the man. He thrived on it."

His young superstar felt the same way. "I thrived under pressure," Bailey affirmed. "If I was going to be the hero, I definitely would have to take the responsibility—and I could be the goat. I would be the one to win or lose the game. I think any good player wants to have the basketball at the end of a game."

Now was the time for Damon to reach the pinnacle of his greatness. He never had lost a sprint in practice during his career. He took great pride in his conditioning. When the game was on the line he still had plenty of gas left in his tank. "Conditioning was a big thing to me," he acknowledged. "It was a big key to my success. I was in such better shape than anybody I played against. For three quarters, I would wear those players out. In the fourth quarter, I was still fresh."

And fresh he was. The frazzled Minutemen desperately tried to keep the ball out of Bailey's hands, but it was impossible. He used strength and intelligence to score his team's last 11 points as they rallied for a stunning 63-60 victory that surely must have been written in the stars. He finished with thirty points to go with eight rebounds and five assists.

As soon as the game ended, Damon bolted into the stands to hug his parents. His father always had told him he never would truly celebrate with him until he won the state title. He normally would just say "good game." This truly was a night for Wendell Bailey to let his hair down, too.

Before he headed home that night, Bailey received the coveted Trester Award for mental attitude and grades (he had a 3.7 average) as well as basketball ability. No better choice ever has been made for an award of this type. Damon Bailey epitomized everything that was good about high school athletics.

Seated among the huge crowd that night was Angelo Pizzo, who was responsible for the famous movie *Hoosiers*. He told the press, "I got cold chills. It's almost like he came out of the script. The last time I saw a championship game was when Hickory played South Bend. But this was better because this was real."

In his final campaign, Bailey averaged a career-high 31.4 points, 9.4 rebounds, and 6.8 assists, as the Stars again set a school record with 29 victories against just 2 defeats. His 3,134 career points (28.4 average) broke Indiana's seemingly unapproachable state record of 3,019 set by Marion Pierce of Lewisville in 1961. "It never even entered my mind," Damon admitted, "but it's definitely something you can be proud of."

He also grabbed 1,011 rebounds during his career, for a 9.2 average, and averaged 5.0 assists. He shot a remarkable .600 from the field and his free-throw percentage was .756.

Bailey always prided himself in being a winner, and the Stars' four-year records speak for themselves: They were 99-11 overall and a perfect 39-0 at home during the Damon Bailey era. Like his idol, Larry Bird, Damon played the game unselfishly, made everyone around him better, and was a winner in every sense of the word.

And the awards continued to pour in. Bailey was named National Player of the Year by *USA Today,* Gatorade, and Naismith. The Gatorade award prompted Bedford to proclaim a "Damon Bailey Day," and he was presented a limestone key to the city. "It's more for me to enjoy today than at the time," he said. "I still had things I wanted to accomplish. I was still playing, and it was kind of mind-boggling."

One post-season award that Damon received, however, was very special to him: Mr. Basketball. "That one definitely was a goal," he freely admitted. "That is the ultimate goal for a high school player in Indiana. It definitely is a great honor. I wanted Mr. Basketball, a state title, and a third goal was to have a good enough high school career to go to a major college." Goals definitely accomplished!

Bailey had a full spring and summer of all-star and AAU games before heading up the road to Indiana University. His debut as a freshman produced 5 points and 6 assists in 20 minutes as the Hoosiers posted a 100-78 victory over Northeastern at Maui, Hawaii. He scored in double figures 20 times with a high of 32 during a wild 97-95 double-overtime loss at Ohio State. On that occasion, he drilled eleven of fifteen from the field, and seven of ten from the free-throw line. He also had four assists, and not a single turnover.

Continuing to live out his dream, Bailey was named Big Ten Freshman of the Year after averaging 11.4 points, 2.9 assists, and 2.9 rebounds. He also shot .506 from the field and .692 from the free-throw line as the Hoosiers posted a 29-5 record.

His numbers went up slightly as a sophomore, and he helped the Hoosiers (27-7) soar all the way to the coveted Final Four, where they lost to Duke, 81-78, in the semifinals. He finished with averages of 12.4 points and 3.1 assists.

The Hoosiers compiled a superb 31-4 record during Bailey's junior year and won three games in the NCAA tourney before bowing to Kansas, 83-77, in the regional finals. His scoring average dropped to 10.1, but his assists rose to 4.1.

To be expected, Bailey's senior year at IU was his best. He was held below double figures in scoring just twice during a 21-9 campaign. He scored twenty or more points fourteen times, with a high of thirty-six. Even though hindered by an abdominal tear late in the season, he finished with career-high averages of 19.6 points and 4.3 assists. He was named first-team Big Ten and third-team All-American.

During his four-year career, the versatile Bailey—who had bulked up to 210 pounds—played point and shooting guard and small forward. He set an IU record with 380 three-pointers, tied for second with 474 assists (3.6 average), and placed fifth with 1,741 points (13.2 average).

Playing four years under Bob Knight, who launched his celebrity status as an eighth grader, had its ups and downs. "Unless you experienced playing for Coach Knight," he said, "you couldn't know how great it was when it was great or how bad it was when it was bad. My relationship with my parents was very similar."

Bob Bridge, the master statistician, dug up some interesting facts about Bailey's IU career. He pointed out that Damon joined Isaiah Thomas and Steve Alford as the only players ever to lead the Hoosiers in scoring and assists during the same year. He was the second-most-efficient scorer per shot taken, and he played in more victories (108-25) than any player except Quinn Buckner.

The Indiana Pacers made Bailey the number forty-four pick in the 1994 NBA draft, and it seemed only natural because he was so loved throughout the state. However, he tore his patella tendon while playing with the Pacers in a summer league and had to spend his entire rookie year on the disabled list. He only did rehab and never touched a basketball.

"As a kid, I always had some problems," Bailey explained. "Some of it was from growth. I did a lot of running on roads and played on cement. I abused my body. I wasn't an exceptional athlete—I looked like a lot of other kids. If I was going to be better, I had to outwork guys. Throughout high school, I had soreness and never got it checked out. At IU, I played with a lot of pain."

The next year, the Pacers cut him. "It definitely took some of my athletic ability away," Bailey said of his repaired knee. "I was talented enough to play at that level, but not to be an all-star."

Though he spent parts of two seasons playing in France and once was invited to the Cleveland Cavaliers' training camp, Bailey's four-year professional career (1995-99) belonged to the Fort Wayne Fury of the Continental Basketball Association. Knee problems plagued him throughout, and by retirement, he had undergone seven surgeries.

The Fury's radio announcer/public relations director, Rob Brown, was Bailey's roommate on the road. He still marvels at the Hoosier legend's grit and ability to play with pain. He recalled a trip to Florida during which Damon got deathly sick from some bad seafood and threw up most of the day. Still, he played thirty-five minutes that night, despite the very strong possibility he would look bad in front of several NBA scouts.

"That hurt him because most of the guys in the CBA were out for themselves," Brown pointed out. "You don't see a lot of that stuff [dedication]. Most guys would have taken the day off."

In the 1997-98 season, Bailey led the CBA in assists (379 for a 7.3 average) and free-throw percentage (.852). He also set the pace in assists (6.8) during the 1998-99 campaign. His career highs were thirty-eight points and eighteen assists. Over 4 years, he averaged 14.9 points during the regular season and 14.0 during the playoffs.

"I was very happy with my career," Bailey said. "I didn't accomplish everything I wanted. Something that nobody can take away from me is that at every level, I was a winner."

The Damon Bailey Basketball Camps were launched following his graduation from college. Today, Damon runs fifteen camps—all in different cities in Indiana—over a seven-week period each summer. He estimates that between 1,200 and 1,500 attend each year. Those attending range from first through ninth grade.

The Hoosier legend wears other hats, too. He is a partner in the Bedford-based Hawkins-Bailey Warehouse, which primarily sells filters and lubricants for cars and heavy equipment. The company, which operates mainly in Southern Indiana, Southern Illinois, and most of Kentucky, grosses around $12 million each year. To make him feel truly at home, his business partner's wife, Emily Hawkins, saw to it that his office carpet contains an interwoven replica of his number 22 IU jersey.

He also wears a third hat that he never expected to even try on—he is the second-year head basketball coach at his alma mater, Bedford North Lawrence High School. His high school coach, Dan Bush, had always told him, "You should never take a [coaching] job unless you can play yourself."

Well, he took it anyway, although it didn't happen overnight. He recalled, "I said no five times before I said yes. I had thought about it if the opportunity ever would come up. This was probably the only job I would have taken because of my business. The time commitment is the hardest."

He took the job just one week before tryouts in 2005. He had "no game plan" and had to clear it with his business partner, be sure he had good assistants to take over if he missed a practice, and assure his family he would not neglect them. His first-year record was 11-10, and his goal is to "get that tradition back. The program is not where I want it now." He admits, "It definitely has been a struggle with time and philosophies. I wrestle with expecting kids to do the same things I did. It's been a huge learning curve for me. This year, I was a lot more prepared."

Following his second year (12-10), Damon resigned as head coach. He explained that juggling coaching with running a business and raising a young family became too much of a drain to handle. "I enjoyed it, but it was just too hard," he conceded.

Now thirty-five years old, Bailey insists he does not fear tarnishing his image if he doesn't make it big as a coach. He emphasized, "I'm not worried much about my image. I'm doing something I enjoy. If you're afraid to fail, you'll never succeed. I still know a lot more about basketball than a lot of people. Will I be a good coach? There is a difference between playing and coaching. I don't put the time in that needs to be put in [because of work], and my family takes time away from coaching. Once upon a time, basketball was at the top, but not today."

Damon's family includes his wife of eleven years, Stacey, whom he started dating in ninth grade; Alexa, a fourth grader; Loren, a third grader; and Brayton, who is in kindergarten. Being the oldest, Alexa already is "pretty good," according to her proud papa. "She's extremely quick. She's a competitor—a lot like me. She really enjoys the game and the competition of it. Loren is more of a cheerleader and dancer. Brayton is just starting to play at the boys' club. He's pretty good, skill-wise. His favorite thing is to come up to me, shake my hand, and say, 'Hi, Damon Bailey, I'm your favorite fan.'"

Bailey said he "grew up in a Christian home" and his family attends Heltonville Christian Church. "It [the spiritual side of his life] is important, but we don't go to church every Sunday because we're on the road almost every weekend, with the girls being involved in basketball and dance."

When—and if—he ever has any spare time, he enjoys playing golf, hunting, and fishing.

No matter how Damon Bailey fares as a coach, he will be a hero forever in his tiny hometown of Heltonville, Indiana. While he was playing in the CBA, Bailey's fans began a drive to raise $4,000 to build a lasting monument in his memory. They raised $6,000 with no sweat whatsoever. The result is a ten-foot limestone tablet in the shape of the state of Indiana, with his picture carved into it. It rests majestically—and quite appropriately—close to the Heltonville gymnasium.

Forever humble, Damon says simply, "It's hard for me to explain. Obviously I can take great pride in that. Everything I did was not for that. It makes you proud that you had a career which merited that type of recognition. I'm proud that they call you their own and put you on a pedestal."

RON BONHAM:
Muncie's Best Ever

The Muncie Central Bearcats have been the dominant power in Indiana high school basketball ever since they captured their first of a record eight state titles in the late winter of 1928. The Cradle of Champions heritage was launched by Charlie Secrist, who drilled a spectacular shot from beyond half-court to nip Martinsville, 13-12, and deny John Wooden a title in his senior year.

The victory was so huge, in fact, that townspeople quickly formed the Public Schools Extension Association and, in less than a year, built the gigantic Muncie Fieldhouse. It was dedicated on December 7, 1928, and was the largest high school gymnasium in the world for more than thirty years.

Since then, Muncie has built other high schools, though Central remains the mecca. The program has developed many great players, but none greater than Ron Bonham—the fabled Blond Bomber.

Bonham's status in Indiana folklore would be much loftier if he hadn't had the misfortune of playing for the best team that never won the state championship. In March of 1960, the Bearcats steamed into the state finals with a perfect 27-0 record, the state's number-one ranking, and a huge favorite's role to take the big trophy home.

What few doubters who may have existed quickly vanished when Muncie massacred number-two-ranked Bloomington, 102-66, in the semifinals. The six-five, 190-pound Bonham was at his best, with a state-finals-record 40 points. Nobody could stop these Bearcats! They had five future Division I college players, and firepower galore.

Then the impossible happened. East Chicago Washington, coached by wily John Baratto, pulled away late to post a simply shocking 75-59 victory in the championship game before a stunned crowd of 14,943. Bonham pumped in a game-high twenty-nine points (fifteen on free throws), but he fouled out for the first time in eighty-five varsity games. His brilliant career ended with 3:07 left and his team trailing, 61-55. The Bearcats shot a woeful 30 percent from the field.

"That was the biggest disappointment in my basketball career," Bonham readily admits. "I still get people who stop me and talk about it. We blew [Bloomington] out of the gym. I don't know if we were overconfident. We had been beating people by thirty points. We just felt invincible and nobody could beat us. I think if we played East Chicago fifty times, we'd beat 'em [every time]. We didn't play a good game. I didn't have any spring in my legs. We were just a step behind. It was just meant for them to win."

Future Indiana Hall of Fame broadcaster Morry Mannies did the radio play-by-play of the Muncie games that day, and he also was greatly affected by the heartbreak of the Bearcats' crushing defeat. "It was one of the saddest nights of my career," he said as he reflected on fifty-one years in the field. "I was near tears. I could have made a million dollars [if he had bet against the Bearcats]."

Prior to the title game, Mannies, then a senior at Ball State University, had talked his boss into letting him interview the champions after the game. Following the defeat, he balked slightly, but his boss barked, "Well, get out there and interview the champions!"

He admitted, "It was a good lesson."

Growing up in Muncie meant attending Bearcat basketball games—if you could get a ticket. People left coveted season tickets in their wills. The Muncie Fieldhouse seated an unheard-of 7,500, and visitors got only 50 tickets, mostly high in the rafters. "There was so much purple and white [Muncie colors] in the stands, it had to be overwhelming for people to come in there," Bonham noted.

"My parents always had season tickets," Bonham continued. "It was a dream of mine to be a Bearcat. The fieldhouse always was packed—standing room only. It's lucky the fire marshal wasn't there. They had the greatest fans in the state of Indiana. It really turned me on."

Unfortunately, Bonham developed a heart murmur at a young age. No basketball! Instead, young Bonham took up tap dancing, which he did for twelve years. He also did acrobatics. All those years were not wasted, however, because he was developing agility and strength, which later served him quite well.

"It was pretty severe," he said of the heart murmur. "But it corrected itself. I was told not to exert myself, but I always was active. When the doctor gave me the OK to exert myself, I used to work out five or six hours a day. I had a basketball goal behind my house, the whole neighborhood came, and we played late.

"I was one of those white fellows who could jump," Bonham continued. "I could dunk flat-footed. Acrobatics as a youngster helped me develop strong legs and helped my turn-around jump shot."

Playing his first organized basketball for the Blaine Hornets in eighth grade, Bonham immediately became the leading scorer. He repeated that feat for the freshman team.

The summer before his sophomore year, Bonham was putting in long hours to fulfill his dream of making the Muncie Central varsity. He and another future Bearcat star, John Dampier, were playing "one on one 'til death," he said, not totally joking. "We were so competitive. I broke my ankle, but didn't know it until the next day. I finished the game [about another half hour], although I was in excruciating pain. I think I won the game."

Was Ron Bonham mentally and physically tough, even at that age? You better believe it! He went through three walking casts that summer [once he fell in the river], but never missed a single day of workouts. He was a teenager on a mission and wasn't going to let a little broken ankle deter him from his lifetime dream.

Fully recovered, Bonham was rewarded for his fanatical efforts with a coveted varsity berth. He was the lone sophomore to make it. Morry Mannies recalls broadcasting his breakout game that year. "Ron came in during the second period, scored twenty-five points off the bench that night, and never saw the bench after that," Mannies noted. "It changed the Bearcat world.

"He was slender, but had great footwork," Mannies described. "Dancing had made him so nimble. He had long nails on his hands. As he grew stronger he was just unstoppable. He was the picture of an athlete. He was tough because of the abuse he took. When it came to the big shot, he was the one who took it. Was he cocky? You bet!"

Playing against one of the state's toughest schedules, Bonham averaged an impressive 18.8 points as the Bearcats posted a 22-7 record and got all the way to the state finals before bowing to Crawfordsville, 53-45. He scored nine points in the game.

Bonham was such a standout shooter that Muncie sportswriter Bob Barnet began calling him the Blond Bomber. Other times, he referred to him as the Muncie Rifle. Every name was appropriate, of course, because week after week, Bonham would gun down the opposition.

How devoted was he to perfecting his craft? "He'd be wringing wet before we'd blow the whistle to start practice," assistant coach Bob Heeter related. "That's how seriously he worked on his shooting. He worked on that turn-around jump shot religiously. He was really dedicated."

As a junior, he stepped up his production considerably, averaging 25 points a game and making first-team All-State, as the Bearcats posted a superb 25-2 record. They just missed a Final Four berth, losing to eventual state champion Indianapolis Crispus Attucks, 64-62, in the semi-state finale.

Despite the crushing final game, Bonham had his greatest year as a senior. He poured in 803 points—with a school-record 53 against Middletown in the regional—for a 27.6 average. Bonham calls his fifty-three-point explosion "memorable. It was in the New Castle gym. You just feel like you could kick the ball in." That fifty-three-point effort still ranks number two in state-tourney history.

He did, however, give his coaches a scare between the semifinal and final games of the sectional that year. "He was very easygoing," Heeter noted. "He was late coming to the fieldhouse [for the title game]. John [head coach John Longfellow] called his dad and found out he was home taking a bath. That didn't set very well with us."

The six-five, 190-pounder finished with a career total of 2,023 points, which still is number 1 in the storied history of Muncie Central. He also averaged 12.7 rebounds. He repeated as a first-team All-State selection, was named Mr. Basketball, and made the *Parade* magazine high school All-American team. The summer before he entered college, he was named Star of Stars in both Indiana-Kentucky All-Star games, scoring a total of fifty-nine points.

Morry Mannies believes that Bonham actually could have finished his career as the all-time leading scorer in state history, had he not played with so many other high Division I performers such as Dampier, Jim Davis, and Jim Nettles. They not only shared the points, but they blew out most opponents early and, consequently, spent a surprising amount of time on the bench. Bonham estimates that he played only twenty-four minutes a game (three quarters) as a senior. It was a high price for success.

"He was Public Hero Number One," Mannies said fondly. "When you ask people who the greatest Muncie Central player was, it's Ron Bonham."

Basketball wasn't the only thing that Bonham excelled in, because he was an outstanding singer, too. His crooning talent and teen-idol looks just added to his popularity, though he was somewhat of a loner. He joined with four other teens to form the Originals, a rock-and-roll group. They wore blue dinner jackets and black tux pants, and were so talented that they drew a screaming crowd of 6,000 for a concert at the Muncie Fieldhouse. They even cut a record which sold more than 5,000 copies.

"I was the only player on the five," Bonham noted. "We harmonized well. We used to go over to my house and practice. I've only got one copy [of the record] left."

Bonham's college saga got off to a controversial start. After sifting through approximately 300 college scholarship offers, he enrolled at nearby Purdue University for three days in the fall of 1960, but never attended a class. He wound up at the University of Cincinnati, where he had a tremendous three-year career.

Longtime Purdue assistant coach Bob King had been recruiting him. "I always thought he was a really good high school player," King said. "I didn't know he was going to be such a good college player. He had great moves, could really shoot, and was a good ball handler."

King said that once Bonham came to the Purdue campus, "I started to show him around. He was worried about where to park his car and if he had to take ROTC. Ray Eddy [head coach] called me at 5 AM the next day and said, 'Bob, get over to Muncie.' By the time I got over there, he was gone."

Ron himself explained what happened. "There was so much pressure to stay in the state of Indiana," he related. "My heart wasn't with it [Purdue], and I had depression at the time. The people were great at Purdue and I felt bad. I wanted to go to a basketball college." He had attended Cincinnati's basketball banquet during the great Oscar Robertson's final year, and was extremely impressed. "[Robertson] won every possible award. They had great alumni, enthusiasm, and tradition."

Larry Elsasser, however, provided the clincher, because he not only played basketball but he also loved the outdoors. They had met when Ron visited the school. He called Elsasser after he left Purdue, and was encouraged to join him at UC. He did and they wound up being roomies for four years. They were kindred spirits. More than once, they ignored classes and sneaked off to go hunting or fishing.

"Nobody could have had a greater time in college than I had in four years," Bonham emphasized.

Adding frosting to the cake, Bonham didn't even have to change mascots, because the UC teams also were named Bearcats. These Bearcats provided him with something that eluded him in high school: a championship ring. Oscar Robertson, a Hoosier great before him, had set the table—not being able to win a title—and Bonham was a thankful benefactor of the feast.

UC won the NCAA title when Bonham was a freshman, but freshmen were not eligible for varsity competition in that era. Even though three starters returned the next year, he cracked the starting lineup as a sophomore and averaged 14.3 points. He finally got that elusive championship ring when the Bearcats (29-2) captured the 1962 NCAA crown with a 71-59 victory over favored Ohio State, led by Jerry Lucas and John Havlicek.

As a junior, Bonham was the leading scorer at 21.0, but the 26-2 Bearcats had to settle for NCAA runner-up, as this time they fell upset victims to Loyola of Chicago, 60-58, in overtime. Still he finished as high scorer with twenty-two points in the heartbreaker. The team record slipped to 17-9 his senior year, but he averaged 24.4 points, still number 6 in UC history.

Bonham made All-America his junior and senior years and completed his career with 1,666 points, still number five in school history. His career scoring average of 19.6 points ranks third in school history, and his free-throw percentage of .831 (458-551) is second. His high game was thirty-eight points against North Texas State.

One championship ring was only the beginning for the Muncie great, because he was the number eighteen pick of the Boston Celtics and played on NBA title teams in 1965 and 1966. In the 1966-67 season, he joined the first Indiana Pacer team that competed in the American Basketball Association. He scored 478 points and pulled down 113 rebounds in 76 games with the Celtics, while he had 245 points and 57 rebounds in 42 games with the Pacers.

"It's humbling," Bonham said of his time with the Celtics. "Bill Russell, John Havlicek—they were the best players in the world. The second year I started [when Satch Sanders got hurt] until I dislocated the thumb on my shooting hand.

"Auerbach [coach Red Auerbach] told us that if Wilt Chamberlain got close to the basket, we should just grab his arm [because he was a notoriously poor free-throw shooter]. He'd lift you up off the floor. I got my thumb between the ball and his arm, and my thumb got dislocated in three places. I couldn't grip a ball for almost three weeks."

Following his abbreviated pro career, Bonham returned to Muncie and has lived there ever since. He is the first to admit, "I was just blessed to play with the talent where you're recognized."

In 1991, he was enshrined in the Indiana Basketball Hall of Fame. "It was probably the top honor I ever had," he said humbly. "In my trophy room, that's the one on top." Some of his greatest athletic souvenirs, he revealed, already are earmarked in his will for the Indiana Basketball Hall of Fame. They include rings for being on a state runner-up team in high school, NCAA and NBA champions, and watches for being on NCAA and NBA champions, and twice making All-America. The NBA watch is gold.

Bonham served twelve years as a Delaware County commissioner and has been superintendent of Muncie's Prairie Creek Park & Reservoir for the past thirty-seven years. Actually located seven miles outside of the city limits, it covers 2,300 acres and is the second-largest city park in the U.S. He and his wife of thirty-three years, J.J., who has been his office manager for thirty-six years, "both are conservation people," he said.

They raise bird dogs and do a lot of fishing and small-game hunting. Ron lost sight in his left eye to melanoma cancer and the ensuing radiation. "I love bird hunting, and I always close my left eye anyway," he said philosophically.

A man with deep spiritual faith, Bonham accepted Jesus Christ as his Lord and Savior as a teenager while attending Normal City EUB Church in Muncie. "I believe in the Lord," he said. "I always have and always will. I feel I'm blessed."

When he left pro basketball, Bonham was asked to sell insurance or real estate, and he readily admits, "I could have made a lot more money." However, the outdoors has always been his first love, and he backed it up big-time when Prairie Creek needed to raise $50,000 to put a pier on the reservoir for the elderly and handicapped.

He put his money where his heart was, as he and J.J. dug up several valuable items from his basketball past and auctioned them off. They included such treasures as his Muncie Central Bearcat jacket ("That was a heartbreaker," he conceded.), Mr. Basketball jersey, and uniforms from the Celtics and Cincinnati Bearcats title teams. "My wife and I were sitting there crying," he mused. "There were good memories there."

The good news is that his mementoes, along with many other donated items, helped raise the entire $50,000 in a single day.

The Bonhams, who have one daughter, Nicole, own a fifty-two-acre property just three and a half minutes from his office. But the Prairie Creek facility is a place where the sixty-four-year-old Bonham is always at great peace. "It's an appointed position," he said. "We've been very dedicated. We've spent a lot of time here and made a lot of sacrifices, but it's been worth it. They'll probably scatter my ashes out here."

DAVE COLESCOTT:

Driven by Defeats

As an elementary school student, Dave Colescott witnessed two of the most crushing defeats in Marion High School basketball history. That frustration was a driving force as he eventually sparked the Marion Giants to their first state championship in forty-nine years as a junior, led a repeat performance as a senior, and completed a Hoosier trifecta by adding prestigious Trester Award and Mr. Basketball titles to his glowing résumé.

Besides Colescott, the only Indiana players ever to win the Trester Award, at least two state championships, and be crowned Mr. Basketball are Chris Thomas (Indianapolis Pike, 2001) and Greg Oden (Indianapolis Lawrence North, 2006).

At 11 years of age, Colescott experienced agony while watching the Giants—coached by his father, Jack—lose a 58-56 heartbreaker in the state semifinals to Indianapolis Shortridge on a last-second shot by Oscar Evans. "I thought he traveled; it was clearly a walk," Colescott still believes. "I saw the referee blow his whistle, but there was bedlam on the floor."

The very next year, his dad's team suffered a gut-wrenching 61-60 loss to powerful Indianapolis Washington—again in the first round of the Final Four. "The clock didn't work, and it was a very nerve-wracking game," Colescott recalled. "We thought we had it in the bag, but we never knew how much time was left.

"I remember the utter disappointment my dad had. He was devastated. Dad was criticized over the losses. I learned a lot from the way he reacted and carried himself. It really motivated me for the rest of my playing days. It taught me never to forget. Those teams meant a lot to me and to all of us in Marion. We mentioned it a lot growing up."

Young Colescott had such empathy for his father that he cut down the net from his small bedroom basket and gave it to him as a symbol of the big one that got away.

Jack and Marge Colescott had three girls before Dave came along. He almost didn't survive, because he was born prematurely and had yellow jaundice. The first six weeks of his life were spent in the hospital. "My dad came in every day because they didn't think I'd make it," Colescott said. "I had three balls in my crib and (in later years) I always had a ball in my hands. I'd even watch TV and be dribbling a ball. Today, kids play video games."

During practice and games, young Colescott would follow his dad and soak up the game from the inside. "I didn't push him a bit," Jack Colescott stressed. "He picked up his love for basketball on his own. At home, he had a basket which fit on the back of the door. He used to drive his mother crazy when he was about five or six years old.

"He was gifted with quickness and speed. He developed strong forearms and wrists [in high school] and that helped his shot. I always said he was one of the quickest players I've ever seen in basketball, but his quickness came in spurts. He was a good student in the classroom and had good basketball knowledge. He read a lot."

Colescott was a football quarterback in junior high, but he read the handwriting on the wall very clearly one day in eighth grade when he was relentlessly pursued by the Logansport monsterman. "He had a skull and crossbones on his helmet and he could outrun everybody,"

Colescott shuddered. "He was 200 pounds and I was 140. He caught me and hit me so hard that I ate grass. On the next play, he hit me with a forearm shiver. He grunted a lot and he scared me. I was a lover," he laughed.

Jim Brunner, now sports director of Marion radio station WBAT-WCJC, got his first look at Colescott as an eighth grader and swears, "He was only five-three. After [varsity] games, he'd be on the floor shooting Coke cups at the rim. Bill Fowler [his boss at the time] would say, 'There's the future of Marion basketball down there shooting Coke cups.'

"By his sophomore year, he grew to be five-eight or five-nine. It was surprising how non-confident he was, almost humble. There was something there that never let him be cocky. After every game, he'd always ask, 'How'd I do?' He was a real great kid. He was like a [Larry] Bird or Magic [Johnson]. He got all the team involved, drove kids to practice, and hung out with them."

Jack coached Dave for a half dozen years in Little League and junior baseball, but retired from basketball coaching to become athletic director before he entered Marion High. "Marion is a tough place to coach," the senior Colescott noted. "I wanted him to play high school basketball and not have to fight that day-in, day-out pressure. I knew him. It kind of hurt him when people talked about his dad. I didn't want to put him in the position of a coach's son."

The summer before his sophomore year, Colescott decided to quit football, so his dad made him go out for tennis. For three months, all he did was hit against a board. "I just hit and hit for hours and hours," he related. The end result was that he greatly strengthened his wrists and forearms and, therefore, greatly increased his shooting range for basketball. He played number three singles as a junior, number two as a senior, and "turned into a respectable player" by his own admission.

As tennis ended, his lifetime dream came true—he made the Marion varsity basketball team. He was a Giant at last! However, he was going to face turbulence, because Bill Green had succeeded his father as head coach. Yes, it was the same Bill Green who had coached Indianapolis Washington to that memorable 61-60 state-finals victory over Marion in 1969. He still was so hated in Marion that people egged his garage and put "For Sale" signs in his front yard.

And Dave Colescott "didn't like him very much. He always said rednecks were going to rule the world, and he listened to country music. I was spoiled, used to my father. [Green] obviously was a great coach, but it was a totally different world. We had to make some adjustments."

Unknown to the sophomore guard, Green already had told his father, "I'm going to ride him. I want the other kids to feel sorry for him." Jack Colescott said that making an example of his son worked like a charm to build team chemistry. He explained, "He wanted the other kids to realize that Dave wasn't special. When they began to feel sorry for Dave, the battle was won. A couple times, reserve players came up to me and said, 'I don't know how he can stand it.' Bill was the perfect coach for him. He demanded a lot out of him and was a motivator."

Colescott scored eight points off the bench in his first varsity game against Wabash and "felt pretty good. The next Monday he [Green] went into me for fifteen or twenty minutes. He said, 'What are you ever going to do for Marion High School?' I had never been chewed out like that." Green described that practice scene this way: "He didn't pick up his man when I told him to. He said something smart back to me, so I sent him to the shower."

Still experiencing shock, Colescott went home and "told my dad I wanted to quit. I wanted to go to another high school and have him coach me. He said, 'If you want to quit, quit, but don't ever do that to me again.'"

Following a sleepless night, Colescott returned to practice. Green slyly told him, "I don't think we have to talk about anything, do we? After that, we became good buddies and still are today. You can't say he was a franchise because he wasn't tall enough (six-one). He was very smart, had a quick first step, and was a coach on the floor without question. They couldn't steal the ball from him. He made fewer mistakes even though he handled the ball 65 percent of the time. Game-wise, he was the best ball handler I ever had."

Of course, Green continued to ride his young star. "Bill made us run a lot of suicides," Colescott said. "He made me dribble the ball and beat all the big guys down the floor. I always thought I was just as fast with the ball [as without]. Sometimes he even made me dribble left-handed. I felt I was in great shape. I used to tell my teammates that I could run for days."

Green's constant prodding undoubtedly drove Colescott to elevate his game, because all he wanted to do as a youngster was simply make the varsity. He admits, "I was satisfied just being an average player at Marion High School. I never thought of myself as a star until my senior year. I got to be the player I became a lot because of his leadership. He was one of the best bench coaches I ever saw."

Colescott eventually became a starter and helped the Giants to a 13-11 record during his sophomore year. He averaged 13.9 points and handed out 54 assists.

During Colescott's junior year, the veteran Giants reeled off victories in their first 14 games and were poised to be named number 1 in the state polls when they were upset, 73-66, by Fort Wayne Snider. "We thought we were going to run the table," Colescott said. "But they wore us out." Marion then reeled off 14 more victories to finish with a sparkling 28-1 record and end 49 years of frustration by capturing the second state championship in school history.

It almost never happened, though, because Colescott was sick in bed with a 103-degree fever the day the Giants were to play bitter rival Oak Hill in the sectional tournament.

"I had the flu or food poisoning," Colescott related. "I had nothing in my stomach and had been throwing up for a day and a half. My dad already was at the gym, and I was in bed. My body ached. I told my mom to tell Dad I was not coming. She pulls me out of bed and takes me to the gym in my pajamas. I met the doctor there and stunk the place up, shooting four-for-thirteen for eleven points. I played about half of the game. I wish I would have fouled out, because I felt so bad."

The bottom line is that he got a crucial assist toward the end as Marion survived to win a 48-46 nail-biter. Even though it was miraculous that he played that night, Colescott had to endure taunts for a long time. He unhappily recalled, "Every Oak Hill person I'd see would say, 'We were a better team and you're not that good of a player.'"

This turned out to be a historic game for several reasons. Bill Green had not yet won even a sectional during his Marion tenure, and some of the natives were getting restless. A loss to Oak Hill possibly could have sent him packing. Now retired and playing golf practically every day in Florida, he can look back on being the only coach in Hoosier history to win six state basketball crowns. On the other side, frustrated Oak Hill coach Jack Keefer soon left for new Indianapolis Lawrence North, where he built a brilliant program that has produced four state titles.

It also marked the Giants' closest call in the entire state tournament. As he prepared to face Lebanon in the state semifinals at Market Square Arena in Indianapolis, Colescott recalled, "My sister [Linda] looked at me and said, 'You're pale as a ghost.' I said I was scared. I went back into the locker room and couldn't come out. It was the worst case of jitters I had in my life."

Colescott admitted to seeing nightmarish flashbacks of heartbreaking losses the previous two times Marion had reached the Final Four. But this time, he had to give Green his due. "Bill always was positive," he conceded. After the national anthem was played, Green said, "Time to go. Isn't this fun?" Finally relaxed, Colescott poured in 24 points and held Lebanon star Brian Walker to 2-for-12 shooting as the Giants rolled to a 73-65 victory. In the title game, Colescott contributed 10 points and his usual superb floor game as Marion defeated Loogootee, 58-46.

"I can't even describe the feeling," Colescott said of the moments following the championship contest. "All I remember is I never felt as good after a game. Let's do it again. It *is* fun." The team was greeted by an estimated 25,000 delirious fans on its return home.

Though all five starters scored at or close to double figures, Colescott still was the leader with an 18.7 average. He also set the pace with 129 assists and an .810 free-throw percentage, in addition to shooting 46 percent from the field.

Four starters graduated in the spring of 1975, but Coach Green still had his star "whipping boy" to build around. Interestingly, Colescott finally figured out what Green had been doing to him throughout his career. "My dad was probably just as much in on it as Bill," he acknowledged. "The middle of my senior year, I finally began to understand. I was loyal, but I thought he was hard on me. If the reserves felt sorry for me, they didn't consult me."

Leading an inexperienced lineup, Colescott faced more pressure than ever before "because of who I was and high expectations. It was hysterical. The crowds [capacity of 7,600 at home]. Tradition was the biggest pressure. Bill always tried to warn us of the fickle nature of fans. He never let us get too high or too low."

The pressure even spilled over into his everyday life at school. "People watched you," he related. "We couldn't go out to eat at lunch. But every day, the school parking lot was only about 25 percent full [during lunch]. One time I went out. The principal and vice principal saw me and called me into the office. They wanted to suspend me. I said to my dad, 'Go out to the parking lot. They bring me back pizza. Why can't I go out?' My dad said, 'I know.'"

Kenny Hill, editor and publisher of Marion's weekly newspaper, *Sports Hotline*, always cites a senior effort against Lafayette Jeff as the finest game of Colescott's career. He scored more than half of the Giants' points (37)—including the winning shot from 27 feet—and grabbed six rebounds in a 55-54 triumph.

In addition to Colescott, however, the Giants had another potent weapon—Bill Green's strangling match-up zone defense.

"Fundamentally, we were so sound," Colescott said. "The second year, it was the most important. The defense helped us stay close. Bill would make adjustments at halftime, and we'd take them out of their game. A lot of it was coaching. Bill did his best job of coaching that year."

There were plenty of land mines to navigate during the Giants' second straight march through the state tournament. The first obstacle was bitter rival Oak Hill in the sectional. Colescott had been waiting for an entire year to get even for all the snide remarks he had heard as a junior. The Oak Hill fans never had cut him any slack—or given him any credit—for heroically rising from a sickbed to help his team win.

Even though his brother-in-law, Glenn Heaton, was seated on the Oak Hill bench as an assistant coach, Colescott was primed, and wild horses couldn't stop him this time. At halftime, the Marion star had outscored the entire Oak Hill team, 29-18, and the final was a laugher, 86-51. He finished with a career-high forty-two points, and estimates that half of his baskets were from three-point range. "They are our most bitter rivals, and I wanted to make sure that they knew I wasn't as bad as they thought," he emphasized.

In the Fort Wayne semi-state, the Giants opened against unbeaten Anderson Highland, and Colescott couldn't throw the basketball in an ocean that day. "I think he missed ten shots in a row," veteran radioman Jim Brunner said. "Every time he looked at the bench, Green would put his hands up and tell him to keep shooting."

Perhaps because University of North Carolina coach Dean Smith was in the audience, Colescott felt like "there was a lid on the rim. I never looked at my dad [in the stands] very often, but he was shaking his head and yelling for me to stop shooting. It definitely was my worst game."

Finally, Green grabbed his shirt during a timeout and vowed, "If you quit shooting, I'll take you out!"

Well, the Giants' leader did keep firing and drilled a 25-foot bomb for a 56-55 lead with 1:04 left. Then he added three late free throws to provide a hard-earned 59-57 victory. He scored his team's final five points to finish with twenty-four, but shot only nine-for-thirty from the field. He also pulled down nine rebounds. That night, he scored 23 points and grabbed seven rebounds in a 69-66 triumph over Fort Wayne North to send the Giants soaring to the Final Four for the second straight year.

The state finals, again drawing a capacity crowd of 17,490 to Market Square Arena, also provided a pair of nail-biters. The Giants nipped Jeffersonville, 49-47, in the first round as Colescott accounted for 26 points and seven rebounds. Then he scored 25 points in the 82-76 title-game victory over Rushville.

"The feeling was different the second time," Colescott said. "It was probably more shock. It was a dream [the first time] before. Right after that, I was given the Trester Award [for mental attitude, grades, etc.]. I just didn't know what to say. I always thought that went to the losing team. The Trester means that you're a pretty good student and athlete."

The well-rounded Colescott carved out a 3.4 scholastic average and ranked ninety-sixth in a class of 700. He also is "proud that I never got a technical foul during my whole career."

The accolades for Colescott's brilliant senior performance still come from every corner. Brunner claims, "He was the whole team. He willed that team to the state championship."

Green says, "I don't know how we won. He was just everything. He never choked. If he had choked, it would have been all over."

Jack Colescott says simply, "With all the pressure he carried on his shoulders, he carried it pretty well."

The six-one, 167-pound guard led the 23-5 Giants with a 26.7 scoring average, 141 assists, and a .720 free-throw percentage. In addition, he grabbed 149 rebounds and shot 47 percent from the field.

Colescott finished his brilliant three-year career with 1,529 points, for a 20.1 average. He also had 330 rebounds and 324 assists while shooting .452 from the field and .742 from the free-throw line. The Giants compiled a 64-17 record during that era.

Not long after the state finals, Colescott was crowned Indiana's 1976 Mr. Basketball. "That was big, because Indiana is such a great basketball state," he said. "It was almost too much to have that all happen to one person in one year. It was like Utopia."

That great honor, however, proved to be both a blessing and curse, because Colescott was then faced with a gut-wrenching decision. He also was one of Marion's outstanding baseball players, but now he was forced to choose between the two sports.

In 1975, Bill Green had acquired a debt while taking an Indiana All-Star basketball team to Russia. So, the following spring, he scheduled several exhibition games around Indiana to pay off his debts from the previous year. That meant that he badly needed Mr. Basketball to lead the current team. Colescott was caught in the middle because the governing Indiana High School Athletic Association would not allow an athlete to play an outside sport while his current sport was in season.

Colescott had been one of the Giants' top two pitchers and a starting infielder for two years. "I didn't have the best stuff, but I had more heart and won every big game," he said of his mound prowess. "Kokomo always was a thorn in our side. My best game was against Pat Underwood [later a pro pitcher]. I hit the game-winning triple and was the winning pitcher.

"I think baseball was my best sport. I had played it since Little League. I didn't play as a senior. We probably would have won the state because they got to the semi-state without me. I kind of let my teammates down. It was probably my biggest disappointment."

Ever since he knew about college basketball, Colescott had expected to attend Purdue. "I was a Purdue fan," he readily conceded. "I went to their camps and football games. I loved Rick Mount. I always played well and felt comfortable there [Mackey Arena]. But they had four super guards, and I knew I wasn't better than any of those four."

The Colescotts received the dreaded rejection from Purdue assistant coach Bob King, who was equally disappointed. "I wanted to recruit him so badly," King lamented. "There was no question he was going to be a great player, an All-American-boy type. He directed traffic, and when they needed something, he could get the points. We had so many good guards at that time that we couldn't take him."

Enter famed North Carolina coach Dean Smith, who told him that he would never face as much pressure in Chapel Hill as he did in Marion. Colescott, now forty-nine years old, still agrees with that assessment. "High school is more intense than college," he affirms.

His career in the rugged Atlantic Coast Conference got off to a rocky start when he had to guard All-American guard Phil Ford every day in practice. Ford was fresh from helping the U.S. Olympic team bring home the gold medal, and had been playing nonstop for the past year. He was hobbled by bone spurs, so doctors slapped a cast on him—supposedly for eight weeks—at the end of August. After about half that time, however, he took the cast off.

"I'll bet you're glad you got that cast off," Colescott said to Ford.

The super guard shocked him with his reply: "Yeah, I'm going to try to play today."

Colescott reasoned, "Obviously, he's going to be hobbling around. I never had a spanking like that in my life. For two years I had to follow him around.

"He was unstoppable. He would take a long jump from the free-throw line to lay it up. I would play tight and he would go around me. The coach would blow his whistle and tell me to get off him. I'd get off him and he'd hit five straight jumpers. The coach would blow the whistle again. I never saw a more dominant player. He and Isaiah [Thomas] were the best players I ever guarded."

Adding to his rookie woes, Colescott broke his right foot early in the season. "I really should have been red-shirted," he believes. "I got hurt in the fourth or fifth game and didn't come back until the ACC tourney. It taught me a little bit more about humility. I never had sat on the bench. I learned something isn't going to be handed to you.

"Injuries hurt me throughout my career. I was concerned about knee injuries. Carmichael Auditorium had the hardest floor I ever saw. It felt like we were playing on concrete. James Worthy shattered his foot and we didn't know if he ever would play again. I was on the floor more than anybody, because I always was diving for balls. I got bursitis in my elbow. The Dean Dome [built later] was much softer. The shoes also weren't very advanced at the time."

Colescott's injury was particularly frustrating because the Tar Heels went all the way to the NCAA championship game before losing to Marquette, 67-59, during Al McGuire's final year as coach.

After chasing Phil Ford for two apprentice years, Colescott became a starter as a junior. While serving as quarterback and assist specialist, he averaged 8.7 points, 1.7 assists, and shot .520 from the field. He had a high game of twenty-one points against Cincinnati. During the ACC tournament, he shot a combined nine-for-thirteen in victories over Duke and Maryland, and made the all-tournament team. As a senior, he averaged 7.5 points, 2.3 assists, and shot .485 from the field.

For his entire career with the talent-laden Tar Heels, Colescott averaged 4.9 points and 1.5 assists, while shooting .490 from the field and .733 from the free-throw line. The Tar Heels were 98-27 during his career. Discounting the year he was injured, Colescott said, "Those were the best three years of my life, playing for Dean Smith, whom I really respected."

During his senior year at UNC, Colescott developed "jumper's knee. It really slowed me down. I needed surgery on my knee. I had two weeks to get ready for a tryout with the Utah Jazz. I made it to the last cut. They knew my knee was suspect. We played two forty-eight-minute exhibition games at Denver. They had me bringing the ball up court to see how long I would last. My knee was double the size. The next day, the Marion paper called and told me I had been cut."

He actually played part of a season with the Philadelphia Kings in the Continental Basketball League. At age twenty-three, he considered taking a crack at minor league baseball, but abandoned that idea because he was older than the man who would have coached him.

Utah offered him another tryout the following year. He was working out in Chapel Hill, playing one-on-one against Matt Doherty, when he broke his right ankle. "I was going to leave [for Utah] the next day," he sighed.

So, he took a job with Hanes Hosiery in 1982, and now serves as vice president of sales for sister company Champion Athletic Wear, based in Winston-Salem, North Carolina.

Colescott said he is grateful for the "God-given" ability he had in basketball. He is a member of the Old Town United Methodist Church in Winston-Salem, and says that the spiritual part of his life "obviously is very important. It's the cornerstone. It puts things in perspective and gives you a good outlook daily on life."

He and his wife, April, have been married for fourteen years. They have three children, Raymond, Ashley, and Jack. Ashley was a three-year starter in basketball at Winston-Salem's Mt. Tabor High School. Eight-year-old Jack—named in honor of his grandfather—is a third grader, who's just getting his tennis shoes wet in his dad's favorite sport.

Though Colescott travels several days a week, he always returns home on Friday to coach Jack's West Central League team at the Community Center. "He really likes it," the proud papa says. "He plays hard. His favorite player is [UNC sophomore] Tyler Hansbrough."

Colescott's place in history was firmly entrenched in 2002, when he was named to the prestigious Indiana Basketball Hall of Fame. "I didn't ever think that would happen," he said humbly. "It was a great way to cap it off and be remembered. Dad went in a few years before. I wanted to be like my heroes. I owe a lot to those guys who carried the torch before me, guys like Rick Mount. It's like a dream and words can't describe it."

MIKE CONLEY:
Premier Point Guard

Though he was born in Fayetteville, Arkansas, Mike Conley Jr. left an everlasting mark at Indianapolis Lawrence North as the finest point guard ever produced in Indiana high school basketball. He was a tremendous passer, ball handler, the best defensive player, and always the clutch guy when a big basket was needed.

Mike inherited great quickness and athletic ability from his father, Mike Conley, Sr., who won the Olympic triple jump in 1992. He also was a fierce competitor, but was so unselfish that he never blinked at playing in the shadows of seven-foot Greg Oden as the Wildcats tied all-time records with three consecutive state titles and victories in their last forty-five games.

All Conley really cared about was winning, and he was driven by a fiery spirit. Oden warned that no one should anger Mike "because he's the greatest player when he's mad. In open gyms, when he's mad, he cannot be stopped."

How valuable was Mike Conley? Well, the Wildcats lost only twice during his final two years—both while he was hobbled by turf toe as a junior. When he was healthy, they avenged both defeats. The LN coaching staff, to a man, thought Indiana's Mr. Basketball should have been a co-award, but it went solely to Oden.

When the six-one, 175-pound guard, along with Oden, signed with Ohio State University, Lawrence North coach Jack Keefer privately told Ohio State counterpart Thad Matta that Conley "is the best player I ever have coached." After all, he was the "Head," the player that longtime Marquette University coach Al McGuire always said a team had to "cut off to kill the body." Mike Conley orchestrated the greatest three-year dynasty in Indiana history.

Fort Wayne Snider guard Ryan Sims may have put it best when he said admiringly, "Mike does the little things that make big things happen."

Indianapolis North Central star Eric Gordon, who played with Conley's summer team, described him as "just like another Magic Johnson. Several times a game, he passes through two or three guys at the same time for a basket."

Conley acknowledged that many have perceived him as being Oden's "caddy," but emphasized, "It doesn't really faze me that much as long as I know the big picture—as long as I have faith in myself."

During the summer before Conley's senior year, longtime basketball camp and all-star game director Sonny Vaccaro put it bluntly, "Michael Conley is an All-American and no longer Greg Oden's caddy. His decision-making is the big difference. He understands and runs things so well. Players have faith in him. He is able to guide a team of superstars, and no egos are involved. His defense always has been tenacious. He has handled being the son of a great athlete and the teammate of a great athlete as well as anybody I ever have seen. He has formed his own identity."

Lake Oswego (Oregon) star Kevin Love played against the Hoosier greats at several major summer events. He said Conley "was what made their team go—Greg's partner in crime. He's a special athlete, a special kid. He would have been great, even without Greg."

Growing up in Arkansas, Conley developed an early passion for basketball and worked at it tirelessly. He was such a prolific shooter that he once poured in fifty-two points as a third grader. After that he began to maximize his other skills and thoroughly enjoyed setting up his teammates. His leadership paid huge dividends as he led his father's AAU teams to five national championships over the years.

Mike Conley Sr. called his son "a treat to coach, because he understands the game so well. He's obviously taken it to another level. If I was as good as him, I'd probably never run track again." Driving him to succeed, Mike Jr. related, was a desire to "be as famous and athletic" as his Olympic-champion father.

"I'd like to say I worked on specific things," Mike Jr. said of his formative years. "But for some reason I already had mastered dribbling, passing—things like that. It just all seemed to come naturally. I was just blessed to be given that talent."

Mike Conley was made for basketball-crazy Indiana and vice versa. He became a Hoosier in sixth grade when his dad took a job with USA Track & Field in Indianapolis. That summer, the heady point guard got his first look at Greg Oden, who was transported from Terre Haute to play for his dad's AAU team. Two years later, the Oden family moved to Indianapolis.

Conley and Oden became immediate varsity starters as freshmen at Lawrence North. Quarterbacking the Wildcats from day one, the rookie point guard—who could shoot equally well right- or left-handed—averaged seven points, dished out seventy-seven assists, grabbed sixty-four rebounds, and made fifty-eight steals. He shot 39 percent from three-point range. LN posted a surprising 21-3 record against tough competition despite its youthfulness.

The Wildcats rolled to a 29-2 record during Conley's sophomore year. This time, they went all the way to notch their first of three straight Class 4A championships with a decisive 50-29 victory over a Columbia City team which had taken them to double overtime earlier in the season. Mike finished with averages of 9.7 points, 4.7 assists, 3.7 rebounds, and 3.0 steals. He also shot 37 percent from three-point land.

Conley's junior year was marred by a foot injury, which caused him to miss several games in the middle of the season. During a 71-37 rout of Indianapolis Brebeuf, his shoe came off and he jammed his toe on the floor. Not realizing the seriousness of the injury, he played five games at what he termed "about 45 percent" efficiency.

Despite the injury, Conley put together a brilliant effort against highly regarded Fort Wayne Snider before 4,564 at the Fort Wayne Coliseum. With Oden in foul trouble, Conley exploded for twenty-one points, eleven rebounds, and nine assists as the Wildcats overcame a ten-point fourth-quarter deficit to win going away, 71-61.

The Wildcats were upset by Indianapolis Arlington, 70-60, as Mike played sparingly. Then he sat out the entire North Central game, which the Wildcats also lost, 69-63.

The Arlington rematch, played before a turn-away crowd in the sectional semifinals, created the stuff of legends. It was a thirty-two-minute war. The lightning-quick Golden Knights slapped on a suffocating full-court press, scratching and clawing from the opening jump ball. The referees let them play, so no prisoners were taken that night. They double-teamed everyone—except Mike Conley. "We knew that he knew when the trap was coming," Arlington star Deonta Vaughn explained.

"There was so much energy being used and exerted," Conley recalled. "It was a rough, physical game. Even though I was tired at some points and didn't want to bring the ball up, I knew they [Arlington] respected me, and it gave me confidence to handle the pressure. It was the most intense game I ever played in."

The Wildcats, who trailed at the half, 32-25, pulled away in the fourth quarter to post a 60-45 victory in what rightfully was billed as the state championship game. Rising to the occasion, as usual, Conley was high scorer with sixteen points, had three assists, and rarely turned the ball over during a masterful performance.

The state title game three weeks later was rather anticlimactic as the Wildcats defeated eight-time champion Muncie Central, 63-52, before a sellout crowd of 18,345 at Conseco Fieldhouse in Indianapolis. Conley led the repeat champs (24-2) with four assists. He also teamed with Trester Award-winner Brandon McPherson to play lock-down defense on the talented Bearcat guards, forcing them far out of their shooting comfort zone.

"I take a lot of pride in my defense," Conley acknowledged. "If they score, I take it personal." An innate sense of anticipation makes him doubly tough on defense and led to a school-record number of steals. "Michael stumbled into more steals than most guys get in a lifetime," quipped Lawrence North JV coach Joe Leonard. "He was phenomenal stealing the ball. It was as if people didn't even see him."

He is so smooth and shows such little emotion that at times he is accused of loafing. "It's just my personality," he explained. "I don't get too high."

Still, Conley insists, "The best part of my game is knowing how to win. Anybody could score thirty points a game if they were put in that situation. I do whatever it takes to win."

Despite his success, Conley "is the only person on the planet more humble than Greg [Oden]," according to McPherson. Adds LN principal Lynn Lupold, "He walked through our halls, and if you didn't know who he was, he'd have been just another kid."

After finishing his junior year with averages of 10.7 points, 5.1 assists, and 3.1 rebounds, Conley was ready for even bigger things.

In the late spring, Conley and Oden reported to the Spiece Indy Heat for their final summer campaign. They won nine games in two and one-half days to capture the championship in the twelfth annual Gym Rats Run 'n' Slam All-Star Classic at Fort Wayne, Indiana. Though he lacked big numbers, Mike was named MVP. In his usual humble manner, he said, "I don't know if I deserved it. The whole team played real well."

Two weeks later, Conley earned MVP honors as the Heat captured the Adidas May Classic in nearby Bloomington, Indiana. No Oden (he was visiting relatives in Buffalo, New York), no problem!

At the Reebok ABCD Camp in New Jersey, Mike outscored the nation's number-one-ranked rising junior, O.J. Mayo, 15-9. They guarded each other, and Mayo shot just three-for-thirteen from the field. Mike also had eleven points and ten assists in the all-star game.

At the close of summer competition, Clark Francis, publisher of the *Hoop Scoop*, called Conley "the clutch player of the summer ... who appeared to have ice in his veins as he made all the big shots in all the big games."

Mike Conley Sr. estimated that his son and Greg Oden played eight hundred games together during the spring and summer portion of their careers.

As his senior year opened, Mike amassed twenty points—drilling five-for-eight from three-point range—had four assists and three steals in a 62-33 victory over neighboring Lawrence Central.

Five games later, he had to step up his offensive output because Oden was sidelined with a swollen jaw from the previous contest. Fort Wayne Snider—ranked number three in the state—was a scary opponent, returning most of its starters from a team which nearly had beaten the Wildcats the previous year. All Mike did was pour in twenty-six points and lead LN to a shockingly lopsided 89-45 victory. Indeed, he could score when necessary!

The point guard supreme really made a big fan of coach Dave Weber when he helped the Wildcats beat defending Illinois Class AA state champion Glenbrook North, 79-61, at Northwestern University. He called Conley, who scored twenty-four points on ten-for-eighteen shooting, "the best player we've seen."

Perhaps for the only time in his high school career, Conley made himself the first option on offense early in the state championship game against surprise returnee Muncie Central. He bobbed and weaved and turned on the jets to score eleven points as the Wildcats raced to a commanding 24-7 first-quarter lead. Four of his buckets came on drives, one after a steal. He had sixteen of his twenty-one by halftime, and LN already held an insurmountable 50-24 advantage. The final score was 80-56, and it wasn't nearly that close. The reign of terror was over at last!

"He put us on his back," Oden acknowledged.

The Wildcats finished with a perfect 29-0 record and were unanimous national champions. Their average winning margin was an impressive twenty-one points.

During the four-year Oden-Conley era, they compiled a tremendous 103-7 record, including a 36-0 record at home. They tied all-time Indiana records with three consecutive state titles and forty-five victories in a row. (Had Mike not been injured as a junior, the win streak could have been sixty-four.) The toughness of their schedule during those years never had been rivaled.

Conley averaged 16.5 points, 4.1 assists, 3.8 rebounds, and 3.2 steals as a senior. During his career, he scored 1,157 points, while setting school records with 449 assists, 290 steals, and 126 three-pointers. He received long-overdue recognition when he was named to the prestigious McDonald's All-American team.

He credits his mother, Rene', for pushing him hard academically, resulting in a 3.5 scholastic average.

The Conleys attend First Baptist Church of Indianapolis. Mike emphasized, "My religious faith is important. I know that none of this would be possible without God."

JAY EDWARDS:

Mr. Clutch

Jay (Silk) Edwards was one of the greatest clutch players—and most underrated long-range shooters—in Indiana prep basketball history. He teamed with Lyndon Jones to spark Marion to three consecutive state championships from 1985-87, tying a record that had stood for sixty-five years.

"We sold out every gym we went to," Edwards said proudly. "We had a talented team that liked to run, liked to rebound and get the crowd into it. We were like the Beatles of high school basketball."

The six-four, 185-pound swingman scored 1,860 points for a 19.0 average, and the Giants lost just 4 of 89 games over 3 years. They were so dominant that they ran off an incredible forty consecutive victories from their sophomore year to almost midway through their junior year. Edwards and Jones befittingly shared coveted Mr. Basketball honors.

Jones, who knew him best, said, "Jay always was a great shooter and a clutch shooter. Whenever we needed a game-winning basket, Jay would take it and make it. He was the best ball player I ever played with."

"He had an incredible amount of confidence," said Jim Brunner, sports director for Marion radio station WBAT-WCJC. "He always wanted the ball. Any time, any game, whenever it was getting tight in the last couple of minutes, he wanted the ball. He was not cocky; he was so self-assured that he could always make the shot."

As a sophomore, Edwards drilled an eighteen-footer with one second left, to nip Fort Wayne Snider, 59-57. As a senior he went coast-to-coast in the last five seconds to sink another eighteen-footer and stun Richmond, 51-49. "He dribbled all the way, shot, and ran off the court [before the ball went in], because he knew it was going in," Jones said of the Richmond game. Continuing his late-game heroics at Indiana University as a sophomore, he drilled last-second shots to beat both Illinois and Michigan.

"I've been like that since I was a little boy," Edwards said. "If I was going to lose a game, let me lose it. When I did win a game, I never said I won it. When I lost it [such as a game at Purdue during his freshman year at IU], I took the blame. I'd rather me take it and miss it."

Edwards credits much of that clutch ability to watching an earlier Marion great, James Blackmon, and University of Louisville star Milt Wagner. "I liked his clutch play—how nothing seemed to bother him on the court," he said of Wagner. "I kind of copied his demeanor. He was cool and collected."

Former Marion coach Bill Green, the Indiana record-holder with six state titles, says, "They can talk about Rick Mount [Lebanon], but had there been three-point shots, he [Edwards] would be ranked very high. He was one of the best jump shooters I ever saw. He had a good follow-through. He was not that physical of a kid, but he knew how to slip and slide and lay the ball in. I didn't teach him very much because he just had it."

Though Edwards was spectacular at times, he was so smooth that often coaches didn't realize what he had done until statistics were compiled after a game. "You'd think he wasn't playing," Green said. "Then you'd look at the book and see that he was second high scorer and led in assists. I'd just say, 'Jay, we've got to get the next three or four rebounds' [and he'd do it]. He was a real quiet kid and I never had any problems with him."

Brunner called Edwards "an incredible outside shooter. At least two of every three shots he took would have been three-pointers [today]. When he let it fly, he had total confidence. You always remember his incredible slam dunks and triple doubles."

Edwards believes his picture-perfect jump shot "came pretty naturally," but it became lethal only after he gained strength, since he was "really, really skinny." Practice obviously was the catalyst because, as he put it, "I shot jumpers until my arm almost fell off. There is no shortcut."

During his high school years, Edwards outshot everybody, including Coach Green following practice. The local McDonald's restaurant gave Coach Green Big Mac cards, but he made his players earn them by beating him. The winner had to sink five in a row from just beyond what is today's three-point line. Jay added to his legend by once drilling seventeen in a row and winning thirty-three of those cards in one year. "I could sit there and shoot pretty good if nobody was in my face," he conceded.

Edwards also was a superb free-throw shooter—as a junior he drilled 103 in a row one day following practice. That talent was forced on him by older brother Jeff, who used to beat him consistently in games of "21" because he always missed his free throws. Again, practice made perfect.

Another Edwards trademark which really turned on the fans was his thunderous dunks. As a sophomore, he rammed home two spectacular dunks at home against Anderson, but the one against New Castle was deluxe. He grabbed the game-opening tip, took three steps, and dunked on Sean Alford. "The crowd was going crazy," he recalled. "I had my elbow over the rim. It was probably the best dunk I ever had. I was so excited that I missed my free throw."

Actually born in Muncie, Edwards moved to Marion at age five. "He always loved basketball," his mother, Rosemary Edwards, said. "He used to roll up his socks, take a coat hanger, and put it over a door. He was usually the tallest boy on his team—tall and skinny. It was always basketball, although he did play a lot of baseball. In high school, Bill Green didn't want him to play other sports."

At age six, Edwards began playing in the Police Athletic League, thanks to the guidance of director Randy Black, who used to transport him to practices and games. "He was just so dominant," Black recalled. "We used to play one-on-one, and I beat him all the time. One day [when Jay was twelve], I beat him twenty to eighteen and I never played him again." The handwriting, obviously, was on the wall that Jay was coming into his own.

In 1979, Black led his nine-and-ten-year-old team to the national PAL championship, with Edwards earning MVP honors. They won the title game by around forty points, and were so dominant that the losing team protested—claiming the players were too old. Not true, of course, but everyone was so amazed this team came from one city because most entries were all-star teams from a large area.

Overall, though, Edwards laughed, "We did a lot of losing. Teams that beat us when we were younger, we beat in high school."

Long a basketball hotbed, Marion also offered residents a Boys & Girls Club where they could play from ages seven through eighteen. Former director Mike McMillan describes Edwards as "always the more scorer-type kid. He had great leaping ability and was a great kid. If I compared him to any other kid, it would be James Blackmon. He was smooth, effortless."

As he got older, Edwards started going to the high school games and "finally realized the tradition that Marion had. They sold out most of their games."

Edwards, then a five-eleven point guard, led in points and assists as an eighth grader at Jones Junior High, while Lyndon Jones and two other future varsity starters were at Justice Junior High. The townspeople were ecstatic because they all sensed something great on the horizon.

"We never got big heads," Edwards stressed. "All we wanted to do was win. If we didn't win, we weren't happy. We saw a lot of close, heartbreaking losses [by the high school teams] and we said that it wasn't going to happen to us."

As a freshman, Edwards got into just enough varsity games to score thirty-four points, but the summer before his sophomore year, he attended the Five-Star Camp in Pittsburgh, and not only improved his play but also gained more confidence. "The confidence thing was really big," he emphasized.

In the fifteenth game of his sophomore year—a 64-63 upset of number-two-ranked Fort Wayne Northrop before 10,000 at the Fort Wayne Coliseum—Edwards noted, "We were number one, and after that, we knew we could win the state."

The Giants finished with a perfect 29-0 record, defeating Richmond, 74-67, to win the state championship. Edwards finished with a 15.4 scoring average. He also picked up a nickname which has stuck with him ever since.

Jim Brunner began calling Edwards "Silk" during game broadcasts, because he literally *was* smooth as silk on the basketball court. "I liked it," Edwards admitted. "Everybody else had a nickname. I think it fit, as far as my style of play. It stuck and it still fits. I didn't show very much emotion when I did something good or spectacular. I just wanted to win. I hated to lose."

Surprisingly, Edwards said their first state title "was not as exciting for Lyndon and me, because we had two more years left. We were thinking about the next year."

Edwards had begun playing baseball at age five, and continued to play through his sophomore year. He played shortstop, first base, and pitched. He had been the top hitter and RBI performer in Little League as a twelve-year-old, and as a freshman on the varsity JV team, he had shown some power with a pair of home runs. However, he gave up baseball at the start of his junior year.

The junior basketball season was quite a bit rockier than expected, as the Giants lost three games by a combined seven points before putting it all together. The losses were to Warsaw (which snapped a forty-game winning streak), 55-52; and back-to-back to Fort Wayne Northrop, 77-75, and Indianapolis North Central, 72-70. Edwards pumped in a career-high thirty-nine points and had four dunks against North Central. He estimates that he would have scored more than fifty points, had there been a three-point rule.

The sophomore title had been comparatively easy, but those junior losses "taught us a lot and kept that hunger," Edwards conceded. Coach Green also motivated his talented junior lineup by pitting them daily in practice against a JV team which went 19-1 every year the varsity was winning the state championship. To make it even tougher, he spotted the JV a 20-0 lead every time. "It wasn't like we could coast," he pointed out.

Following the loss to North Central, the Giants won their final fourteen games, including a 75-56 rout of Anderson in the state-title contest, to finish at 27-3. Edwards wound up with what would be a career-high 24.6 average. He also averaged 8.4 rebounds while shooting .528 from the field and .820 from the free-throw line. His high game was thirty-nine points.

Each summer, Edwards played with a Marion AAU team. They were playing the Russian Junior National team one night at Anderson when six-ten Shawn Kemp (Elkhart Concord) came down for a tryout. Coach Mike McMillan recalled that Kemp "shot zero-for-five from the field and fouled out in five minutes. Jay teased him in the locker room, and that didn't go over too well. Rick Fox jumped in too. Jay was kind of sly to rib you, but he got his points across. Kemp didn't make the team."

At the beginning of Edwards's senior year, the Giants were ranked number one in the nation by *USA Today*. They would have gone all the way had they not stubbed their toes one time, a 78-74 setback against Lexington, Kentucky, Lafayette on the road. "I wish we could have kept number one," Edwards said with regret in his voice. "That number-one ranking meant a lot to me. That upset me. The team that beat us was not that good."

So "Silk" took it out on the rest of his Hoosier opponents. The Giants won their last twenty-three games, including a 69-56 championship-game triumph over Richmond. Edwards never was better, exploding for thirty-five points and sixteen rebounds in his final high school contest. He averaged 21.4 points during his senior year as the Giants finished 29-1. He also shot .518 from the field and .750 from the free-throw line.

Looking back at the string of titles, he says, "It was incredible. It didn't really hit me until ten years later." Just as impressive in his mind was going unbeaten three straight years in the North Central Conference. "That's probably never been done before (or since)," he said. "That conference is, hands down, the best in the state." It would be hard to dispute, because each of Marion's state-title wins was over an NCC opponent.

Few people know that Edwards originally planned to attend the University of Louisville. "I already had committed to Louisville," he revealed. "It was basically between me and [Coach] Denny Crum. It was not in the paper. I just loved the Louisville basketball team. I had been to their camp three years in a row."

Indiana University also was among the dozens of major colleges recruiting Edwards, and about that time, he said, "I found out that he [IU coach Bob Knight] was really high on Lyndon, too. He said he wouldn't recruit over me. He said I would have the [Steve] Alford role. I would be in a system where I could use my talent."

Bill Green was in on the discussion when Knight visited. Knight later told him, "This is one of the best recruiting jobs I've ever done. These two kids really are going to make a big splash in our program."

But before he headed for IU, Edwards played in the Indiana-Kentucky All-Star series (scoring thirty-four points in one game) and then made a huge splash in the annual Back-to-School Tournament at Muncie. Jerry Freshwater recalled, "He scored seventy-three points in the championship game. They couldn't stop him. We had all no-name players, but we won four games."

Never having to lift weights in high school, Edwards was able to add 25 pounds at IU, to reach 210. After about a month and a half, he had a breakout effort, pouring in nine points in the closing minutes of a game against Notre Dame. "Dick Vitale [ESPN] said, 'Here he is. He's arrived,'" Edwards paraphrased.

"I thought they were so much bigger, stronger, and faster and it would take me a couple years," Edwards believed. "Once I got my confidence, I was off on a roll." He went on such a roll, in fact, that he finished with a 15.6 scoring average and was named Big Ten Conference Freshman of the Year. He led the conference in free-throw percentage, a sizzling .917, and three-point percentage, .571. His overall .908 free-throw percentage ranked number six in the nation. His high game was thirty-six points against Minnesota, when he set a Big Ten record with eight three-pointers (eight of nine).

Edwards was even better as a sophomore, averaging 20 points and 3.7 assists and earning MVP honors as the Hoosiers won the Big Ten title. "We were out-talented," Edwards admitted. "We should have been fifth or sixth. Coach Knight should have gotten Coach of the Year easily that year. He is a great coach. Without him coaching me, I wouldn't even have been Freshman of the Year or MVP. We beat Michigan twice and they later won the NCAA."

Despite his brilliant on-court performances, Edwards drifted into drugs. "I got into the wrong crowd," he related. "When you are a star, a lot of good and bad people want to be around you."

He totaled 1,038 points for an 18.2 average in his two years at IU, and then was bitten by the NBA bug. "I was young and everything was happening so easily," he explained. "In my mind, it wasn't going to be hard stepping into the NBA."

So he entered the draft and was the number-three pick in the second round by the San Diego Clippers. He got off to a rocky start when he injured a tendon in training camp. He added to his own miseries when he was caught with drugs and suspended for two months.

He believes NBA officials held his past against him because he "was already coming in with a mark—basically being a dumb, dumb, dummy. After the first year I never had a problem or flunked a drug test. I definitely had the talent." He averaged around eleven points during two years with the Clippers and then was cut.

An amazing twelve-year odyssey followed, during which he played in the Continental Basketball Association, then starred in such countries as Spain, Israel, Venezuela, Canada, and the Philippines. He estimates he averaged around eighteen points during his pro career.

Despite the continual language barrier, he "loved going to different countries. You get to see the world, too. The weather was beautiful in Venezuela. In Israel, the people took care of me. I hurt my Achilles and that was it. I retired at age thirty-two in 2002."

Edwards currently is selling cars at Luxury Motors in Downers Grove, Illinois. However, he returns to Marion as often as possible to watch his son, Jay Edwards, Jr., follow in his footsteps. The six-four junior is "getting better and better," according to his father. "He's more athletic than me. His dribbling has to get better. Right now he's a mid-major. If he really works at it, he could be big-time Division I. He's definitely big-time football. He had nine interceptions as a free safety."

LYNDON JONES:

A Born Leader

When Lyndon Jones was in seventh grade, he was moved to the point guard position on orders by Marion High School varsity basketball coach Bill Green. Previously he had been playing inside because he "was so much bigger than kids growing up," he recalled. "I was five-nine or five-ten, and I thought I was going to be a big man."

Green, who already had coached three state champions, made the astute move because he "knew that he wasn't going to be big. He handled the ball very, very well and he could go right or left real well. He also was a natural-born leader and took a lot of pride in it. He was the guy they [other players] listened to. I did the strategy and he did the chewing and beating up [on the floor]. I didn't teach him much, because he just had it.

"He was very, very close to David Colescott [who led Marion to state titles in 1975 and 1976]. He had more physical ability. He could jump a little higher, but was not as quick as David. He was able to take the ball one-on-one. David couldn't do that, because as a senior, he had to do it all. Lyndon had more talent with him."

Jones was flattered by the comparison to Colescott. He noted, "That's a great comparison. He did very well in high school and college, and is doing a fantastic job in the business world. He is a tremendous role model, and I always am happy to come back and help at Marion."

That magnificent leadership ability enabled Jones to quarterback Marion High to three consecutive state championships, tying a sixty-five-year-old record, then help Indiana University to a pair of Big Ten Conference crowns. Today, he is responsible for 300 employees as second-shift coordinator at engine-maker Cummins in Columbus, Indiana.

Playing at six-two, 180 pounds as a high school senior, Jones finished his brilliant four-year career with 1,711 points for a 15.1 average. His sharp-shooting teammate, six-four Jay Edwards, took scoring honors during the title years with 1,860 points. Together they formed a lethal combination—one of Indiana's best-ever one-two punches.

Edwards called his longtime buddy "a very strong point guard. He could get to his spot anytime and score. He was good on defense. He had the heart and desire to win. He knew when to give me the ball," he laughed. "It was always nice to know that if I had a bad day, I had him beside me. Without him, I'd probably have gotten 3,000 points. Without me, he'd probably have gotten 3,000 points."

WBAT-WCJC sports director Jim Brunner called Jones "the steady anchor for four years. He never made mistakes. Look at the tight games, and who had the basketball in his hands? He was not flashy or spectacular, but he was the real backbone of the team. He always lived by Bill Green's motto that they were living in a glass house. He tells kids [today] to put their academics first. He has really got a head on his shoulders."

The "glass house" image paid huge dividends for the triple state champs. "Everywhere we went in Marion, people knew us," Jones related. "Even outside the city of Marion, people would know us. It made you have self-awareness of what you were doing. And our parents did a good job, too. People still recognize us today, because people in Indiana love basketball."

Jones got his basketball start in the Police Athletic League at age six. His father, Alfonso, soon gave him the nickname "Smoke," which has stuck with him over the years. He explained, "My dad said my first step was so fast—like a puff of smoke." He didn't like it at first, because he thought people would believe he smoked cigarettes, but he admits, "It stuck and it grew on me."

Youngsters in PAL played on eight-foot baskets and used a somewhat smaller basketball. Director Randy Black remembered Jones as a little guy who just couldn't get enough court time. He said, "When other teams were playing, he'd run out on the floor [during timeouts or quarter breaks], pick up a ball and shoot. He couldn't stand seeing a ball out there and not shooting it."

Jones pled guilty. "It was just love of the game," he confessed. "It was always about trying to improve and get better. It was instilled in us—you were in the gym, so just work. Randy would chase us off the court. For punishment, he would get the brooms out and make us sweep off the floor."

The Marion Giants never seemed to run out of great basketball players. Jones's parents were season ticket holders, and he began going to high school games at age seven. "When you're growing up in Marion and love to play basketball," Jones related, "your childhood dream is to be a Marion Giant. You try imitating their games. There are three seconds left and you're Joseph Price ..."

Edwards and Jones were the same age as three other future Marion starters: Kyle Persinger, Eric Ewer, and Daric Keys. This group—all destined to play Division I college basketball—was so talented that it won the PAL National Championship for boys ages nine and ten in 1979. The PAL competition ran during the school year.

In the summer, the PAL players switched to the Marion Boys & Girls Club, where they were able to play in national AAU age-group tournaments. Director Mike McMillan said, "We could see that ball-handling skill he had. He could see the court well. We could see he was going to be a true point guard. He was very reserved, quiet, a good leader for the younger kids. They looked up to him. He was a team player, a very dedicated young man who always looked out for his community."

Of course, Jones had his own heroes. He looked up to Marion High stars such as James Blackmon, Joseph Price, and Morris Tyson. Jones said that the lesser-known Tyson "took me under his wing. During the summers, he would pick me up and work with me." Price and Blackmon took him to camps at Notre Dame and Kentucky, respectively. "James was bigger than life—a superstar to us," Jones said. "He put Marion on the [national] map. We wanted to be James Blackmon."

Great things were expected of this group, and the anticipation grew greater each year as they advanced in age. They were split in junior high, some going to Jones and some to Justice. When the two teams met, regular season or playoffs, they packed the gym, drawing standing-room crowds close to 1,500.

Junior high games would be plugged during varsity radio broadcasts and the Marion weekly newspaper, *Sports Hotline*, gave the youngsters plenty of ink. "From a young age, we had so much success," Jones noted. "After you get used to winning, that's what you expect. We really didn't feel the pressure. It's kind of crazy—just like it was meant to be. But we had people around us who kept us level-headed."

The "level head" definitely was needed, because when they were in eighth grade, these future Giants were given a large—premature—spread in the *Marion Chronicle Tribune*—against Coach Green's wishes. He got both junior highs together at Christmastime to put in some varsity plays and read them the riot act.

"Now I've got to tell them they're not very good," Green admitted. "I brought out every weakness I could. I said Jones was a little chubby. Jay was skinny. They took it well. I had control because I had a good reputation."

In the 1983-84 season, Jones started on the freshman team. "I was crushing people the first couple of games," he described. Shortly afterward, he was allowed to skip the JV team and go straight to the varsity, where he became a starter at mid-season. That made him the first freshman to start a Marion varsity game since Harold Curdy in 1961. He played in 25 games that year, scoring 115 points for a 4.6 average.

The next year, Marion's best-ever sophomore class joined forces with a few key seniors, and the result was a tremendous 29-0 record, and their first of three consecutive state championships with a 74-67 victory over Richmond. Jones, who really came into his own as a ball handler, scored 416 points for a 14.9 average. His best game was against Fort Wayne Northrop, a night on which he drilled nine straight shots. "I felt good, so I kept stroking it," he recalled. "I made a variety of shots, mostly mid-range."

"They got a lot out of their size and mobility," Green pointed out. "They were maximum every game. They never had a bad game. Our match-up zone helped a lot of these kids reach great heights. We got an awful lot of mileage out of it."

Green's match-up zone was so effective that even college coaches asked him to help them install it. "It was big," Jones conceded. "My role as a point guard was to play at the top of the zone and direct the ball in the direction I wanted it to go. I tried to send it to the weaker person. There were several variations. It was man-to-man and zone mixed together. I got a lot of my dunks that way. I would steal the ball and it was off to the races. For some reason, they [opponents] couldn't figure it out. We had smart ball players. We practiced it and perfected our roles."

It was the beginning of a golden era for the Giants. ESPN's Chris Fowler, who visited Marion three straight years, gave the Giants national publicity on his popular *Scholastic Sports America* show. "That was big-time," Jones affirmed. "The whole town was hyped about that. I can remember wearing one of my best sweaters the day we were being interviewed. It was a half-hour program and everybody taped it."

Looking back, Marion *Sports Hotline* editor and publisher Ken Hill says, "It was amazing, because Marion became the focal point of the national prep world. We were on *SSA*, in the *Christian Science Monitor*, and ranked number one in *USA Today* [preseason in 1986]." Bill Green even recalls being sent a Japanese-language U.S. magazine which included a story about his team.

The next year, the Giants' all-junior lineup won its first eleven games, extending the school's winning streak to a sizzling forty in a row. But then disaster struck—they lost to Warsaw, 55-52. "Looking back, it [the streak] did put extra pressure on us," Jones analyzed. "All Warsaw had was Rick Fox."

After two more victories, they were stunned in back-to-back games by Northrop (77-75) and Indianapolis North Central (72-70). Following the second loss, Jones knew he had to do some serious chewing out. "I felt the team slipping," he explained. "Nobody was safe at that meeting, from Jay on down. I told him, 'We need you to score, but to take good shots.' I remember going all the way around the room. Even the reserves were there. I told them, 'You need to get ready. This will be you next year.'

"It's not hard to be that person. On a basketball team, there's always a person to have that role. I just welcomed that role. I was groomed for that role from a young age. That's why I think I excel at that role now at work. It's hard to manage 300 persons."

The Giants obviously took their leader's words to heart, because they reeled off victories in their last fourteen games and won their second consecutive state title with a 75-56 victory over Anderson. Jones poured in 584 points for a 19.5 average, as the Giants posted a 27-3 record. He also shot an excellent .528 from the field.

The awesome string of titles never would have been possible, however, without Jones's brilliant performance during a heart-stopping 83-82 victory against powerful Michigan City Rogers in the Fort Wayne semi-state finale. He scored thirty-one points against Rogers after bagging thirty-seven earlier in the day during a 79-72 victory against Fort Wayne Northrop. "That was the time that I really shined," Jones said proudly. "We always thought that the Fort Wayne semi-state was the state championship because of teams like Michigan City Rogers, Northrop, Concord, and Warsaw.

"Jay was in foul trouble [against Rogers] and I said, 'Hey, I've got this.' I really took over. I didn't feel anybody could guard me. We were down about five points when Jay went out. I think I hit eight or nine shots in a row. You're in that zone and don't feel anybody on the court can stop you. I put my team on my back."

Edwards was quick to add, "Watching Lyndon against Michigan City Rogers was something special."

The Giants really were ecstatic when they opened their senior year ranked number one in the country by *USA Today*. However, after winning their first six games to raise their latest winning streak to twenty, they stubbed their toes in Kentucky, being upset by Lexington Lafayette, 78-74.

"We thought we were deserving of that [number-one ranking]," Jones said. "We were the best team in the country. Mentally, we thought that we automatically would win. Jay was in foul trouble and I couldn't get my rhythm going. It definitely hurt us [to lose the top spot]. I wish we could have done it over. Our main goal was to win our third state championship and go out with a bang, but it would have been icing on the cake."

Still, the veteran Giants recovered quickly and steamrollered their final twenty-three opponents. For the second time in three years, they defeated North Central Conference opponent Richmond in the finale, 69-56. Jones had his greatest year, scoring 596 points for a 19.9 average, and averaging 7.0 assists as the Giants finished 29-1. He shot a superb .583 from the field. Their three-year record was a dominating 85-4.

Now retired and playing golf nearly every day in Sebring, Florida, Bill Green still occasionally pops in an old tape of the Giants' three-year reign of terror. "I didn't realize we were so good," he said. "I was on the kids all the time. We did things that I don't see college kids doing."

Jones originally was "dead set" on attending North Carolina State, but when Indiana University's legendary coach, Bob Knight, showed interest, he began to waver. His thought process was interesting. "One thing that always was a goal was to be Mr. Basketball in the state of Indiana," he explained. "If I went to IU, I would help solidify myself [in the voting]. We [he and Edwards] really thought that way. Then we visited IU and realized their rich tradition.

"I always tried to think ahead," Jones continued. "If I graduated [from IU], that would help me in the next stage of my life. I would have that on my résumé. Coach could help. There have been a few occasions that I had to call on the coach and get his assistance. He always has been there for me."

Well, Lyndon and Jay realized their final high school dream by being named co-Mr. Basketballs. "It was special wearing that number one jersey," Jones said. "Your name gets called last. It definitely was even more [than he expected]. You get all that attention and people still remember you today."

Before they signed the IU letter of intent, Jones and Edwards were warned that Bob Knight would be super-tough. "To be honest, I was shocked," Jones admitted when he first reported to practice as an IU freshman. "You're eighteen, and he's not going to talk that way to me. He's consistent. It was like night (no pun intended) and day. Coach Green was laid-back. Coach Green is a player's coach. He would let me run practice. Coach Knight—it's his way. It was an adjustment."

The adjustment got even tougher when the Marion duo reported late for their first-game walk-through. The upperclassmen failed to tell them that they had to be EARLY. "When we got there, they were coming off the floor," Jones sighed. "We did not get to play, and then we had to run the Assembly Hall stairs. You definitely go through some trials and tribulations. As I look back, I can definitely respect what Coach was trying to do. I realize he had our best interests in mind."

One night, Jones and Edwards invited their PAL mentor, Randy Black, to attend an IU game, and later brought him into the locker room to meet Coach Knight. "This is the guy who taught us how to play basketball," Jones said.

"You did a lousy job!" Knight fired back.

"We knew he was just kidding," Jones claimed.

Jones started 15 games his freshman year, averaging 4.9 points and shooting 51 percent from the field. He had seventy-three assists. "I knew my role as the leader of the team was to get everybody involved," he said.

The next year was to be his best as a collegian and the last time he would play with longtime teammate Jay Edwards. The team was struggling early in the year. Jones had a breakout effort against Notre Dame, scoring more than twenty points and playing a strong floor game. That earned him a starting berth, and Coach Knight soon went with a three-guard offense. The Hoosiers then took off on a thirteen-game winning streak and wound up winning the Big Ten Conference crown. He averaged 8.4 points and 3.4 assists and started 29 games—all career bests.

As a junior and senior, Jones averaged 6.1 and 3.9 points, respectively, but was able to start only a total of 22 out of 56 games. The Hoosiers did share the Big Ten title his senior year. During his career he averaged 5.9 points and 2.6 assists while shooting .458 from three-point range and .767 from the free-throw line.

The game he'll remember most was one against Michigan when he was a sophomore. "Jay hit the winning shot," he noted. "They had missed a free throw. Eric Anderson rebounded and got it to me. Time was clicking off the clock. I delivered a bounce pass to him and he hit nothing but net with one second left. That was a key win to get the Big Ten title.

"Jay and I always had that connection. I always knew where he'd be and he always knew where I'd be. I would always know when to get Jay the ball. It was just a special relationship from all the years that we had played together."

Following graduation from IU in 1991, Jones played a year and a half in the CBA. A broken wrist spelled the end of his distinguished basketball career. He told his father, "I've had enough. I don't want to chase my dream anymore. I have a degree and I want to do something different."

So, he took a job with General Motors, which he held for almost eight years. He then moved to Savannah, Georgia, where he and his father opened a small trucking company, which his father still runs. He has held his current job at Cummins for the past year and a half.

Lyndon and his wife, Sophia, have two daughters: Lark, age six, and Lyric, age five. Both already are playing organized basketball. The proud papa says that Lark, who is quite tall for her age, "reminds me so much of myself. First starting out, she is really reserved and shy. She is really nervous because there are so many people there."

As long as Lyndon Jones is alive, he'll be attempting to give back for all that he has been given. He will be working with Jerry Freshwater, who currently is Marion High's head girls' basketball coach, each year at a summer camp in Marion. They grew up in the same neighborhood, though Jones was older.

"I looked up to Lyndon," Freshwater said. "You could see and touch him. He was my hometown hero. He treated us great, like our big brother. He helped and guided us. He made sure we kept out of trouble and kept us hungry to play for the Giants."

And so the cycle continues. As each summer camp comes and goes, many aspiring Marion Giants will be looking up to Lyndon Jones, much as he did in the case of a James Blackmon or a Joseph Price. And they could never choose a better role model.

GEORGE MCGINNIS:

The Franchise

A very strong argument can be presented that George McGinnis not only was the strongest teenager ever to play high school basketball in Indiana, but also the premier two-sport athlete.

Indianapolis Washington varsity basketball coach Jerry Oliver got a call one Saturday morning from his freshman coach, Howard Leedy, who was refereeing an eighth-grade game. He exclaimed, "Jerry, you've got to get over here! There's a kid you can't believe."

The "kid" turned out to be George McGinnis. "He was six-oh or six-one, but strongly built and so quick," Oliver recalled. "He broke to the top of the key, got a bounce pass, grabbed it with one hand, turned, took a drop step, one dribble and laid it in. I told him, 'Be a good student and person and you can make a living [from basketball].'"

"I remember him as a man playing with boys," said longtime Purdue University assistant coach Bob King. "He was so big and strong at an early age. He had size, strength, and agility. He did a lot of things that smaller guys did. He was a tremendous football player, too. He took advantage of the opportunities he had. He was already a grown man [when he turned pro after two years in college]."

Garry Donna, who has been editor and publisher of *Hoosier Basketball* magazine for thirty-seven years, noted, "He did something I never had seen happen in Indiana high school basketball. He cut so hard to the basket one time that his shoe exploded. He was an incredible physical specimen who had skill. He was the most skilled power player I've ever seen."

McGinnis is the first to admit, "I never lifted weights. It was all genetics. My dad [Burnie] was six-six and my mom [Willie] was six-oh." Despite his huge physical advantage, McGinnis insists he didn't use intimidation as a weapon. "I could see some fear in their eyes," he conceded, "but I never tried to use that. There was no psychological game—I just went out and played."

Longtime friend and teammate Steve Downing didn't exactly see it that way. He said, "Growling—intimidation—in high school was part of his deal."

Bill Green, who won a record six Indiana state basketball titles, coached McGinnis in his senior year at Washington and has been a believer ever since. Now retired and living in Florida, Green said, "He had the most talent of any kid I ever had—dexterity, agility, and strength. Our track coach tried to get him to run. He ran the 440 under 50 seconds in a pair of tennis shoes. That's how much talent George had.

"He was the all-around high school athlete. He could have done anything he wanted. He was not cocky; he was just good. If I was going to build a franchise, I would have to choose George McGinnis first over Oscar Robertson. I've gotten into a lot of arguments over that, but I stand by my guns."

Because McGinnis was such a dominant basketball player, his superb football talent has been somewhat forgotten. He actually made the prestigious *Parade* magazine High School All-American team in football and basketball.

McGinnis, who was a muscular six-eight, 218 pounds, and wore a size 14 shoe when he graduated from Washington High in 1969, started both ways at end for three years. The Washington record during that period was an excellent 26-3-1. His sophomore year, his 10-0 team was declared mythical state champion. He had an outstanding senior year, leading the Continentals to nine straight victories before they lost their final game. Despite playing on a running team, McGinnis made 22 catches for 418 yards and 6 touchdowns. He also made seventy-seven tackles.

Washington football coach Bob Springer recalled, "George, by far, was the most dominant player we had. He could catch the ball, block downfield, and play defense. He was so competitive, big and strong. He had no fear of anything. He probably was the most fearless player we ever had. He practiced just as hard as he played. He went all-out. He would kill our little guys [in practice], so we had to call him off."

"I was just so tall that they could lob the ball in the air and I'd out-jump everybody," McGinnis pointed out. "Coach Springer had as big of an effect on my life as any coach. He instilled a sense of toughness I didn't know I had. I was so big that I could get by on three-quarters effort."

Because his family was not well-off financially, McGinnis constantly had to battle his father for the right to play sports during his elementary and junior high years. "He was totally against it," George said. "He would raise his voice to my mother, telling her I should work. At sixteen, I did get a job with the construction company he worked for. I worked summers for two years. It was hard work. Man, I never felt in better shape. We had to carry ninety-pound boards for eight hours a day."

McGinnis got his basketball start playing pickup games at the famed Lockfield Gardens and Dust Bowl, which spawned the likes of Indianapolis Attucks superstar Oscar Robertson. "Oscar definitely was our idol," McGinnis said. "He was all everybody talked about. I assumed I was going to go to Attucks."

However, busing started while McGinnis was in junior high and his neighborhood was designated as part of the Washington district. "To me, it was a win-win situation," he said. "But it would have been really historic to go to Attucks."

An even more competitive place to play on weekends and all summer long was Meadowood in Speedway. "You could be out there all day if you wanted," McGinnis pointed out. "We went from daylight to dark. We would stay out there for four, five, or six games in a row, but you got so worn out that you were [finally] ready to get beat."

Steve Downing first got to know McGinnis when they were eighth graders playing pickup football in a park. "He was always the biggest guy and I thought he was too old," Downing admitted.

By the time McGinnis was a freshman at Washington High, he already stood over six-four. For much of his life, he had heard the whispers, particularly from parents of boys whom he dominated: "That kid is too big and too good—he's got to be overage." He tried not to let it bother him, and looked to his coaches as his role models.

That same year, McGinnis and Downing became basketball teammates. However, they first had to experience a few rocky moments. They were in a locker room when George spotted Steve's watch and grabbed it. "It was more of a prank," George insisted. "I had never had a watch in my life. I was six-four-and-a-half and he was only five-eleven [he grew to six-nine as a senior]."

Downing came out of the shower and saw what was happening. "You going to fight me over this?" McGinnis asked, according to Downing, who now is the senior associate athletic director at Texas Tech University.

Downing replied, "I'll have to, because that's my brother's watch. I had to swallow hard, because I had no intention to fight. He gave it back and my heart rate came down after that."

McGinnis admits today that he probably was bluffing anyway, because he knew that Downing had four or five older brothers who undoubtedly would have come head-hunting, had he kept the watch.

During his sophomore year, McGinnis met sixty-year-old Allie Dragoo, who was to become one of the most influential persons in his life. He was taking her speech class when one day, she pulled him over and said, "If you're going to be a big basketball star, you're going to learn how to speak."

He explained, "I had gotten on TV for the first time in my life after a big game. There's a camera and mic in my face, and I just froze. I said, 'Ah, ah.' She made me write speeches and told me there was no such word as *ain't*. I just loved her class. By the end of the year, she had me writing speeches and giving five-minute talks on persons or topics. I got a B-plus in her class.

"After I took her class, she still remained very close. We had a terrific relationship. She was just so proud of me. She would write me at IU and send me little care packages. She'd say, 'I think you finally got it.' Take all my coaches, and she played as big a role in my development as any of them.

"As a sophomore, nobody really knew me. She put her arms around me and embraced me. That's why I think it's so important to stay involved in this community. [He still lives in Indianapolis.] If I can help one person, I can make a difference. That's what made me want to serve."

On the court, George McGinnis was something special to behold from day one, because he combined his fantastic physical ability with an equally formidable work ethic. He related, "I would dribble left-handed, then right-handed until my hands got sore. I would shoot right-handed hooks, then left-handed hooks. Normally, big guys at that time couldn't do all of that. It really gave me an edge. I was a prototype guy—one of the first big guys able to put the ball on the floor, make plays, and play away from the basket. I loved contact, because football brought that out in me."

That all-important sophomore year also helped a dream to grow, because McGinnis was old enough to get his driver's license. McGinnis, Downing, Wayne Pack, and Jim Arnold would play evening pickup games in the off season. On their way home, they would detour to the famed Butler Fieldhouse—the legendary site of the Indiana state finals—stop in that vast, empty parking lot for close to an hour, and let their imaginations run rampant.

The Washington foursome would "broadcast" the state-championship game in which their team never failed to win. Whoever was doing the play-by-play at the moment, of course, always scored the winning basket at the buzzer. "I'm almost embarrassed to say that," McGinnis said sheepishly. "We took turns. We said, 'Man, we're going to be in there.' That's how important it [winning the state] was to us. It was just a big dream then."

Downing added, "[Butler] was the mecca. We had seen and heard so much about it. It was the mystique. They were all jump shots and the clock was expiring. That says something about our egos," he laughed.

McGinnis played varsity ball for Jerry Oliver until he took a job as an assistant coach at nearby Indiana University just before their senior year at Washington. Oliver, who had won the state title in 1965 with Billy Keller, admits, "I knew they had potential to win the state championship. If I hadn't won the other one, I wouldn't have done it for sure."

Under Oliver's tutelage, McGinnis got into fourteen varsity games as a freshman, but scored only nineteen points. He averaged fifteen points and eight rebounds as a sophomore and the Continentals compiled a 16-7 record. They were 24-3 during his junior year as his averages rose to a highly impressive 27.6 points and 21.4 rebounds.

Oliver noted that McGinnis "could do so many things kids six-eight at that time couldn't do. He had guard skills. We did not have strong guards. When we got pressed, I just said, 'Get the ball to George and get out of the way.' It was no problem. One-on-one, nobody could guard or stay with him. He taught me some things."

Enter Bill Green, who had been Oliver's assistant. He took over and replaced Oliver's strict man-to-man defense with a newfangled match-up zone, which was to be instrumental in winning an eventual six state championships.

But, wait a minute! Green also had been offered a college assistant's job for more money at Oklahoma State. Wisely, though, he turned it down and recommended John McLeod, who later became a distinguished head coach, not only in college but also in the NBA.

McGinnis, Downing, and company couldn't have been happier to have the young, easygoing, redheaded coach as their new leader. "We had good rapport with him and he was terrific," McGinnis said. "The match-up zone wasn't that hard [to learn], because the man-to-man was a lot tougher. The zone was really tough and drove people nuts. We [he and Downing] were like two redwood trees, trapping people in the corners."

Despite a new coach and a new offense, the talented Continentals were on a relentless mission because of their failure as juniors. With their state-title dreams a possible reality that year, they were upset in the regional finals, 72-60, by Indianapolis Shortridge.

"We were cocky, because we had beaten them earlier," McGinnis admitted. "We felt we had let ourselves, our coach, and our school down. That was a long summer. We were determined. The next year we never, never let up. We were just pounding them. Our average winning margin of victory was around twenty-seven points a game."

Whenever Green thought practices weren't intense enough, he put McGinnis and Downing on opposite scrimmage teams. "They called them apples games," according to Carolyn Sfreddo, whose husband, Basil, was the assistant coach that year. "The winners got the apples. Those were the best games in the state of Indiana that year. It was Katie bar the door. It was war. They almost came to blows. That's how they kept their competitive edge."

McGinnis exclaimed, "Talk about competition! I never liked to lose. We [his team] did not win many of those scrimmages. [Downing] was relentless. We played tennis when we were in our forties and I'd beat him. He'd get mad and go home. He'd call me later and apologize. He usually played second fiddle, but I never saw any jealousy. He did it with class and grace. He was just as important to the team. All he wanted to do was win."

They apparently formed a mutual admiration society, with victory being their ultimate goal. Take no prisoners. "I always liked that he wanted to win," Downing praised. "At halftime of games he'd grab guys' shirts and try to get them motivated to play because we were so far ahead. George wanted to play. Even if we had a forty-point lead, he'd ask Coach Green to put him back in.

"He was one of the greatest. I played against him every day in practice. I was smart enough to know if I could play [well] against him, I could play against anyone. He was absolutely the most talented person I ever played with."

Mrs. Sfreddo was a keen observer of the basketball scene during the McGinnis years and noted, "Every young lady had her eye on George, because they knew that he had a special future."

She used to make chocolate chip cookies, laced with butterscotch chips, and George couldn't get enough of them. He ate so many of them, in fact, that she gave them a special name: the Big George Cookie.

Chewing up opponent after opponent, the Continentals roared into perhaps the greatest Final Four ever as their dream approached reality. The four teams combined had an incredible 110-1 record. The field included the number one, two, three, and five teams in the final state poll. Number five Gary Tolleston, which had lost to an out-of-state team, had the only blemish on its record. No Final Four—before or after—ever matched this glittering record.

Washington drew the Marion Giants in the semifinals and, shockingly, trailed by ten points (56-46) with six minutes left. With their dream about to go up in smoke, McGinnis recalled, "Coach Green said, 'Pick 'em up full court.' Every play we just dogged 'em. It was a tremendous comeback and we sneaked by those guys [61-60]. They actually outplayed us and deserved to win that game. To me, that was the best team Marion ever had."

The Continentals then put Tolleston away at night to complete their three-year quest, though the final score (79-76) was not indicative of their dominance. "We had the game under control," McGinnis said, "but not the last two minutes." After scoring twenty-seven points against Marion, Big George was at his dominating best in the finale, amassing thirty-five points and twenty-seven rebounds as he pulled down the curtain on a magnificent high school career. Washington finished with a flawless 31-0 record and still ranks among the greatest teams in Indiana history.

Despite his numerous college and pro honors that followed, McGinnis still affirms, "There was nothing like taking a ride on that fire truck around the Circle and then the bonfire. The whole state tuned in. That was the greatest feeling I think I ever had, and I never recaptured that feeling at any level."

When the numbers were added up, McGinnis had probably the greatest year ever—up to that time—by a Hoosier basketball player. He poured in 1,009 points (still number three in state history) for a lofty 32.5 average and was second on the team with 120 assists. His field-goal percentage was an excellent .540. He also averaged a superb 21.7 rebounds. His only flaw was free-throw shooting (.581). He had high games of fifty-four points against Lawrence Central and thirty-three rebounds against Southport.

McGinnis totaled 2,075 points and 1,638 rebounds during his brilliant career, and broke all of Oscar Robertson's Indianapolis city records except for his one-game mark of 62 points. He was named National Player of the Year by *Basketball News*.

"I had read everything ever written about [Robertson]," McGinnis related. "I watched him on TV when he was in the NBA. He was so smart and the basketball looked like it was on a string when he handled it. I met him personally when I was a senior. We were at a function at City Hall. I've still got a picture of me and Oscar standing behind the mayor's chair. Just being mentioned in the same breath was amazing."

Told that Bill Green still rates him over the great Robertson, McGinnis replied humbly, "I don't know about that. I was a lot bigger, but it would be hard to take anybody over Oscar."

His name again was linked to Robertson when he was crowned Indiana's 1969 Mr. Basketball. "It was tremendous," McGinnis said. "It was the only thing a kid could look forward to except the *Parade* magazine All-American team. It was the dream of every kid in Indiana."

Throughout their hectic senior year, McGinnis and Downing were being hounded by college recruiters. Carolyn Sfreddo recalled, "The kids would come out the back door of the gym. I had a little Nash Rambler. They were a sight, with their knees almost under their chins. I would take them for hamburgers at White Castle."

McGinnis actually had well over 200 college scholarship offers for football, but he and Downing quietly had planned to attend nearby Indiana University since their junior year. When Jerry Oliver left the previous year, he said he was confident that his twin towers would be back with him soon in Bloomington.

But before McGinnis moved on to college, he had one more mission: defend his state's honor in the annual Indiana-Kentucky All-Star series. In the first game—a 91-83 Hoosier victory—he had "only" twenty-three points and fourteen rebounds, prompting Kentucky player Joe Voskuhl to tell media members that George was overrated. Those numbers, of course, would constitute a career day for thousands of players.

"What had happened," McGinnis explained, "was that there had been so much buildup, comparing me to Oscar, etc. That kid fueled my fire. The next week, we were goofing off in practice and our coach, Angus Nicoson, threw a chair across the room. It was extra motivation."

McGinnis was so sky-high for the second encounter that ... well, let him tell the story. "I was wearing Chuck Taylor Converse shoes. I was six-eight, 218 pounds, and was really sweating. It was so hot in Freedom Hall. All the players were starting to cramp up. I made a cut and—boom—one of my shoes literally exploded. It was like a shotgun went off. I had to borrow a shoe [from one of the reserves] to finish the game."

What remained of that shoe apparently became a collector's item, because in the summer of 2006, McGinnis was playing in a golf tournament when a man from southern Indiana offered to give what was left of his size-fourteen-and-a-half shoe back to him. He declined.

Despite the stifling humidity, Big George wound up pulverizing the Bluegrass boys to the tune of a game-record fifty-three points and thirty-one rebounds, and the Hoosiers romped to a 114-83 victory. Now prepared to eat his share of proverbial crow, Voskuhl was one of the first to shake his hand. He told him, "I take back everything I said about you. You're the greatest player I've ever seen."

"A few years back, he called me," McGinnis related. "What a great call. We laughed about it."

McGinnis still was cramping up on the long drive home, and had to ask his father to stop the car every twenty or thirty minutes to let him stretch out his legs. That long ride home from Louisville is frozen in George's memory forever. His father, who once screamed at his mother for buying him a pair of tennis shoes, "was so proud of me," George recalled. "I finally had won him over. He said, 'Man, if you ever make the pros, I want a Cadillac—no, I want a helicopter.' That was one of the best games I ever played and the last game he ever saw," McGinnis said sadly. His father died two weeks later after falling six stories from a scaffold.

Due to freshman ineligibility, McGinnis sat out his first year at Indiana University. He warmed up for the varsity the following summer by leading the U.S. in scoring and rebounding at the 1970 World University Games in Torino, Italy. Then he took the country by storm as a sophomore, averaging 29.9 points for number 4 in the nation as the Hoosiers posted a 17-7 record. He also ranked twelfth in the nation with a 14.7 rebound average.

It was one and done for McGinnis, however, because he declared hardship at the end of the season. He received a $15,000 signing bonus from the Indiana Pacers of the American Basketball Association and put a down payment on a house for his mother, who still lives there. "It is well-kept and she is so proud of that house," George said. "I've tried to get her out [to a newer house], but it has sentimental value."

After McGinnis had declared hardship, Indiana hired Bob Knight as its new basketball coach. Steve Downing couldn't help but summon up visions of a televised college basketball game they had watched while being recruited in high school. West Point was playing and its coach, Bob Knight, had just drawn a technical foul. He told me, Downing said, "Hey, wherever we go to college, I don't want to play for a guy like that."

Now Bob Knight was in charge at Indiana. "He came on the campus and he never talked to George," Downing said. "I had talked to Coach Knight and I knew he was going to be good. I tried to convince George to talk to him because I thought he could help him."

They never actually did meet until George was in the latter stages of his professional career. Downing brought him to a game and they went into the locker room. "Coach Knight was reading a book," he said. "He never looked up. When he stood up, he was bigger than you would think. He never smiles. Finally, he says, 'McGinnis, glad to meet you,' and they shook hands."

Today, McGinnis says, "We've got a great relationship. I think he finally understood that I didn't want to see my mother struggle for two more years. I've been to Texas Tech several times and to Kansas to see his teams play. He has had me talk to his teams over the years."

Downing adds, "Coach Knight has made him so much a part of his family. But he can't tell when Coach is kidding. It gets his blood pressure up."

Similar to his splashy college debut, McGinnis walked into the professional ranks and very quickly became an impact player, even though the Pacers were a veteran outfit. "I walked in pretty wide-eyed," he conceded. Still, he had to fill a reserve role for only about the first third of his rookie year before he became a regular. He wound up averaging 16.9 points and 9.7 rebounds, was named the 1972 ABA Rookie of the Year, and the Pacers won the ABA championship.

That summer, George took on a new role: physical therapist to Steve Downing, who had knee surgery as a junior at IU. "He had a boat and took me out all summer," Downing said. "He would throw me off the end of the boat. Water therapy was good and helped me rehab my knee."

George added this little footnote: "He didn't really want to go in, but he was going in!"

McGinnis said that during his rookie year, he "learned so much. The second year, I was pretty confident and we repeated our title."

It wasn't long before an *Indianapolis Star* sportswriter tabbed George as the "Baby Bull." He confided, "I didn't like the name, but it got pinned on me. Slick [Coach Bob Leonard] had a nickname for all of the players. He called me Jiff. To this day, he never calls me George."

Even on the professional stage, McGinnis was a powerful force. He once bent a steel rim in Denver, delaying a playoff game for twenty minutes. "They presented me the rim, but I never kept it," he laughed. Despite his size (six-eight, 235), he consistently won all the sprints at the Pacers' training camp.

McGinnis's biggest problem in the pros was drawing charging fouls. Because he was so famous for his strength, smaller players tended to fall down whenever he got near them, especially on fast breaks. The champion "flopper" of them all was George Karl, who later became an NBA head coach.

"It was frustrating," McGinnis admitted. "Karl was a tough, hard-nosed kid who didn't back down to anybody. One night, he drew two charging fouls on me. I was so mad. I got a rebound and headed down the court. All I saw was him. I knew I could get by him, but I slowed down and knocked him into the third row of the bleachers. I handed the ball to the referee and said, 'Now that WAS a charge!'"

In 1975, McGinnis flashed his all-around brilliance and shared MVP honors in the ABA with Julius ("Dr. J.") Erving. He was the league's leading scorer at 29.8, third in assists (6.3), fourth in rebounding (14.3) and in three-point percentage (.354).

"That was my greatest year," McGinnis said proudly. "[Erving] was playing for Virginia and was kind of the star of the league.

We were rivals but friends. Our league was built on a shoestring budget. We knew we were all in this together. The NBA thought we were a joke."

Joining the Philadelphia 76ers, McGinnis left no doubters as he made first-team all-NBA in 1976. In 1977, teaming with former rival Julius Erving, he helped the 76ers reach the NBA finals. He later played for the Denver Nuggets and returned to the Pacers to finish out his career. He scored 9,545 points for the Pacers and set club records with single-game highs of 58 points and 37 rebounds.

The Pacers have retired his jersey, number 30, and it hangs proudly today from the Conseco Fieldhouse rafters. "I feel pretty good," McGinnis said. "It finally hit home when a guy said, 'Even after you're gone, nobody is ever going to wear that number.'"

Over the years, McGinnis has enjoyed such activities as water- and snow skiing, breeding horses, and even competing in barrel racing. "I finally figured out that all my horses were becoming swayback because I was so heavy," he analyzed.

McGinnis has his own company, GM Supply, which deals heavily with the automobile industry. He also is extremely active in community affairs throughout Indianapolis and the entire state. His name constantly is linked to such charitable institutions as the Muscular Dystrophy Association, the March of Dimes, and Meals on Wheels.

In addition, he has served as co-chairman several times to help Indianapolis land the NCAA basketball championships; is chairman of the Governor's Council for Physical Fitness; he helps formerly incarcerated people find jobs; and he also helps out with the Boys & Girls Club. "I'm probably involved with every organization that has something to do with kids," he said. "I've always got some meeting to attend."

Indiana governor Mitch Daniels watched the towering McGinnis and Downing demolish his Indianapolis North Central basketball team when he was a senior. "We'd just never seen anything like it," he admitted. "It was almost like watching a tip drill. Even at that age he was so far beyond anybody else.

"We've become friends in a variety of ways. He's been a great citizen of the state. He's lost a lot of weight and looks great. George steals the show [on fitness TV ads]. He's a ham. By chance we live in the same neighborhood. When you're with him you wouldn't know you're with a Hall of Fame player. He's still much in demand. I try to be sensitive and not ask too much of him."

The fifty-six-year-old McGinnis, who is a member of Friendship Baptist Church, continues to give back. "I've always been a firm believer that you don't ever forget where you came from," he summed up. "The things you are given, you give back two-fold. I've been blessed. I really have."

RICK MOUNT:

Picture Perfect

The Scripps Howard News Service once took a poll of thirty current and ten former college basketball coaches to find out who they believed to be the greatest outside shooter in history. Rick "The Rocket" Mount was the number-one vote-getter. There's no doubt that the Lebanon legend had the prettiest, most lethal, picture-perfect jump shot ever seen in the sport.

"Rick Mount was the best shooter I ever saw in my life," longtime Purdue University assistant coach Bob King affirmed. "Rick had the advantage of being able to shoot over people. He had great spring, and that was really important. He developed shooting into a science. He'd shoot 500 shots a day and he still does it."

"He not only was an excellent shooter, but he was a lot bigger [at six-four] than most guards at the time," explained Billy Keller, who teamed with him for two years in the Purdue backcourt. "He shot the ball really high—like he was six-seven—and faded away. He probably came off screens better than anybody I've ever seen. He shot before anybody could get to him. Steve Alford was really good coming off screens, but he used a lot of them. Rick only needed one."

As an assistant coach for fourteen years at Indiana State and St. Joseph's College, Jerry Hoover rarely traveled the main highways when he was scouting a high school player. He loved to take the back roads, find a small store where a few old-timers congregated every day, and after making friends, get the inside scoop on the player he was going to see.

Just before walking out the door, however, Hoover would casually comment, "Hey, you guys are pretty knowledgeable about basketball—who was the best shooter in Indiana history? They all said 'Rick Mount.' When I asked who was second-best, they'd give three or four answers."

The most surprising thing about Mount's jump shot is that nobody taught him how to shoot. He started at around age five by shooting a tennis ball into a bottomless cashew can which was nailed to his back porch. He then moved inside to a bent coat hanger and net which was placed inside a door jamb. "I cut up my dad's fish net and got a spanking for that," Rick recalled.

Later he moved his fish-net basket into the garage, and this was the true beginning of his picture-perfect jumper, because he had to launch his tennis ball over the high beams. "It got me jumping and lifting," Mount explained. "It was lift, jump, extend, and follow through. I never shot much on a ten-foot basket until I was in fourth grade. I had an eight-footer on the garage, but only used a volleyball. By ninth grade, I had a jump shot from anyplace on the floor."

Rick's love for basketball came naturally. His father, Pete Mount, a wiry six-three center with great moves, had set many school records while leading Lebanon to state runner-up honors in 1943. After serving in the U.S. Army, he played briefly for the Sheboygan Redskins in the National Basketball League, the forerunner of the NBA.

"What got me fired up," Rick related, "was that dad had a silver ring [from the state runner-up team]. When I was seven or eight years old, I'd get it out of his jewelry box and put it on. He caught me one day looking at it. He just jumped on me, got right in my face, and I thought he was going to whip me. He said, 'You don't deserve that!'

"Two weeks later, I got it out and there he stood in the bedroom door. It was the same stuff. Here, you take your ring! I'm going to get the gold ring. He didn't say another thing. Down the road, I know he was just prodding me to be a competitor. That drove me to beat him and just play, play, play."

And play he did. His fifth-grade games drew up to 1,000 fans—some from as far away as 100 miles—as his fame began to spread throughout Central Indiana. Everybody, it seemed, wanted to get a firsthand look at the phenomenal son of the great Pete Mount. His grandfather, John Mount, heard a fan say, "Pete's son could be a pretty good player." To which John quickly replied, "He's going to make everybody forget Pete Mount!"

The Mounts also bonded through their love for hunting and fishing. John and Pete often would take young Rick so he, again, could serve as an apprentice. "They'd take me rabbit hunting," Rick recalled. "I'd always have to carry the rabbits. They'd shoot them and I'd carry them."

On the basketball court, father and son would go at it tooth and nail when Rick was "around eight or nine. He'd beat me and I'd go inside crying. I was real competitive and hated to lose. In the summer, I knew what time he got home. I'd wait on the porch with my ball. I finally beat him, and that was the last time he played me."

Rick averaged between eighteen and twenty points, and his elementary school team lost just once in two years. He averaged twenty in junior high, with a high game of twenty-eight, playing six-minute quarters.

His parents divorced when he was in seventh grade. Admittedly shy and somewhat of a loner because he had no brothers or sisters, he pointed out, "I spent a lot of time by myself. I didn't want highs or lows in the game. I wanted to stay at a relaxed level. You've got to keep your emotions in check. There's too much emotion out there. Inside, I had high intensity."

These circumstances, which shaped his life, caused some people to view him as rather aloof and anti-social.

Looking up to such superstars as Oscar Robertson and Jerry West, Mount was prepared to begin earning his niche among the greats as he approached his freshman year at Lebanon High School. His career was aided greatly by a new coach, Jim Rosenstihl, who saw immediately that Lebanon Memorial Park needed a major facelift.

The park was the spawning grounds of Lebanon basketball, but it was in disarray. Rick described the setup as "two bars, a wooden backboard and playing on dirt." Rosenstihl, who later staged outdoor tournaments which drew as many as 4,000 fans, eventually built two lighted courts, complete with bleachers and an electric scoreboard. It was first class, indeed, and attracted great competition for his players from throughout the state.

Mount had not yet played his first varsity game when Rosenstihl took him to demonstrate shooting at a coaches' clinic in Huntington. A mixture of 500 high school and college coaches sat there amazed as the freshman guard went through the Tigers' one-minute drill with incredible precision. From twenty feet, he would take one dribble and shoot. He made his first eight shots, missed two, and then drilled his final twelve for a mind-boggling twenty-of-twenty-two performance. "I was a little nervous at first," Rick conceded, "but I ran that drill every day in practice."

In his first varsity start, he battled jitters, but finished with twelve points against Brownsburg. His debut was good enough, though, to ensure that he would never be held under double figures in four years with the Tigers. The next game, at home against Crawfordsville, he shot 11-for-18 from the field, scored 24 points before a standing-room crowd of 2,300, and he was off to the races.

During the sectional tournament that year, Mount exploded for twenty-four points in the first half against Granville Wells. In the second half, however, he got only four shots. Years later, a teammate told him about a halftime discussion during which several players agreed that "Mount is getting too much publicity. It's Rick Mount, Rick Mount, every time we pick up the paper. We're not going to pass to him in the second half."

"There was a lot of jealousy," Rick admitted. "The publicity came back to bite me and kind of bit our team, too. It happens to a lot of really good players. It was bad, too, with my classmates. I could have been in a fight every day."

Still, Mount completed a sparkling freshman year with a 20.4 scoring average and a high game of 30 points against Anderson Madison Heights, as the Tigers posted a 16-6 record.

During the summer leading to his sophomore year, Mount took a job as a lifeguard at Memorial Park. He would work an hour and be off an hour. With his favorite outdoor court beckoning just 150 yards from the pool, he decided to ask a junior high student, Joe "Joby" Roberts, to rebound for him. The reward: a nickel ice-cream cone for one hour's work. A second round later on would earn another cone for an additional hour.

"Two sessions would cost me a dime and I'd get 400 jump shots," Mount related with relish. However, it wasn't all that peachy in the beginning. "The first time he was really bad," he moaned. "He'd throw it behind me and at my feet. I got mad and really got in his face. He started crying and took off. The next day his mom thanked me and (eventually) he got really good at it."

That was just the preliminaries, of course, because Rick still would play three or four hours every night against top-flight competition. The park was a magnet and a great proving ground. He met each challenger head-on and never backed down. "Guys would come from all over," he noted. "We'd have three, four, or five teams standing there from out of town. Some were college players."

That same summer, he received his first visit from a college coach, well-known Bruce Hale from the University of Miami (Florida).

During Mount's sophomore year, he was dubbed "The Rocket" by his future father-in-law, Richard Cadger. "I guess it was because I had a high-arching shot and when I left the floor, I exploded so quickly," Rick explained. Whatever the reason, the nickname was perfect and permanent.

To neutralize double-teams, Rosenstihl began starting Mount at the high post, and from there he could move outside. The new offense helped him raise his scoring average to 23.6 points (high of 32 against Tipton) as a sophomore, and the Tigers compiled a 20-5 record. He shot .490 from the field and .763 from the free-throw line. Purdue later used some variations of that same offense.

That summer, Bruce Hale paid his annual visit to Lebanon. Rosenstihl enjoyed promoting basketball, and Hale helped him schedule a game at Butler University against New York City's Power Memorial High School and its famed seven-foot center, Lew Alcindor. IHSAA commissioner Phil Eskew gave his blessing, and thousands of tickets were sold. It was being billed as the mythical national championship contest.

However, just a few weeks before the game was to be played, a story appeared in the *Indianapolis Times* that questioned why Lebanon—and no other Hoosier school—was able to play a game of this magnitude against a team from a faraway state.

"Phil Eskew kind of lost his backbone and canceled the game," Mount said. "It would have been a great game. It was sold out. Rick Mount vs. Lew Alcindor. We were ready to play the number-one team in the nation." Instead, the Tigers played Lafayette Jefferson and carved out a wild 109-89 victory.

Mount received a surprise visit during his junior year from former Purdue All-American Terry Dischinger, who was playing in the NBA at the time. The big guy wanted to play some one-on-one, and the competitive teenager never passed up a challenge. The Rocket scored well on his patented jumpers, while the six-foot-seven Dischinger was quite effective backing him in and lofting baby hook shots. "I won a few and he won a few," Rick said. "I wondered why he was there. Probably Purdue asked him to do that."

In back-to-back games as a junior, he scored a record fifty points against Danville and forty-three against Indianapolis Attucks, the school which spawned the great Oscar Robertson. The Tigers posted a 15-6 record and his average soared to 33.1. He shot a sizzling .505 from the field and .854 from the free-throw line.

The following summer was memorable for several reasons. For example, one Saturday evening, he drove past Memorial Park with a date, intending to see a movie at the drive-in, but several players from Indianapolis Pike High School caught his eye.

"We waved at each other and I came to a stop," Mount said. "I told my date, 'You won't believe what I'm going to do, but I'm going to take you home.' She slammed the door on me [at her house] and I never had another date with her. I went back and played for two hours.

"That's dedication," he continued. "I ask kids at my camp, 'How many of you would take your boy- or girlfriend home?' None of them raise their hands. I don't see much dedication out there."

Then there was the Fourth of July carnival that came to town. He decided to shoot baskets for teddy bears. It cost $1 for two shots, and you had to sink them both. The odds always were in favor of the carny because no warm-up shots were allowed, the rims were small, the balls always were overfilled with air, and shooters usually were dressed in street clothes and shoes.

Well, Mount, who had been shooting earlier and was wearing his regular gear, decided to "see if I could break the bank. A crowd started forming. People started giving me money and saying, 'Hey, Rick, win one for my daughter.' It took about forty-five minutes and I won twenty-eight teddy bears. At the end, I had to hit eight in a row for a dollar. I looked down the midway and all these kids had teddy bears."

After he had cleaned the carny out, Mount was asked, "What's your name? I know I should have had you stop. How'd you like to go on the road and shoot for money?" Rick still laughs today and says, "They could have put a wig on me and a mustache."

The epilogue to that memorable night is that during one of his camp sessions as an adult, he was approached by the mother of a camper who told him, "I'm one of those little girls whose dad gave you money [to win a teddy bear]."

Since Purdue already had gotten an unofficial recruiting jump with Dischinger's visit to Lebanon, Indiana University entered the picture that summer when NBA players Tom VanArsdale and Jon McGlocklin stopped by to play a little game of "scuttle" with Rick. In that game, two players guard the third and the first to score twenty-one points is the winner. Now the state's two major colleges were on equal footing, so to speak, in the Rick Mount sweepstakes.

Throughout his senior year, Mount was constantly tested by assistant coach Bob Purkhiser, a former all-Big Ten player from Purdue. "He guarded me every day in practice, which was great because no one else could guard me," Rick said. "He pushed me." They played one-on-one games to ten (you had to win by two points) and sometimes they would go to fifty until a winner was determined.

If he could score on Purkhiser, Mount surely would be able to score at will against high school players. It never was truer the night he broke his own school record by torching Crawfordsville for fifty-seven points. He bombed in twenty-four-of-forty from the field and nine-of-ten from the free-throw line. "The whole game I was on fire," he affirmed.

The Tigers always played Crawfordsville home and home each year. The Athenians elected to move their home game against Lebanon to Butler University because their team bus was wearing out. They drew a crowd of 9,500 that night, and Rick still is blown away that they made enough money to buy a brand-new Greyhound bus. That was just one example of the star power possessed by Rick the Rocket.

Everybody's meal ticket was a lot more than a shooter. It's just that his shooting overshadowed every other dimension of his game. Rosenstihl always called Rick "our best passer and ball handler," as well as shooter. Former Purdue assistant Bob King observed, "Rick was a fine passer. He had great instincts. On defense, he knew where the passing lanes were."

Mount's mystique even reached all the way to New York City-based *Sports Illustrated* magazine. *SI* basketball writer Frank Deford, then twenty-seven years old, pointed out, "I proposed an idea to do a story about a classical high school star from some small town. I thought immediately of states like Indiana and Kentucky. We sent out queries to our stringers, and a guy in Indianapolis said he had the perfect kid for us. It was like it was laid out for me. It was not a typical story, but I was delighted to do it. I've never seen Rick since then. I did send him a telegram when he got married."

So Deford and photographer Rich Clarkson paid a visit to Lebanon, Deford picking the brains of local basketball fans and Clarkson taking hundreds of pictures. After all, they were coming to make Rick Mount *SI*'s first-ever cover boy from a team sport.

Told ahead of time, Rick had said to Rosenstihl, "I don't want to do it!" Replied Rosenstihl, "You're going to do it!"

One Friday, they were shooting pictures in downtown Lebanon (population 9,523), but were constantly being bothered by cars passing by. Pistol Sheets, owner of the local pool hall, exclaimed, "I'll stop 'em, Rick," and quickly returned with a gun in his hand. Now everybody knew where he got his nickname!

Clarkson followed the Lebanon teenager everywhere he went, taking picture after picture. "He followed me to class, down the halls," Rick recalled. "The grief you would have to take from your classmates. They would make faces when he was taking pictures. He even tried to follow me into the bathroom."

Though Mount lived in the city, he was taken out in the country for the cover shoot—to put a rural Midwest touch on the story. "That was a big deal," Rosenstihl affirmed. "We went all around the county to find a red barn. Rick was not a farm boy."

The Lebanon legend still vividly recalls the day of the cover shoot. "It was snowing and it was cold," he shivered. "They had me running up and down that driveway for two hours. I was frozen. I had to get in the car [periodically] to warm up."

The end result, however, was a spectacular boost for all concerned. "That article was a good thing for Lebanon and myself," he agreed. "It put us on the map nationally. Looking back, it was a neat thing."

When the February 14, 1966 issue of *SI* hit the newsstands, Rick was pictured on the cover, wearing his warm-up suit and holding a basketball in his hands. The much-sought-after red barn, of course, was lurking in the right background.

"That particular copy sold well not only in Lebanon, but all over the United States," Rosenstihl said proudly of the thirty-five-cent issue.

All that really remained now for the Lebanon superstar was to bow out with that coveted but oh-so-elusive state championship. He drove the Tigers all the way to the semi-state at the old Purdue fieldhouse. They faced a formidable Logansport team in the first round and trailed 50-39 entering the final quarter.

What followed was probably the greatest exhibition of shooting in Lebanon history. The Rocket lived up to his name by firing ten missiles and connecting on nine of them. They weren't all long jumpers, either. He was pretty ambidextrous throughout his career and his incredible display included right- and left-handed hooks. He poured through twenty points in eight minutes, and the Tigers pulled out a scintillating 65-64 victory. He finished with a remarkable forty-seven points and fifteen rebounds.

"I was in a zone," Mount understated. "Even the Logansport announcer started rooting for me. I asked their coach [Jim Jones] why he didn't call a timeout and he said, 'I got caught up in your shooting and forgot.'

"Anytime I played two games in one day, leg cramps got me in the fourth quarter," Mount revealed. Unfortunately the Tigers had to play again that night. After he sparked the Tigers to a thirteen-point lead against East Chicago Washington early in the fourth quarter of the title game, sure enough, the inevitable happened. He cramped up big-time, sat out most of the final period, and the Tigers suffered a heartbreaking 59-58 defeat. Playing barely more than three quarters, the exhausted superstar still finished with twenty-nine points and thirteen rebounds.

Mount's longtime dream ended—unfulfilled—in frustration and heartbreak. Even though he had been named the number-one high school player in the country by *USA Basketball Yearbook* and soon was to receive the same honor from *Parade* magazine, he admitted, "Back then, it was a good honor, but it kind of went in one ear and out the other. I tried to keep a level head. All I thought about was winning state, getting that gold ring, and beating my dad." He could take solace in one thing, though—he did break all of Pete Mount's school records.

The Tigers had their best year under Mount's leadership, with a 21-6 record, and he matched his junior scoring average of 31.1 points per game. He also shot .503 from the field and .828 from the free-throw line.

The six-four, 185-pounder finished his magical four-year career with 2,595 points (27.3 average), still number 4 in Hoosier history. He shot .480 from the field and .808 from the free-throw line. His career low was eleven points as a freshman, and he missed just one game—due to blood poisoning as a senior—while leading the Tigers to a 72-23 record.

Jim Rosenstihl made sure no one ever would wear Mount's famous number 10 home uniform by never ordering that number again. In 2007, Rosenstihl received his own reward when the Lebanon gym was named in his honor.

Adding to his many laurels, Mount was named Indiana's Mr. Basketball. "It was a big honor, more of an individual honor," he acknowledged. "What I liked about it was that it was for charity [the Indianapolis Star Fund for the Blind]. On paper, we were really good, but we got beat both games [by the Kentucky All-Stars]. We sold out Freedom Hall and Hinkle Fieldhouse."

The next order of business was college, and since Bruce Hale had been visiting him throughout his career, Mount announced he was going to attend the University of Miami [Florida]. Well, all heck immediately broke loose in Lebanon.

"Right afterwards I was at a baseball game and no Lebanon people would talk to me," he said in dismay. They obviously disliked his decision because they hoped to continue watching him play—near home—at the next level.

The Lebanon boycott continued into the summer. At that time, the NCAA did not have a binding national letter of intent. During an outdoor tournament that summer, Rosenstihl approached Rick with Big Ten Conference letters of intent for Purdue and Indiana. "Why don't you sign one in case you want to go to the Big Ten?" he asked innocently.

However, as Mount pictures it in his mind, Rosenstihl held the Purdue letter in his right hand, which was closer to him. He bit and signed the Purdue letter. A couple weeks later he indeed did decide to switch. West Lafayette was close to home and Purdue was building a new arena to replace its antiquated fieldhouse. "I was more of a homebody and it was just forty-five minutes away," he explained. "If I wanted to come home, I could come home. Bruce Hale was a gentleman and wished me luck. It worked out really good."

Freshmen were not eligible for varsity competition at that time, so they scrimmaged against the varsity and played against other freshman teams. Their first dress scrimmage drew an amazing 9,500 fans, and Mount poured in 33 points. He wound up setting a freshman record with 490 points for a lofty 35.0 average.

Lebanon fans bought 1,000 Purdue season basketball tickets and were part of the capacity crowd of 14,123 who showed up for the dedication game of spanking-new Purdue Arena, which later was named Mackey Arena. The opponent was none other than UCLA, led by its superstar, Lew Alcindor. This was the dream match-up that had been denied when they were in high school. Mount did not disappoint, scoring twenty-eight points, but UCLA nosed out the inspired Boilermakers, 73-71. It was the first of numerous sellouts during the Rick Mount era.

Unknown to most onlookers, Mount had suffered a stress fracture in his left foot three weeks before the opener, and played the entire first half of the season with an aluminum insert in his shoe. "I had a lot of pain and no pain pills. It ached and ached and took a couple hours to calm down [after a game]. It was hard for me to move laterally," he admitted. "It [the insert] would bend when you'd go up on your toes. Later on, I cut it so my toes were free. I was averaging twenty-three points and a sports writer said, 'Hey, you're not doing so good.' I said, 'Hey, I've got a broken foot!'"

The Boilermakers played Wisconsin in their first Big Ten game and he took the insert out. With his foot pretty well healed, he exploded for forty points that night, shooting sixteen-for-thirty-two from the field and eight-for-eight from the free-throw line.

Unfortunately, Mount faced some of the same ugly jealousy that had plagued him in high school. One day during his sophomore year, the Boilermakers were doing lay-up drills when Herm Gilliam, instead of passing to him, slammed the ball into his stomach. He retaliated by firing the ball back at the head of Gilliam, who had led Purdue in scoring the year before. Coach George King saw only Mount's retaliation and quickly barked, "Mount, go home!" Taking it literally, Rick cleaned out his locker and headed back to Lebanon.

When Athletic Director Red Mackey got wind of what had happened, he was livid. He told Assistant Coach Bob King that he and George King "can find another job if you don't get Rick Mount back on campus by this evening."

Mount, who did return, of course, noted, "It made an impression on my teammates, too."

Mount finished his sophomore year with a 28.4 scoring average, an .846 free-throw percentage, and he made several All-American teams as the Boilermakers posted a 15-9 record.

His junior year was to be his best as a Boilermaker. He revealed that the relationships on the team still "were bad until Christmas. For some reason, he [Gilliam] decided he might like me. He started talking to me. I guess he figured it out. That's why we went to the NCAA. Before the season, there was no way because we were not on the same page. Chemistry is so important. A lot of good teams went down the tubes due to egos."

Another teammate, Billy Keller, explained, "Rick was somewhat misunderstood. He was always good-hearted and friendly, but kept to himself. He didn't want to spend time with us. He went home a lot. People misread that."

Well, once the Boilermakers raised their chemistry level, they were on their way to the Big Ten championship (13-1) and a number-six ranking in the nation with a regular-season record of 20-4.

In the regional finals, Purdue led Marquette by one point with two seconds left in regulation when the Warriors' Ric Cobb drew a two-shot foul. As he prepared to shoot his first free throw, Cobb stared confidently at Mount and said, "It's over!" His first shot tied the score, but he missed his second attempt and the game went into overtime.

In the overtime session, Mount drilled the most famous shot in Purdue history when he hit a twenty-two-foot baseline missile with two seconds left, to sink Marquette 75-73 and send the Boilermakers soaring to the coveted Final Four. He finished with twenty-six points.

Years later Mount ran across Marquette assistant Hank Raymonds, who told him, "That shot hurt [head coach] Al McGuire the worst I'd ever seen. All summer he was miserable."

Mount's chance meeting with Cobb ten years ago was even more satisfying. Cobb saw him coming and hollered those infamous words, "It's over!" The ex-Marquette player shook his head and sighed, "I had a chance to put us in the Final Four and choked."

In the semifinals, Mount fired home thirty-six points on fourteen-of-twenty-eight shooting as Purdue routed the highly-regarded North Carolina Tar Heels, 92-65.

The Boilermakers had another shot at mighty UCLA, and this time it was for all the marbles, the NCAA championship. Purdue fans were so giddy that a carload drove to Lebanon and stole the sign which read, "Home of Rick Mount, Mr. Basketball, 1966." They planted it firmly on the campus as they awaited the title clash. Unfortunately, UCLA rolled to a 92-72 victory, despite Mount's twenty-eight points.

The citizens of Lebanon later reclaimed the famous sign and put it back in its rightful place. A year later, they dedicated an outdoor court in his name. The six-foot sign, however, was desecrated time and again by Mount's detractors.

"The first day it was up, someone painted it black," Mount sighed. "They would clean it up, and the second day, someone would paint it black. It's been in a shed in my mini-barn for a long time."

The Purdue star completed his junior year with a superb 33.3 scoring average, .515 field goal percentage, and 847 free-throw percentage. He was named Big Ten MVP and was a consensus first-team All-American. Purdue benefited with a school-record 23 victories, 93.0 scoring average, and 120 points against archrival Indiana.

The Rocket really blasted off during his senior year, and was particularly dominant against Iowa. He poured in fifty-three points in the first Iowa game, then smashed the Big Ten record by exploding for sixty-one in their second meeting. On the latter occasion, he shot twenty-seven-for-forty-seven from the field. Thirteen baskets were from beyond what today is the three-point line, which would have made it a seventy-four-point game. He also had a fifty-three-point game against Michigan.

"I murdered a lot of guys," Mount pointed out. "For some reason, my eyes got real big [in games against Iowa]. They went undefeated my senior year."

Mount averaged a career-best 35.4 points as a senior and shot .831 from the free-throw line as the Boilermakers posted an 18-6 record.

During his brilliant three-year career, Mount set a Big Ten and school record with 2,323 points for a 32.2 average. He shot .483 from the field and .843 from the free-throw line. He also repeated as Big Ten MVP and a first-team All-American. Purdue lost just three home games during his career, and he looks back fondly on those days.

"It was a great place to play," he acknowledged. "What was so great was the fans. They would scream and yell. When we played UCLA and almost beat them, that set the tone. If we'd had 20,000 seats, we probably could have filled it."

Retired Purdue assistant coach Bob King noted, "We still call Mackey Arena 'The House that Rick Built.' [The Mount era] was the revival of Purdue basketball."

Though Purdue does not retire uniform numbers, Rick probably believed nobody ever would wear his famous number 10, because it was sent immediately to the Naismith Hall of Fame, where it has rested since 1970. But in 1989, Coach Gene Keady allowed Richmond's Mr. Basketball, Woody Austin, to wear number 10. Rick was unhappy, basically because Keady had not given him a "respect call," and started his personal boycott of Purdue games.

As soon as Austin graduated, Keady took the number out of circulation again. Ten years later, Rick received what he at first thought was a crank call. He finally realized it was from a current Purdue player, Brandon McKnight, who was asking permission to wear number 10. He told him to "wear it in good health" and he did wear it proudly from 2002-05.

At the height of his glory, Rick Mount made the biggest mistake of his life—he signed a contract as the number-one draft pick of the Indiana Pacers, who then belonged to the American Basketball Association. The problem was that the Pacers were a winning, veteran outfit and Coach Bob "Slick" Leonard didn't want Rick Mount. General manager Mike Storen drafted him anyway and signed him to a $250,000 contract—not for $1.5 million as was reported—for five years.

"It was the wrong place at the wrong time," Mount emphasized. "[Leonard] already had his team. My signing was on television. Someone asked, 'Where's Bobby Leonard?' Storen just rolled his eyes. I wanted out of this contract and then Storen goes to Kentucky.

"In a camp game, I hit three or four threes in a row and Leonard says, 'We're not at Purdue now, Mount.' I said, 'Trade me.' He said, 'You're going to sit here [on the bench] and eat s--- ...' I had twenty-four points in the first half against Pittsburgh and he said, 'You're not starting [the second half].' You start doubting yourself and you lose a little edge mentally."

Then there was the night that he never got off the bench until the last five seconds. Enraged, he jumped into his GTO and roared 115 miles per hour toward Lebanon. Noticing a police car in his rearview mirror, he took the first Lebanon exit. He explained why he was driving so recklessly. The state trooper, who knew him, responded, "I'd be going 115 miles per hour, too." The trooper didn't have the heart to give him a ticket, so all he received was a warning.

Eventually he got sent to Kentucky, also played for Utah and wound up his five-year ABA career with Memphis. Each of the three teams he played with reached the ABA finals. He was averaging 21.6 points, shooting a sizzling 67 percent from the field, leading the ABA in three-point shooting, and ranked among the top ten in assists for Memphis when he separated his shoulder. He missed most of that season, then attempted a comeback the following year with Utah, but tore his hamstring so badly in the preseason that he was forced to retire.

He actually did sign with the Houston Rockets in 1978, but he had been out of the game for two years and hated airplanes, so he never went to training camp.

Rick and his high school sweetheart, Donna, had been married since the summer before his senior year at Purdue, and they elected to live in Lebanon, despite the way some ungrateful residents had treated him. He explained, "I had lived there all of my life. It's a small town and both sets of our parents were there. It's a good place to raise kids, and is close to Indianapolis and Lafayette."

They had a son, Richie, who was to add to the Mount legend. When Richie was making waves as a junior high star, Rick received a call from Lafayette Central Catholic, asking if he would like a head coaching job. As soon he got interested, however, he was told by IHSAA commissioner Gene Cato that all head basketball and football coaches in Indiana had to have a college degree. He was twelve credit hours short and never did get his degree. Today, that rule has been altered.

Similar to his father, Richie also was drawn into controversy when his parents attempted to red-shirt him by having him repeat eighth grade.

"We felt he needed a little more maturity," Rick explained. "We probably should have held him back before kindergarten. Because of my name, they were going to make an example of me. It got blown all out of proportion. I took a survey and I found principals, superintendents, and teachers who had held their kids back."

Finally, the Lebanon school board ended the heated controversy by voting three-to-two in the Mounts' favor. But the Indiana Department of Education then passed a rule that no repeats would be allowed strictly for athletic reasons. It's called, of course, "the Richie Mount Rule."

Interestingly, Rick had been held back in second grade due to a long illness, and Pete had been held back in the same grade, due to "orneriness," Rick claimed.

Rick and Richie used to go one-on-one, creating instant replays of Pete and Rick from years earlier. And with the same results. "We'd always get in fights," Rick admitted. "He was just like me—he didn't like to lose. We never played much. He beat me one time when he was in college. I'm really proud of him."

As expected, Richie Mount was heckled by fans sporting the color red during his stellar four-year career at Lebanon. Richie fought back the best way he knew—the Mount way—by pouring in point after point. Rick and Donna watched him faithfully from the bleachers for two years. Finally, Rick couldn't take it anymore, and he spent his son's final two years listening to the radio.

"I never was a great spectator," he conceded. "My wife would grab me, because I was going to go up and get somebody. The Mount name really bothers people a lot."

Nevertheless, Richie created his own niche in the Mount legend by scoring 2,139 points during his four-year career, which at the time, placed him with his famous father among the top ten scorers in Indiana history.

Then Richie completed the circle when he was named an Indiana All-Star in 1989. His father had made it in 1966 and his grandfather in 1944. Thus the Mounts joined the Shepherds of Carmel as the only families in Hoosier basketball history to have three generations named to the prestigious Indiana All-Star team.

They probably do have one distinction that belongs solely to them. They once all played in a fund-raising exhibition game staged by Jim Rosenstihl. Playing against the Boone County All-Stars, Rick poured in twenty-five points, Richie had twenty-two, and Pete was put in just long enough to fire a last-second hook shot.

Today, Richie is a policeman in Lebanon, and has two sons, Jordan, a third grader, and Derek, who is in kindergarten.

Rick boycotted local games until 2000, when he was asked to help out with the Lebanon High girls' basketball team. Since then, he has eased gradually back into the scene and is thoroughly enjoying himself.

Long an avid outdoorsman, Mount has shot seventeen turkeys (the biggest at twenty-six pounds), six deer (including a twelve-point buck) and landed an eight-pound largemouth bass.

Mount has spent most of his adult life selling athletic equipment of some type. For the past twenty years, he has sold the Shoot-A-Way, which is a ball-return device.

But his true love is the Rick Mount Shooting School, which he started nineteen years ago. He was working a Nike camp in Denver one year when he got to asking himself, "When I leave, who is going to reinforce this stuff?"

He had long ago broken down his own picture-perfect jump shot and made a demonstration video of it. Why not start his own camp, break down the teenagers' shots the same way, and send them home with a voiceover video of their own? "When they leave my camp, that will be their coach at home," he said triumphantly. It's his voice on the video, and he is in the middle of everything that goes on at each camp.

Today, Rick and partner Jerry Hoover operate ten three-day shooting camps in Ohio, Illinois, Indiana, and Kentucky from June 8 until August 15. Approximately 16,000 boys and girls from ages 10 to 18 have received his instruction. Players have come from as far away as Japan, Russia, and England, and sixty-eight players from Germany are scheduled to come this summer.

"He's the best there is and ever was for teaching shooting," says Hoover, a former college assistant coach. "If kids do what he tells them, they eventually will become good shooters. He's got wonderful terminology. Everything he teaches has a unique phrase."

Jim Rosborough, associate head coach at the University of Arizona, took his son, Jon, to Mount's shooting school in Fort Wayne the summer before his senior year in high school. He became an instant believer.

"It was a tremendous camp," Rosborough said. "He was out there shooting, doing demonstrations, everything. It was an amazing display. He was very personable and it was well-run and organized. The big thing was repetition. He charted every single shot, and they each had 2,500 shots. They videotaped eight or ten shots. He gave them a written and verbal critique."

One year, a man from Charlestown, Indiana brought his son to Rick's camp at St. Joseph's College. He improved his scoring average from 8.0 as a seventh grader to 20.0 as an eighth grader. Hoover told him to "bring a carload" that next summer. The father definitely surprised Hoover when he replied, "I'm not going to do that, because then everybody else will know about your camp."

Charles Halterman of Petersburg, West Virginia wasn't afraid to share the wealth. He brought his son, a rising freshman, the first year. He was so happy with the boy's improved shooting that he brought twelve kids the next year, then twenty the following year, then fifty-one kids in a caravan of fifteen cars the fourth year. Mount and Hoover later held a camp in West Virginia that drew seventy kids.

Jim Rosenstihl agrees that his former high school superstar "is a great teacher. He can back it up. He can still shoot. There's nobody who shoots like him, not even today. He never smoked or drank. He still looks like he's forty years old."

The sixty-year-old Mount indeed still can shoot with the very best, even though he had knee surgery ten years ago. He long has been ambidextrous and never ceases to amaze campers when he drills ten straight three-pointers right-handed, then swishes twenty consecutive free throws left-handed. He really was on fire one night at Millikin University, sinking an incredible ninety-four of a hundred three-point shots.

"There aren't too many that can outshoot me," Mount said without boasting. "You've got to be in shape. If I hit 45 of 100 shots, they aren't going to listen to me."

So he puts up at least 200 of those patented jumpers every day—weather permitting—on his driveway court. "I can't get in a gym at Lebanon," he said. "When they changed the locks, I never got a key."

Rick estimates that he easily would have scored more than 3,000 high school points with today's three-point rule. He says the line (nineteen feet, nine inches) "is too close. It's hurt because it's taken the mid-range shot away. Nobody guards the mid-range. If you make a shot fake and take one or two dribbles, you can get all the shots you want. It should be twenty-two feet in high school."

Mount's biggest competition for the title of Indiana's greatest outside shooter always will come from Jimmy Rayl, Kokomo's Splendid Splinter. Jim Rosenstihl gave this comparison: "Rick had better moves to get open and he had a true jump shot. He got up over his man. Rayl was almost a push shooter, but he did give you more range."

They never faced off in high school or college, but they did tangle as adults once in a memorable game of H-O-R-S-E on Rayl's driveway court. However, the game ended with each player having four letters and will forever remain a tie. "He was way out there," Mount said of Rayl. "He had really unlimited range. They'll still be debating when we are dead and gone."

STRETCH MURPHY:

Gave Giants Their Name

Charles "Stretch" Murphy was Indiana's first outstanding big man. He was born on April 10, 1907, in Marion and grew to be six-seven. Though average by today's basketball standards, Murphy literally was a giant in his day. Most boys his size in that era lacked coordination and didn't even try out for basketball. Few coaches wanted to put forth the effort to develop them. It was a time still dominated by the quick, little man.

Reinforcing the beliefs of his era, Murphy once told a Tampa, Florida sportswriter, "I was considered a freak to most people. I wasn't supposed to be able to do anything. The first time that I played ... I didn't know a basketball from a football. Growing up in Indiana, it was an instinct for boys to play basketball."

He definitely was a giant to his half-brother, Bill Merkert, who was thirteen years younger. "I used to have to sleep with him and he always was kicking the covers off," Merkert laughed. "I didn't get to see him play much, because there was just too much difference in our ages."

As a junior high performer, Murphy, ironically, played for the Marion Midgets, and was coached by Miss Dorothy Lynch.

Several years later, Murphy began playing for Marion High School, which at that time had no nickname or numbers on its uniforms. He lettered for three years and was dominant with the center-jump rule in effect at that time.

As a sophomore, Murphy appeared in fourteen games, scored thirty-nine points, and had a high game of ten points. He started to dominate as a junior, scoring 254 points for a 10.2 average, and posting a high game of 16 points as Marion compiled a 21-4 record. He was even more dominant as a senior, pouring in 411 points for a 14.2 average and exploding for a career-high 30 points on one occasion. He finished his career with 704 points, for a 10.4 average.

Murphy and his teammates had a special incentive entering the 1926 state tournament, because Marion sportswriter Bern Boxell had picked Kokomo to win the title.

Well, the Giants steamed past Kokomo, 24-8, at the Kokomo regional. For the state finals, they traveled to Indianapolis in taxicabs and had to huddle under wool blankets because the cabs had no heaters.

Longtime Lafayette, Indiana sports editor Gordon Graham got his first look at Murphy during his final prep tournament. Years later, he wrote, "As usual, there were many great players to be seen, but on this occasion only one word was on everybody's lips—'Murphy.' They gasped, groaned and cheered. Stretch didn't even lead the tourney in scoring, but he got all of the tips, rebounds, etc., and was a general nuisance to all opposition as Marion High School won its first and only state championship."

While closing out his career, Murphy became linked with Martinsville star Johnny Wooden, who was two years younger. They met for the first time in the state championship game, won by Marion, 30-23. Murphy scored five points and made the All-State team as Marion finished with a 27-2 record. Wooden was held scoreless.

After the title game, an Indianapolis sportswriter called the newly crowned champions "the giants of Marion"—basically because of Murphy's towering size, though he was a string bean at 160 pounds. The tag stuck, and Marion finally had a nickname for its athletic teams.

During the state tournament, which included 719 teams, the Giants trailed only once—by a single point in the semifinals against Evansville Central. They would not win another state title until 1975. The Giants were coached by Eugene Thomas, who later guided Kalamazoo to a pair of Michigan state championships.

Marion's superb season inspired Harold M. Sherman to write a book, entitled *Get 'Em Mayfield,* which was a fictitious account of a Hoosier high school basketball team that beat all the odds to capture a state championship. It was part of a "Mayfield" series and, perhaps, provided readers an early glimpse of the Milan Miracle which surfaced twenty-eight years later.

In the book foreword, Sherman wrote, "Dedicated to Indiana High School Basket Ball and more especially to coach Eugene Thomas and his Marion Giants, state high school champions of Indiana, 1925-6, whose exploits on the court have furnished much of the inspiration for this new story of 'Mayfield's Fighting Five.'"

"He was extremely agile," recalled Wooden, who became his teammate two years later on an outstanding Purdue University squad. Showing the awe he still has today for Murphy's size, Wooden said, "I think he could have looked down at the basket. He was thin but strong. He was the most unselfish player. He was wonderful and gentle. He would have been outstanding in any era."

The lanky Murphy was rated one of the nation's premier defensive players and became a more dominant scorer in college under the tutelage of Hall of Fame coach Ward "Piggy" Lambert. He also was a powerful rebounder, even though he weighed just 173 pounds. His quick, accurate outlet passes enabled the Boilermakers to launch a running game not familiar to many colleges at the time.

Murphy was such a talented center that when he arrived on the varsity as a sophomore, he pushed six-two Wilbur Cummins—who had led the Big Ten Conference in scoring the previous year—to a forward position.

He lettered three years and set a Big Ten Conference record with 143 points in 1929. He almost matched that total with 137 points in

1930—his senior year—during which he served as captain and led the Boilermakers to the Big Ten title with a 10-0 record (13-2 overall). In that final campaign, he set Big Ten records with a 28-point game against Ohio State and a 13.7 season average. He graduated with a career total of 562 points for an 11.2 average. Purdue was league co-champ in 1928 and 1929. He was named Helms Athletic Foundation All-America in 1929 and 1930. The Boilermakers posted a 41-8 record during his career.

Nicknamed "Long John" during his high school days, Murphy was given the permanent tag of "Stretch" by a Chicago sportswriter because he "stood out in a crowd" during his dynamic college career.

Wooden, who was a great player in his own right, still credits Murphy for many of his own national honors. "He got me recognition from the beginning," the humble Wooden said. "We liked to walk behind him in hotels to hear what people would say. It would be like walking behind a seven-footer today."

Longtime Purdue assistant coach Bob King, now retired, agrees with Wooden that most onlookers viewed Murphy's size with awe. As a youngster, King attended some of Murphy's college games. "I thought he was the tallest guy I ever had seen," he admitted. "Six-foot-seven guys were like giants in those days. He rebounded well and set a lot of screens. For a big guy he could keep up with all the little guys [running the court]."

Fully grown, Murphy wore a size fifteen shoe. The only problem was that basketball shoes at the time were not bigger than size twelve. "I just had to wear them," he told a Tampa, Florida sportswriter, "but I don't think that I ever paid attention to the pain. I didn't have any choice." As he aged, however, he had many problems with his feet.

After graduation, Murphy played for the George Halas-owned Chicago Bruins of the American Basketball League from 1929-30. He was paid between $25 and $50 per game. Then he played for the Independent League Indianapolis Kautskys from 1930-33.

Murphy seldom played against anyone his height, because the average center in his day stood only about six-two. Therefore, he was the master of the center jump. He once told a sportswriter, "That was naturally down my alley. I could get the tip-off 99 percent of the time against anybody they put in at center. The tip-off was quite a thing then. We had plays from it."

He also coached basketball for three years (1931-34) at Edinburgh High School, where he compiled a record of 27-39. His second season was his best, posting a 15-9 record and finishing second in both the Johnson County Tournament and the sectional. He then earned a master's degree in physical education from Columbia University and launched a very successful career directing boys' clubs. In 1938, he began a twelve-year tenure at the Bristol, Connecticut Boys Club. He received national recognition there, because he helped turn around the lives of many young, disadvantaged boys. In 1950, he moved to Florida where he directed the Tampa Boys Club for twenty-two years until his retirement.

Murphy was enshrined in the Naismith Memorial Basketball Hall of Fame in 1960. He was chosen for the Indiana Basketball Hall of Fame in 1963, the second year after it was opened.

Marion won back-to-back state titles in 1975 and 1976 and Murphy, who was living in Tampa at the time, had been able to listen to some radio broadcasts of Marion games on a Fort Wayne radio station. He returned to his hometown both years to speak at pep sessions, give inspiring locker-room talks, and sit in the front row at state-finals games. "He'd get everybody fired up," said Jim Brunner, veteran sports director of WBAT-WCJC radio station in Marion.

In 1976, Murphy talked to the Marion players the day of the state finals. Jack Lake wrote in the *Marion Chronicle* that during his talk to the team, he observed, "I see you guys still are wearing Converse All-Star basketball shoes. I remember how hard I had to work to save $3.75 to buy a pair of Converse shoes."

Murphy noted that his team had to play one game Friday and three Saturday at the state tournament. The pace was somewhat slow because a center jump was called after every basket. However, he was quick to point out, "That didn't give me any rest, because I was the center and I just had to keep on jumping."

The Marion great said he didn't like the way coaches of the 1970s were always jumping off the bench. He explained, "Eugene Thomas [his coach] always told us to have fun and let the other team worry. Then he sat back on the bench and watched."

When Murphy finished his pep talk, the Marion players "exploded in cheers."

Lake reported that Murphy practiced what he preached. "He was seated at the far end of the bench. He would stand only during quarter intermissions to take pictures."

The Hoosier great died in 1992 at the age of eighty-five.

GREG ODEN:

Unassuming Superstar

Greg Oden ranks as the greatest defensive player and the most gifted big man in the history of Indiana high school basketball. He was Bill Russell in a teenager's uniform. And to top it all off, he probably was the most humble superstar ever to grace a Hoosier basketball court.

Along with point guard Mike Conley, Oden sparked Indianapolis Lawrence North to the most incredible three-year dynasty in the proud history of Indiana basketball. The Wildcats tied state records with three consecutive Class 4A championships and forty-five victories in a row. They were unbeaten in 2005-06 and crowned unanimous national champions.

Oden matched the great LeBron James when he was named two-time National Player of the Year by Gatorade, *USA Today*, and *Parade* magazine. He also received the Morgan Wootten and Naismith trophies, other symbols of being the nation's number-one player. An "A" student, he also captured the two most coveted honors in Indiana: Mr. Basketball and the Trester Award for mental attitude.

Greg Oden was talented enough, experts said, to be the NBA's number-one draft pick after his JUNIOR year in high school.

Retired Purdue University assistant basketball coach Bob King has watched most of Indiana's great players over the years, and he calls Oden "the best and most athletic big guy I ever have seen in Indiana high school basketball. His hand-eye coordination is as good as I ever saw for a big guy. He also makes some outlet passes like [former NBA star] Wes Unseld used to make. He does things that a guy six-three does."

Bill Green, who won a record six Indiana state championships, observed, "I think this kid has brought back the interest in high school basketball."

Reaching a shade over seven feet and weighing 260 pounds as a senior, Oden dominated the paint throughout his prep career. After all, he had a vertical reach of 111 inches to go with his eighty-six-inch wingspan. He was blessed with the innate ability of being able to block a shot without fouling and often keeping the ball in play. His mere presence intimidated many shooters.

Lawrence North, always a superb defensive team under Coach Jack Keefer, could gamble by sending its guards out high to put great pressure on three-point shooters because Oden—the Great Eraser—always was lurking in the background, ready to stuff any shooter lucky (?) enough to get near the basket.

Oden actually was born in Buffalo, New York, and lived there until his parents' ten-year marriage ended in divorce. His mother, Zoe, then took him and younger brother Anthony to live with relatives in Terre Haute, Indiana. Though tall for his age, he was just a normal kid who never had dabbled in basketball.

Ironically, his father, Greg Sr., had just put up a basketball goal at their home before his sons were whisked away. It was a near miss! Still, Greg and The Game were destined to become one. It was merely a matter of time.

As a fourth grader at Fuqua Elementary School in Terre Haute, Oden was asked to try out for a talented age-group AAU basketball team coached by policemen Jimmy Smith and John Gilmore. Giving up his beloved Saturday morning cartoons for basketball practice was bad enough, but the five-eight youngster couldn't even make a lay-up. For the next year or two, he shot lay-ups endlessly.

Despite rarely getting into a game, Oden never complained. He just kept working, learning the game, and getting better one day at a time. As a six-two sixth grader, he started to show some potential. Smith, who had become Greg's mentor, was asked to share him with Mike Conley, who was coaching an AAU team in Indianapolis, seventy miles north.

Conley, the 1992 Olympic triple jump champion, teamed the lanky Oden with his son, Mike Conley Jr., who already was an extremely polished point guard, and the families became very close.

"He was really uncoordinated and didn't have much skill at that time," Mike Jr. said kindly. "The last thing I would have thought was that he would have a chance of going to the NBA."

The Odens moved to Indianapolis when Greg was a towering six-eight eighth grader. He teamed with Conley to lead Craig Middle School to an unbeaten season, and they were on their way to becoming the finest inside-outside combination in Hoosier prep history.

They received their first taste of national exposure the summer before their freshman year when both were invited to the prestigious Nike Jamboree Camp in St. Louis. Greg told Mrs. Conley (Rene') that he didn't want to go because "I can't dribble or shoot." She talked him into going, but as they left she recalled that he "had a long face."

Surprise! Surprise! Oden wowed camp director George Raveling, who told Mrs. Conley that the young center had been "awesome. He's been the talk of the camp."

Oden became an immediate varsity starter as a freshman at Lawrence North because he not only was talented, but he was a great hustler and unselfish to a fault. During scrimmages he often was the first to dive on the floor for loose balls.

As a six-ten, 210-pound freshman, he averaged a modest nine points and nine rebounds, but blocked seventy-four shots to help the Wildcats post an impressive 21-3 record.

Oden came into his sophomore year at six-eleven, 245 pounds. Coach Keefer got his first eyeful of the young giant's enormous potential during an early practice session. Irritated by a series of passes thrown below Greg's chest, Keefer ordered him to show his teammates how high he could jump. Taking just one step, he leaped so high that his entire hand touched above the square (eleven feet, seven inches). Everybody—Keefer included—gasped because they never had seen a player soar that high.

In late December, the Wildcats nipped ball-control-minded Columbia City, 56-55, in a double-overtime thriller to win the prestigious Hall of Fame Tournament at New Castle. Oden showed his teammates and coaches that he had an unselfish streak a mile wide when, after being named MVP, he gave his trophy to teammate Brandon McPherson, who had scored nineteen points while nursing a painful leg injury.

Oden climaxed his sophomore campaign by leading the Wildcats to a lopsided 50-29 victory in a rematch with Columbia City for the Class 4A state title. He called the title "your ultimate goal. There's nothing bigger, except graduating. I dreamed about it because I wanted it bad."

He completed his sophomore campaign with averages of 13.9 points and 9.8 rebounds as the state champs compiled a 29-2 record. He shot .722 from the field and blocked ninety-five shots.

ESPN analyst Tim McCormick got his first look at Oden during the summer of 2004 while running the NBA Players Association Top 100 Camp. He called Oden "the best junior we've ever had at our camp. I was really impressed with his maturity. He exceeded my expectations. The intangible I liked so well is that he's very coachable. He reminds me of Tim Duncan and David Robinson."

The fall of his junior year, Greg was elected Homecoming King by the student body. As expected, the shy superstar did not want to be nominated at first. Still, after he won, he confessed, "It turned out to be pretty cool. I knew all the dudes and the girls [other candidates]."

As a seven-foot, 240-pound junior, Oden had several memorable performances. The first came during a 56-40 victory over defending Missouri state champion Poplar Bluff before a crowd of 7,000 and a national TV audience on ESPN2. Finishing strong against six-nine University of North Carolina recruit Tyler Hansbrough, Greg scored sixteen points, which included four consecutive dunks.

He did, however, hit rock bottom during a 69-63 upset loss to arch rival Indianapolis North Central in the Marion County Tournament. He took only five shots and was held to ten points. Keefer then threatened his ultra-unselfish star with losing his starting position should he not take at least fifteen shots a game from then on.

In the very next game, a rematch against North Central, Oden exploded for a career-high thirty-seven points, shooting sixteen-for-twenty-two from the field, as the Wildcats romped to a 76-47 victory. North Central Coach Doug Mitchell said, "He all but eliminates what I consider a good fifteen-by-fifteen swath of the floor. You can't get him off his feet."

The Lawrence North star faced every gimmick defense known to man. He took it all in stride. "I just like playing my game and let the scoreboard do the talking," was his eloquent reply to everything thrown at him.

The greatest game during Oden's high school career was the rematch against Indianapolis Arlington—which had upset the Wildcats, 70-60, earlier in the year—in the sectional semifinals. Arlington came in undefeated and ranked number three in the country. Hundreds were turned away from the 3,000-seat Lawrence Central gym.

The Golden Knights elected to constantly drive at Oden, hoping to foul him out. However, he blocked shot after shot back in their faces. When the smoke cleared from the fiercely contested game, the Wildcats had posted a deceiving 60-45 triumph.

What definitely was not deceiving, though, was Oden's school-record eighteen blocked shots. *Hoosier Basketball Magazine* publisher

Garry Donna charted the game and noted that the young Bill Russell clone also altered another eleven shots with his great intimidation. Arlington had only fifty-six shots, so Greg literally had a hand in more than half. The state championship game came early that year.

Three weeks later, the Wildcats won their second 4A title in a row with a 63-52 victory over eight-time state champion Muncie Central as Oden dominated with twenty-nine points, nine rebounds, and six blocks. The Wildcats finished with a 24-2 record and were ranked number six in the nation by *USA Today.*

Oden, meanwhile, had his most productive year, averaging 20 points, 9.7 rebounds, and 3.7 blocks while shooting .675 from the field.

Later that spring, Oden won his first Gatorade award and his family threw a party in his honor. Greg Oden Sr. and his father, Eugene Oden, who saw Greg play two or three times a year, came from Buffalo. Greg Sr. admitted that when his ex-wife first took their sons to another state, "It sucked. I was mad." On this night, however, he stood up and "thanked the Indiana people—I thanked them all. He never would have gotten all those opportunities. Buffalo is not youth-oriented."

Demonstrating his fierce family loyalty, Greg gave up his prom and basketball banquet to attend the graduation of his cousin, Steve Bufford, from the University of Buffalo.

Every summer, Oden spent his spare time working for LN assistant coach Ralph Scott, who has a lawn-care business. Each day, he would don his protective goggles and plug in his earphones before boarding the riding lawnmower. With arms and legs protruding and music filling his ears, the gentle giant was able to live in his own private world for a few hours and pick up some extra spending money, too.

During his last summer as a high school player, Oden dominated in every tournament and at every camp.

At the nation's premier summer tourney—the Reebok Big Time in Las Vegas—Oden paced the Spiece Indy Heat to the championship for the second year in a row. On one occasion, he held six-ten, 255-pound Oregon star Kevin Love to twelve points, causing *Long Beach Press-Telegram* veteran writer Frank Burlison to call him "the most dominant low-post presence in high school basketball since Shaquille O'Neal." Love, who succeeded him as National Player of the Year, says Oden "is so big and athletic and has great hands. The thing he does better than other big men is that he really runs the floor and gets position early. That's what really separates. On every shot, I had to use my body control and leverage. He jumps so high and is so strong. You have to change most everything you do."

The Heat defeated the D-I Greyhounds, featuring O.J. Mayo and Bill Walker, 73-67, for the Big Time title. Oden had eighteen points, thirteen rebounds, and eight blocks and fouled out three post players while repeating as MVP.

Long-time game director Sonny Vaccaro was blown away. Vaccaro noted, "He was the first guy down the court about 60 percent of the time. He sprints. That's what makes him so great. Greg Oden is the best high school big man that I've ever seen. I've seen back to Kareem [Lew Alcindor], Alonzo [Mourning], and Patrick [Ewing]. It's a much different game [today] and he is so dominant. He's the most humble superstar I've encountered in forty-two years." After he had coached Oden for the last time, Mike Conley senior said proudly, "The bigger the kids, the better he plays. When he plays against seven-footers, he becomes the fast one. He now can take over a game OFFENSIVELY and defensively."

Despite all of his basketball exploits, Greg would be the first to admit his greatest thrill of the summer was being nominated for an ESPY and receiving a free trip to Hollywood. He was able to walk the famed Red Carpet (think Oscars) and mingle with such celebrities as Peyton Manning and Kevin Garnett. The next summer, he was invited back and won the top high school honor.

In his final go-round as a senior, Oden sparkled in two nationally televised contests on ESPN2. He put together impressive totals of twenty-three points, seventeen rebounds, and nine blocks in a 69-

54 victory over eventual Ohio state champion Dayton Dunbar at Butler University. Due to a snowstorm, the game drew only six-hundred fans.

Remarkably, Oden was even more dominant in the second TV game, a 78-59 victory before a capacity crowd of 3,200 at arch rival North Central. He finished with thirty-three points, twelve rebounds, four blocks, and three assists while shooting a superb thirteen-for-eighteen from the field and seven-for-eight from the free throw line. The audience included most of Greg's relatives from Buffalo, each sporting a hat with his name and uniform number: "Oden 50."

Later the Wildcats traveled to Northwestern University to challenge defending Illinois Class AA state champion Glenbrook North. Co-promoter Bob Rylko quickly discovered the magic in the big guy's name when fans began calling for tickets to the "Oden game." Greg did not disappoint during the ballyhooed contest, which drew an overflow crowd of 8,494. He finished with thirty-three points and eleven rebounds in an impressive 79-61 victory.

Early in the state tournament, Oden tore a ligament in his right wrist when he was submarined on a dunk, but played the final six games of the season before having surgery in June.

Remarkably, he made all eighteen shots in regional victories over tough Carmel and Pike.

The Wildcats defeated Muncie Central for the second straight year, 80-56, for the 4A state title before another capacity crowd of 18,345 at Conseco Fieldhouse in Indianapolis. Oden did his share with twenty-six points and eleven rebounds as the Wildcats (29-0) sewed up the national championship with a flourish.

Oden's final campaign was his best as he averaged 22.1 points, 10.5 rebounds, 2.8 blocks, and shot a sizzling .736 from the field. He also shot a superb .783 from the free throw line.

During his four-year career, he scored 1,773 points and grabbed 1,058 rebounds. He set school records with 341 career blocks and 619 points in a single year. He also shot .710 from the field.

Though he has a rather fierce physical appearance, Greg speaks softly and is ultra polite. Best friend Mike Conley cites his "humbleness and demeanor. He doesn't brag. He's just a normal kid. He's always happy."

Oden easily could be nicknamed the "Rip Van Winkle of Basketball," or the "Sultan of Sleep." He was famous for stretching out on the floor in an athletic department office and catching a few winks. However, according to Conley, who roomed with Oden on the road, "He sleeps TOO much! When we tried to stay up late, he was the first person to fall asleep. If we wanted to go to the mall, he wanted to go back to the hotel. He would pull down the shades and turn on the air conditioner. In the middle of the afternoon, I was forced to go to sleep."

Greg acknowledges that he has been greatly blessed by God and he attends a local church as often as possible, either with his girlfriend or close friend Jason Weigel.

Terre Haute South coach Mike Saylor puts Oden's future in perspective when he says, "He's going to be a low-post phenomenon. Greg Oden is a franchise. He makes you from a pretender to a contender. His value in getting drafted [by the NBA], I'll bet, will be a total package [including shoe contract, etc.] over $200 million. I'll eat my hat if he doesn't get over $200 million."

BOBBY PLUMP:

Humble Hero

Bobby Plump made the biggest shot in the history of Indiana high school basketball when he drilled a fifteen-foot jumper to stun mighty Muncie Central, 32-30, and give the small-school Milan Indians the 1954 state championship before a capacity crowd of 15,000 at Butler Fieldhouse in Indianapolis.

On the high school level, "The Shot" ranked with Bobby Thomson's famous walk-off home run which enabled the New York Giants to win the 1951 National League pennant.

It was David vs. Goliath all over again, and the underdog's victory sent reverberations not only throughout the state but the entire nation. Milan was the smallest school (161 students) to win the Indiana championship since Thorntown in 1915.

Television was in its infant stages in 1954, and the Final Four was telecast statewide in living black-and-white for only the fourth year. Since the finals had been sold out for many years, it drew a large audience. The spine-tingling title game kept entire families spellbound in their living rooms, most of them rooting for the underdog Indians as the incredible drama unfolded.

At least one man was known to have died of a heart attack while watching the game on television.

Longtime Purdue University assistant coach Bob King said, "[Plump] was in the right place at the right time. He took the shot that immortalized small-town basketball. If they played ten times, Muncie would have won the majority."

The unexpected triumph was so awe-inspiring that Angelo Pizzo and David Anspaugh later used the Miracle of Milan as the model for their number-one-ranked sports movie *Hoosiers*.

Plump was asked to attend a preview of *Hoosiers* before it was released nationally in 1986. "The *Indianapolis Star* asked me to write a review," he said. "I wrote two sentences and got so engrossed, I forgot to write any more. I loved it. Angelo asked me, 'Did we get the last eighteen seconds correct?' That was the only factual thing they got right in the whole movie."

When you're dealing with Hollywood, obviously, you can't let facts get in the way of good entertainment.

Had Plump missed that final shot and Muncie Central rolled to its record fifth state title, he definitely would not have ended up "pumping gas in Pierceville [his hometown]," as *Indianapolis Star* sportswriter Bob Collins wrote facetiously. However, some things would have been different.

– Milan's 1954 team picture would not be resting in the Naismith Hall of Fame in Springfield, Massachusetts.

– There would be no large picture of Plump taking The Shot at the Indiana Basketball Hall of Fame in New Castle.

– Plump's 1954 letter jacket and his first backboard and goal would not be displayed in the Indiana State Museum.

– The movie never would have been made, of course. And the fiftieth anniversary of the game never would have been celebrated by an ESPN Classic rebroadcast of the game plus a live match-up of the same schools.

– There would be no Milan '54 Museum, Inc., which still draws tourists from all over the country.

– Even in high school, Plump had been painfully shy, and he pointed out that had he not become a hero, "I wouldn't have gotten over my shyness as quickly." He began making public speaking appearances that spring and was forced to start coming out of his shell. The number of speeches—if any at all—would have been minimal, too, had he misfired.

– Following college, his high school fame also opened many doors in the business world that might otherwise have been closed.

– The team has had an annual reunion over the years, but Plump concedes it probably wouldn't be nearly as big if the Indians had not won their first—and only—state championship.

– The Indians never would have been featured in *Reader's Digest* or been offered a story in *Look* magazine, which Coach Marvin Wood turned down.

– They never would have been offered a three-week paid-vacation in Europe by an advertising firm. That was rejected by the IHSAA because it would have taken away their amateur standing. "That would have been a nice ending," Plump laughed.

– A very interesting, but seldom-mentioned, by-product of Plump's clutch shot was the immediate increase of Milan students going to college. Few had been taking the college route (an estimated sixteen in the previous four years), but ten of the twelve players on the tournament roster eventually enrolled in college, and six became coaches. Inspired by the basketball success, seventeen of the thirty seniors moved on to higher education. There were 161 students in grades nine through twelve. The educational bar definitely was raised, and it no longer was a question of "if" but "where" a boy or girl would go to college.

Rollin Cutter, two years younger than Plump, related, "I was just talking to a group and told them, 'We didn't have a star player until the last ball went in.' I looked at all of my teammates as equal. I really felt that way. After that we can say he WAS the star. I was on the bench and didn't see it because Woody [Coach Marvin Wood] jumped in front of me."

Ray Craft indicated that there was no jealousy on the team. "Bobby seized the opportunity, and it was a perfect ending to a

Cinderella story," the longtime IHSAA assistant commissioner, who later roomed with Plump in college, said. "He wrote a book, and I applaud him for that."

Still very humble and unassuming at age seventy, Plump said, "I never thought of myself or anybody else as a star. I knew I was good. I've got an ego like everybody else. We won games and that was what the whole thing was about. In my speeches, I say we didn't have a star. Do you know the definition of star? It's a large, encased mass of gas."

Bobby Plump, born at home in Pierceville (population forty-five), was the youngest of six children, and didn't have a name for five days. Finally, a neighbor girl, Helen Dunn, named him after a boy she admired, and the family used it. "I guess they ran out of names," Plump said philosophically. "I thought she picked a pretty good name," he laughed. The family did not have a telephone or indoor plumbing.

His mother, Mabel, died when he was five years old, and his twenty-year-old sister, Dorothea, helped raise him. His father, Lester, devoted himself to his children and never remarried. In fact, Plump does not recall his father even having a date.

As a youngster, Plump participated in basketball, baseball, and track. Basketball always seemed to take the front seat, though. "I found out I was pretty good at basketball, so I enjoyed it," he said. "I had good feet [quick first step] and good hand-eye coordination."

At age eight, he also owned the town's first outdoor basketball goal—a nine-foot-high hoop attached to the family smokehouse—which was a Christmas present from his father. He had to battle dirt and rocks every day, and became an adept dribbler.

Three years later, Roger Schroder's family, who owned the town store, put up a court that actually had a flat, level surface. It was situated in an alley, and the kids who played there became known as the "Pierceville Alleycats."

Glen Butte noted that Plump "was king of the court in the alley. We always wanted to be on his team because he was going to be a winner. His quick first step always was his forte through high school and college. He was the guy we wanted to take the shot with the game on the line."

The big hazard at Schroder's was a manure pile, which was perilously close to the left side of the court. Players never called fouls, and Plump admits he landed in the manure pile "many times. But they didn't guard you too closely after that."

Playing in such extreme circumstances gave the Pierceville kids a special toughness. Making them even stronger were the elements such as snow and rain that they played in. They would pour sawdust over the snow. The skin on their hands often would crack and bleed. All they did was tape their fingers together and continue the game.

Pierceville students all attended school in Milan, which was three miles away and had a population of 1,150. Milan seemed like a "metropolis" to them. Plump first tried out for the basketball team in sixth grade and was cut. "I didn't know I was any good," Plump admitted. "I didn't have any confidence."

He did make the team in seventh and eighth grade, where he came under the tutelage of Marc Combs. "He was so important," Plump acknowledged. "He taught us fundamentals and footwork." He had his players dribble around chairs and shoot free throws blindfolded. He also taught them how to play a zone defense, which later came in quite handy at Milan High.

As a freshman, Plump became intrigued watching varsity reserve player Bill Gorman shoot a jump shot in practice. He observed, "You can get that shot off pretty easily. At the end of the year, Mr. Grinstead [varsity coach Herman Grinstead] told me, 'If you keep practicing that, you might be able to make the varsity.' I practiced all summer, going left, right, stopping, faking, and shooting."

In the fourth game of his sophomore year, Plump cracked the starting lineup because Grinstead kicked seven seniors off the team following an 82-40 thumping by Osgood. (He later brought the best two back.) Plump debuted as one of the top scorers in an upset victory over Batesville, and was shocked the following day when he walked into his first class to a standing ovation. "That was almost as good as winning the state tournament," he conceded. Milan finally had accepted the shy "outsider" from Pierceville.

Plump averaged 9.89 points as a sophomore, and the Indians finished with a 14-6 record. But then Grinstead was fired and twenty-four-year-old Marvin Wood was hired to take his place. The town was in an uproar because Grinstead had been a popular figure.

It didn't take long to convince Plump that Wood was much more than an adequate replacement. "The only reason we won the state [a year later] was Marvin Wood," he affirmed. "He taught me more the first two months than anybody, except Mr. Hinkle [future college coach Tony Hinkle]. He could demonstrate everything."

The youthful coach was obviously ahead of his time, because during his first two years at Milan, he taught his team a four-corner offense, which was dubbed the "cat and mouse," and a match-up zone. In later years, Dean Smith became famous for his four-corner offense at the University of North Carolina, and Bill Green won six Indiana state titles with a baffling match-up zone.

Plump said he "loved" the cat-and-mouse offense, which made Milan famous. "Number one, it was guard-oriented," he pointed out. "Number two, it was an extremely successful offensive weapon or a slow-down game." Twenty-five years later, Wood told his former star that he never found another team that could run the "cat and mouse" like the 1954 state champs.

Coach Wood also made Bobby better by guarding him every day in practice. On one occasion, the junior guard banged into Wood and broke his own nose. "He was pretty good [on defense]," Plump acknowledged.

Bobby was born with a quick first step. He would crouch low, then spring past his defender for a driving lay-up, or leap high for a surprise jump shot. "Mr. Hinkle said I had the quickest first step of anybody he ever coached," he said proudly. He also is proud that he had the "only true jump shot in the Final Four" his senior year.

He wasn't quick enough, however, to avoid Coach Wood's wrath one night when he was caught outside of his house five minutes past curfew. After fixing a flat tire, he was sitting in the car with his girlfriend. "It takes a long time to say good night at that age," Plump pointed out.

Wood's unbending reply to the flat-tire story: "You should have planned on it." A three-game suspension was in order for Plump and teammate Jim Wendelman, who claimed he was taking a babysitter home at 3:30 AM. They missed just one game, though, because they agreed to run a hundred laps around the gym.

During the one game that Plump missed, Gene White had the highest scoring night of his career. According to Marv Wood's wife, Mary Lou, years later as a coach at Franklin High, White reportedly told his players that he—not Plump—made The Shot to win the state title. Of course, we all know he was just kidding, though age does dim the memory somewhat.

Bobby poured in twenty-seven points in his next outing, an 81-60 victory over Rising Sun. Earlier in the year he had exploded for thirty-two points in a 64-43 victory over the same team. He averaged fifteen points during a six-game winning streak.

One week, Coach Wood noticed Plump was moping around in practice and asked twenty-six-year-old assistant coach Clarence Kelly to find out what was wrong. Kelly took him over to the bleachers and found out that he was blue over the loss of his steady girlfriend, who had begun dating a player from rival Aurora. Kelly thought he might quit basketball.

"I told him if he quit, he'd be nothing but a clodbuster," Kelly related. "I laid it on him. The kid was beaten down. He looked like a lovesick dog. I said, 'Man, there are too many chicks out there.'"

Kelly also called Plump "the finest drag-dribbler I've ever seen. He could put the ball on his hip and protect it. He was a great shooter. I never saw such talent in a little dinky town. It had to be more than luck. My wife always said it was God."

"I wasn't about to quit the team," Plump stressed. "It was kind of devastating to me. I didn't have much confidence anyway. Honestly, [Kelly's pep talk] really helped me." Bobby quickly rebounded and found a new girlfriend.

Between girl trouble and the everyday pressure of Indiana basketball, it's no wonder that Plump drank an entire bottle of Pepto-Bismol before most games. "If I wasn't nervous in the dressing room, I wasn't ready," he affirmed. "Once the ball was thrown in, all that goes away and natural instincts take over."

Milan won the sectional and went after its first victory in regional history. The Indians appeared beaten by the Knightstown Morton Memorial Orphans, but the game lasted nearly an extra fifteen seconds because it was not immediately discovered that the scoreboard plug had been accidentally kicked out. The Indians were able to rally for a thrilling 53-51 victory on Plump's two free throws (he finished with twenty-one points) in the second overtime. Milan fans went wild. Several of them jumped in the showers—clothes and all—to help the Indians celebrate.

The Cinderella team then nipped number-six-ranked Connersville, 24-22, for the championship. Plump held the ball for twelve minutes, enabling the Indians to rest from their exhausting victory just a few hours earlier. Now the townspeople really had something to celebrate.

Because of the extra time the Indians had received against Morton Memorial, a newspaper headline the next day proclaimed, "Milan steals from Orphans."

In the semi-state, the Indians held Shelbyville to incredible two-for-fifty-one shooting en route to a 43-21 victory behind Plump's sixteen points.

When the small-town Indians got their first look at vast Butler Fieldhouse, the longtime home of the state finals, Bob Engel quipped, "They can put a lot of hay in this place."

Plump noted, "We always called it the Big Barn. It's the best floor I ever played on and still is the best, bar none. It's the same as it was in 1946. When you dribble the ball, you can feel the vibration in your feet. At Madison Square Garden [New York], it doesn't come up in some places."

At the Final Four, however, their bubble burst, as they were soundly beaten in the first round by eventual champion South Bend

Central, 56-37, despite Plump's game-high nineteen points. "That was devastating—they beat the heck out of us," Plump said. "We never got close enough to use our four-corner offense. We had to change the tempo and get them to play our game, but we weren't physical enough."

Plump completed his junior year with a team-leading 14.2 scoring average as the underclass-dominated Indians (nine of the twelve would return) compiled a sparkling 24-5 record.

During his senior year, he scored twenty-eight points in a 53-46 victory over Versailles and twenty-five in a 74-60 victory over Rising Sun. The Indians posted an 18-2 regular-season record, losing only to Frankfort, 49-47, and to Aurora, 54-45.

Milan reversed the Aurora loss with a 46-38 regional victory. The semi-state brought the challenge of Indianapolis Crispus Attucks and its rising sophomore star, Oscar Robertson. The Indians, who were more experienced, ran away with a 65-52 victory as Plump poured in twenty-eight points. That was to be the worst loss in the brilliant seven-year career of Attucks coach Ray Crowe, who compiled a 179-20 record and won the next two state titles.

The Final Four was sold out as usual, and scalpers were getting $50 for a single ticket. This time, Milan was the veteran team, and it disposed of Terre Haute Gerstmeyer, 60-48, in the opening round as Plump scored twenty-six points.

That brought the Indians to the pinnacle—the state championship game against mighty Muncie Central, a school which had over eight times more students than Milan.

In the first quarter, the Bearcats' six-five center, Jim Hinds, "kind of ran over me," Plump said. "I don't remember being hurt. It was the worst game [ten points] I played in the tournament in two years. But I don't attribute the bad game I had to that."

Nevertheless, the underdog Indians were up, 22-17, at halftime. When they later went to their "cat-and-mouse" offense, however, it failed for the first time ever, and Muncie Central was able to grab a 28-26 lead early in the fourth quarter.

"That's why I stood for 4:15," Plump said of the stunning period during which he held the ball on his hip near mid-court and never moved a muscle. "Because the momentum was going the other way." He missed a shot with a little less than three minutes left, but the Indians' brilliant zone trap press produced a turnover, and Ray Craft drove for a lay-up to tie the game at twenty-eight with 2:12 left. The press forced another turnover, and Plump hit two free throws for a 30-28 lead.

A third consecutive steal enabled Coach Wood to instruct his players not to take another shot. However, Craft saw an opening, sped down the lane—and missed a lay-up. Gene Flowers' short jumper made it thirty-all with forty-eight seconds left.

Plump again held the ball until just eighteen seconds remained. During the timeout, center Gene White suggested that four players should go to one side of the court, leaving Plump isolated against Jimmy Barnes. Coach Wood bought it.

Craft was told to throw the ball in to Plump, but—caught up in the emotion—Plump passed it in to Craft. Luckily, he quickly got it back and prepared to do or die on the final shot.

"I have no idea what was going through my head," Plump confessed. "I knew they weren't going to get the ball from me and I was going to get a shot of some kind. I wasn't afraid to take it." (At that point, he had shot two-for-ten from the field, with three turnovers and no assists.)

At the eight-second mark, he faked left, went right, and Jimmy Barnes gave ground just enough to allow him an open shot from the free-throw line. "I did know it was going in," he said as he recalled the flight of a shot which he had taken literally thousands of times during his career. "My thought was 'We better get back on defense because there's still three seconds left.'

"There was pandemonium. It took us two hours before we went down to our dressing room." During that period, Plump, who had a B average, became the first player from a championship team to win the coveted Trester Award for mental attitude. He admits he never had heard of the Trester Award. He also admits he never had heard of Muncie Central. He was, after all, from a very small town!

Following the game, *Indianapolis News* wordsmith Corky Lamm wrote, "It started out as a fairy tale and ended as an epic." Truer words were never written.

Years later, the team was watching the *Hoosiers* movie for the first time, and Ray Craft quipped, "I'm the guy who made Bobby famous" (because with a four-point lead, no last-second shot would have been necessary). Plump quipped, "I have thanked him ever since."

Riding in Cadillacs, the Indians made a triumphant trip around Monument Circle in downtown Indianapolis—backward—then started their eighty-mile journey home. They were mobbed all the way. There were so many people walking along the highway that the players thought there must have been an accident. When they finally reached Milan, they were staggered by an estimated 40,000 fans, many standing on rooftops to get just a glimpse of their young heroes. The throng reportedly included people from at least five states. The Miracle of Milan already was big news in the entire country.

The six-foot, 148-pound Plump again paced the Indians with a 15.2 scoring average as a senior, and they finished with a sparkling 28-2 record. He also shot .712 from the free-throw line.

One day, Bobby heard a scraping noise outside his house and discovered a young boy cutting off a small piece of wood for a treasured souvenir. Once he received a letter addressed simply to "Plump, Ind." He has answered numerous phone calls at midnight or 1 AM from bars all over the country wanting to settle a bet over the final score or how much time was left when The Shot slew the mighty Bearcats. Not too long ago, he turned down a $15,000 offer for his coveted state championship ring.

When the call came to inform Bobby that he had been named Mr. Basketball, he had to take it at Schroder's store because his family still did not have a telephone. The little guy from Pierceville thus became the first player in history to get Hoosierland's Trifecta: a state title, Trester Award, and Mr. Basketball.

No wonder Plump admitted, "It was kind of a blur from the start of the state tournament until the end of the school year."

The last order of business was picking a college. He could have gone to the likes of Indiana, Purdue, Michigan State, Notre Dame, or UCLA, but he chose nearby Butler University "because of my fear of largeness. I wanted to play for Mr. [Tony] Hinkle and I knew the Hinkle system. I wanted to play as a freshman. Besides that, the floor was nice to me and continued to be nice."

Before Plump enrolled at Butler, he participated in the Indiana-Kentucky All-Star Game. His experience was very similar to the Muncie Central game, because he scored only ten points (8-8 free throws). He grabbed a rebound and drilled a twelve-foot jumper with forty-five seconds left as Indiana eked out a 75-74 victory. It was his only basket, but it proved once again that Bobby Plump truly was "money" in the clutch.

The Hoosier hero's first year at Butler was marked by an illness which caused him to miss the first nine games. He became a starter in the eleventh game, and finished his freshman campaign with a 12.6 scoring average and a .768 free-throw percentage. His high game was twenty-eight against DePauw.

As a sophomore Plump averaged 12.3 points and shot .825 from the free-throw line—fourteenth in the nation—as the Bulldogs posted a 14-9 record.

During his junior year, Plump broke the school record with 470 points (18.8 average), but classmate Ted Guzek was even better with 531 points. He also placed fifth in the nation with an .860 free throw percentage and earned his first of two team MVP awards—always chosen by Hinkle. As a baseball shortstop, he batted a solid .301.

As would be expected, Plump saved his best for last. He had some big games as a senior: a Butler record forty-one points against Evansville, in which he shot twelve-for-eighteen from the field, and seventeen-for-seventeen from the free-throw line; and thirty-three points against Purdue. The Bulldogs even earned an NIT berth, but Plump was held to fourteen points in a 76-69 loss to eventual champion St. John's.

As a senior Plump, set a Butler record by sinking seventeen consecutive free throws, and placed third in the nation in free-throw percentage at .838. He averaged 19.6 points as the Bulldogs posted a 15-10 record. He also set Butler career records with 1,439 points (16.4) and 477 free throws (still number one).

When Bobby got engaged to Jenine Ford in 1958, the announcement ran on the front sports page of the *Indianapolis Star*. When their son Jonathan, one of three children, was born five years later, that announcement—accompanied by a picture—ran on the front (not sports) page of the *Indianapolis Times*. By then, it was a foregone conclusion that whatever Bobby Plump did for the rest of his life was going to be big news.

Before he graduated from Butler, Bobby faced a very tough situation. He had an opportunity to play in the prestigious East-West All-star Game at Madison Square Garden in New York. If he did, though, he would miss Butler's athletic banquet and be forced to give up $100 a game to play eighteen exhibitions with a college all-star team against the famed Harlem Globetrotters.

Hinkle advised him to play in the all-star game, because he already had his standout guard penciled in to play with the Phillips 66ers of the tough National Industrial Basketball League. It turned out to be a wise choice, because even though he had a chance to make the Minneapolis Lakers or the St. Louis Hawks of the NBA, the 66ers gave him a good job with a higher salary, and the side benefits also were better.

Plump played three years for the 66ers, based in Bartlesville, Oklahoma, and was an assistant coach the fourth year. He averaged 5.9 points and shot .804 from the free-throw line during his first year. The next year he averaged 5.1 points, but set NIBL records by shooting a sizzling .930 from the free-throw line and sinking forty-seven in a row. A collapsed lung cost him much of his third and final season as a player.

While assisting Coach Bud Browning during his fourth year with the 66ers, Plump accompanied the team on a seven-week tour of the Middle East. His teammates nearly went into shock when someone recognized his face in Beruit, Lebanon. The Milan Miracle apparently had an impact that even reached far beyond the borders of the U.S.A.

In 1962, Plump moved to the Indianapolis area as a sales representative for Phillips 66. A year later, he went into the insurance business. In 1980, he began concentrating more on investments.

In 1981, Plump received the ultimate honor for a Hoosier when he was inducted into the Indiana Basketball Hall of Fame. "It's hard to describe your emotions because it's such an exceptional honor," he said.

Bobby Plump is so popular in Indiana that he once was urged to run for governor, but turned it down. "I didn't have enough confidence or money," he explained.

Throughout his professional career, Plump has been in great demand as a public speaker. "It was very difficult for about fifteen years," he confided.

Enter good friend Joe Wolfla, who had been a classmate at Butler. "Everybody thought he was stuck up," Wolfla said. "He was just shy. Even to this day, Bobby Plump still is the same person he was in high school and college. He's not only my friend, but also my hero. I'm sixty-nine years old and I've never seen a guy who treats people so kindly."

Wolfla became his manager and made sure that he got paid for his speaking engagements, which he had done free for many years. For the past fifteen years, Wolfla has gone on the road with Plump and served as the "warm-up act. I'm the dog and he's the Shetland pony," Wolfla quipped.

In 1995, Bobby opened a restaurant/sports bar in northeastern Indianapolis and named it, appropriately, "Plump's Last Shot." It is filled with his memorabilia and is frequented by celebrities and people from all walks of life.

His restaurant soon became the headquarters for "Friends of Hoosier Hysteria," as he valiantly fought against Indiana's move from a single-class state tournament to four classes. "We had CLASS basketball," he said of Indiana's much-envied, one-class tourney. "Now [as of 1998] we have MULTI-class basketball."

Bobby had a double bypass at age fifty-eight, and received a pacemaker four years ago. Today, at age seventy, he takes seven pills a day, but is healthy enough to play four-on-four, half-court basketball once a week in a fifty-and-over league. "I can still get around some people," he said proudly. "I don't do it very often, but it's kind of nice to be able to do it. Everybody likes playing with me, because I'm still a pretty good passer."

Does he still have that last-second lightning in his magic jump shot? "Oh, yeah," he replied. "Some go in. I get guarded pretty heavily when it gets down to the last shot."

Current and future generations always will have the movie *Hoosiers*—rated the best-ever sports movie by many—and the "Milan '54 Museum, Inc.," operated by Roselyn McKittrick.

She recalled a couple examples of why this story never will die. On one occasion, a couple in their seventies came all the way from Kansas to visit Milan because of the movie, which they claimed to have seen sixty-seven times the first year that it reached the big screen. "They knew every word that was said in the movie," she marveled. "I showed them all of the kids' homes."

McKittrick was particularly amazed by a couple who visited from northern Indiana. The wife said to her husband somewhat disgustedly, "Well, you're finally here! Are you satisfied!"

Her husband then explained that as a high school student, he had attended the 1954 state finals with three friends. After the morning round, they all agreed that Milan was going to be murdered by

Muncie Central, so they went to a movie and passed up the title game. Twenty miles out of Indianapolis, they had a flat tire. They walked until they found some gas, but when they returned to their car, someone had stolen all four tires.

"I've been waiting fifty years to tell this story," he said proudly of his own unique memory.

The legend of Bobby Plump and the Milan Indians apparently is destined to live forever.

JIMMY RAYL:
Long-Range Bomber

Jimmy Rayl probably had the greatest shooting range of any Indiana high school basketball player in history—and he took advantage of it often. Many times during his brilliant career at Kokomo High School, he would cross the half-court line and cut loose with reckless abandon. The ball would rise majestically toward the rafters, then descend like a rocket, hitting nothing but net. The Green Light always was on, making him a spectacular crowd-pleaser from day one.

Nobody else shot from half-court in that era. Heck, even today with the addition of the three-point shot, nobody shoots from half-court. "A lot of times, people wouldn't guard you that far out," Rayl explained. "My coach [Joe Platt] treated me like everybody else. He never got on me. I was just awfully lucky."

Longtime Purdue University assistant coach Bob King said Rayl was "really an outstanding player. Joe Platt let him crank 'em up whenever he wanted. He has to be one of the best shooters and probably had the best range of any shooter I ever have seen."

Bob Collins wrote in a December 8, 1988 edition of the *Indianapolis Star*: "They usually start with Jimmy Rayl [when discussing Indiana's finest shooters]. Ol' Skinny still ranks as the best pure shooter I've ever watched. Last summer in a shootout of former stars [in his late forties], he dropped nine straight from three-point territory. When Jimmy was hot, he was an object of wonder. Short of a sledgehammer, nothing could stop him when he got that wild shooter's look in his eye."

Ray Pavy, a high school opponent and later a college teammate, agrees. "He had a bigger range than anybody I ever saw," Pavy said. "[Rick] Mount was a good shooter, but he didn't have Jim's range."

Pavy and Rayl hooked up as seniors in the greatest two-man duel ever staged in the fabled history of Hoosier prep basketball. It took place on February 20, 1959 in New Castle's tiny gym, and has been immortalized as the "Church Street Shootout," because the gym was located on Church Street. The ballyhooed contest drew a standing-room crowd of 1,800. It marked the last regular-season game there, before New Castle began using what still today is the largest high school gym in the world.

The dynamic duo combined for an incredible 100 points. Pavy poured in fifty-one points, many coming on swirling drives which either resulted in baskets or free throws. Incredibly, he missed seven lay-ups in the first quarter, but still wound up shooting twenty-three-for-thirty-eight from the field. Meanwhile, Rayl fired mostly from outer space for forty-nine, shooting eighteen-for-thirty-three. Pavy also earned the victory, 92-81, in a key North Central Conference game. They later became teammates and good friends at Indiana University.

Pavy explained that the Trojans couldn't keep the ball from Rayl because "he was quick. Both of us were quick, but Jim was in the air quickly. If a high school kid tried to guard him, nobody would believe [how quickly he got his shot off]. He wasn't bashful. It's my guess that if you put a high school kid on him today—and he's sixty-five—he'd still get his shot off. He was a high-archer. People tried to get under his skin and I don't know anybody who did."

Two days after the game, Bob Collins wrote, "Two of the greatest shooters of our generation (or any generation for that matter) met head-on at New Castle Friday. The result was an epic standoff that will be discussed as long as Hoosiers maintain their reckless romance with basketball. New Castle won, 92-81, but the game was lost in the sheer beauty of watching two tremendous shooters practicing their trade as no two boys ever did before in one game."

"A lot of people still talk about it," Rayl noted. "Somebody gave me a piece of the floor [after the gym was torn down]. Ray and I autographed it. I put it in my [new living room] floor last summer. It's about seven inches long and it fit perfectly."

Perhaps it was prophetic that Rayl's mother, Lucille, grew up on the very ground where Kokomo's High's 7,500-seat basketball palace, Memorial Gym, would later be built. Two years before he began playing basketball seriously [age six], however, he got hooked for life on automobile racing. He attended his first Indianapolis 500 race in 1947 and missed just one until 2000.

"My dad was a Pontiac dealer in Kokomo and we'd go everywhere," he said. "I got to know a lot of drivers. I admired those guys. They were brave. A couple bought cars from my dad. I drove fast—I'm ashamed to say it—when I was in my mid-twenties. I've got a Porsche now, and I'm a good driver."

At age eight, Rayl began playing basketball in his neighborhood. "All we would do was play basketball," he said. "I shot from the side at first, then moved toward the middle. I always was the best shooter in the neighborhood."

Nobody taught Jimmy Rayl how to shoot a basketball. His biggest enemy was his lack of strength. As the old saying goes, he literally was skinny as a rail. Thus, it was only natural that during his years at Kokomo High, he was given the nickname "the Splendid Splinter," because he spread only 138 pounds across a bony, six-one frame. Some fans claimed he even could cut a defender with his razor-sharp elbows. *Kokomo Tribune* sports editor Bob Ford gave him the popular handle. "We'd shoot baskets together and he'd rebound for me," Rayl said of their close friendship.

He was painfully shy off the court, but between those lines, he was a fiery competitor, giving no quarter and asking for none. "Size had a lot to do with it," Rayl admitted. "I always had a kind of chip on my shoulder due to my size. People thought they could push me around."

Rayl scored just ninety-four points in limited roles as a sophomore. However, as he got physically stronger, he really became a dominant force as a junior, scoring points in bunches and helping Memorial Gym overflow its 7,500 seats every night. He averaged a sparkling 25.6 points that year while leading the Wildcats to a 23-4 record. They got all the way to the Fort Wayne semi-state before being upset by Elkhart, 59-57. His high game was 46 during an 88-85 loss to fabled Indianapolis Attucks.

Despite the heartbreak, the loss to Elkhart brought relief of a sort, because Jimmy was extremely superstitious. On a winning streak, he would walk (never ride) to home games and take the exact same path every night. He would wear his "lucky pants" (blue jeans with big holes) and eat the same type of food. It turned out he also had a "lucky toothbrush," and it contained only two tiny bristles the day the Wildcats bowed out of the tournament. Finally, he was free to purchase a new toothbrush! "I'm still a little that way," he confided at age sixty-five. "I put my shoes on the same way, my tie the same way and when I walk through the house I know where every light switch is."

That same year, he made an astounding 532 consecutive free throws in a church gym. He and his partner would shoot ten in a row, then rotate, so he never got into a set position for very long. He was such a great free-throw shooter that once as an adult, he shot one with each hand at the same time (one arched and one a line drive) and both balls stuck in the net.

He was even better as a senior. It seemed that every game he did something incredible—like the day against Logansport when he bent over at the free-throw line and while off balance in midair, banked in a hook shot for a stunning two-point victory.

In that final campaign, Rayl had his best year, averaging 29.6 points—40.0 over his last eight regular-season games—and setting a school record with 1,632 career points. The Wildcats compiled a 23-6 record and got all the way to the state-championship game, where they ran out of gas and were routed by—that team again—Indianapolis Attucks, 92-54. However, Jimmy took home the coveted Trester Award for mental attitude, and later was crowned Indiana's 1959 Mr. Basketball.

Kokomo's biggest barrier to the finals had been Fort Wayne South, which had a superstar of its own, six-four leaper Tom Bolyard—also destined to be Rayl's college teammate. They had a shootout of their own, won by Rayl (40-33), and the Wildcats eked out a wild 92-90 victory in the first round of the Fort Wayne semi-state.

"We'd been wanting to win the semi-state for years," Rayl said. "We called a timeout with five or six seconds to go. I drove to my right and shot [a thirty-footer]. It went through so clean [at 0:02] that the net flipped up and stayed there. If they had beaten us, he [Bolyard] probably would have gotten Mr. Basketball."

Throughout his career, Rayl constantly was harassed by players and fans alike. "In games, people would get on me like crazy," he admitted. "They'd do whatever they could to upset me. Some were dirty—giving me elbows to get me mad. I could put it into an extra gear."

He reached full throttle after being injured while playing at home against Muncie Central late in his senior year. "I went for a loose ball going out of bounds and jumped high in the air," he described. "A player ran underneath me. I came down on the side of the scorer's bench and hit my left eye." He exited the game only long enough to get some stitches and a patch placed so close to his badly-swollen eye that he barely could see.

What happened next still is quite vivid in the memory of Muncie star Ron Bonham, who was to succeed Rayl as Mr. Basketball, "He came back and hit four or five in a row." Bonham said. He also made two free throws at the end of a 79-77 victory, which handed the number-one-ranked Bearcats their first loss. He finished with forty-five points.

Corky Lamm of the *Indianapolis News* was so inspired that the next day, he wrote these immortal words: "Sickly, spindly Jimmy Rayl caught a Bearcat by the tail; wouldn't let him out alive; shot him dead with 45." No more poetic or descriptive words ever have been written about an Indiana high school basketball player.

Rayl was named Star of Stars in the annual Indiana-Kentucky All-Star Game that summer before heading to Indiana University.

As a collegian, he twice made All-America and twice exploded for a Big Ten-Conference record fifty-six points in a single game. (It still ranks third behind Purdue's Rick Mount (sixty-one) and Dave Schellhase (fifty-seven).) He also converted a school-record thirty-two consecutive free throws and was the Hoosiers' MVP in 1963. He finished his three-year varsity career with 1,401 points for a 20.6 average. His career free-throw percentage was a sizzling .835.

Freshmen were not eligible for varsity teams in this era, but the Hoosiers always kicked off their season with a frosh-varsity game. The varsity won, of course, but the Splendid Splinter fired home a game-high twenty-five points.

That same rookie year, Rayl got to know former IU star Archie Dees, who was playing for the Detroit Pistons at the time. They were shooting at opposite ends of the IU fieldhouse one day during the off season. "I was in awe of him," Rayl confided. "The next thing you know, we got to be good friends. We'd play H-O-R-S-E, and I was beating him so often that he made a rule that if my shot didn't swish, it was a letter. If it bounced or touched the rim, even if it went in, it was a letter."

He picked up a new superstition—and had a little fun along the way—when he moved to the varsity as a sophomore. He thought it was bad luck to make his last shot in pre-game practice. "Warming up before games, I would act like I was shooting a lay-up, hit the bottom of the rim and miss on purpose," he revealed. "The fans on the road would laugh and get on me."

Rayl's junior campaign produced 714 points, including a Big Ten-record 56-point explosion in a wild 105-104 overtime victory against Minnesota. His twenty-five-footer tied the game at the end of regulation, then he won it all in the extra session with a thirty-five-foot sizzler.

That same year, he and Archie Dees pulled a fast one to get into an NCAA tournament game at Louisville's Freedom Hall. They came without tickets, so when a team bus started unloading players, they walked right through the turnstiles with the players, undetected because of their size. The only downside was that they had to stand up all night.

Late in his senior year, now playing at a robust six-two and 145 pounds, Jimmy tied his record by dropping a 56-point bomb on Michigan State. It could have been much more because Coach Branch McCracken took him out with three and a half minutes left.

Reflecting on that game, he pointed out, "The year after I graduated, they stopped the clock for traveling. [Before then the clock continued to run as the ball was taken out of bounds.] Games are five minutes longer now." He can only dream about how many more points he could have scored under the new rule.

After graduating from IU in 1963, Jimmy played for the Akron, Ohio Wingfoots, who captured the national AAU championship and won the World Cup gold medal in Rome in 1966.

In his first year (1967-68) with the Indiana Pacers of the American Basketball Association, he averaged 12.5 points and fans voted him most popular player on the team. "I changed my style and tried to pass more," he pointed out. "I was second in assists." He also had managed to boost his weight to 170 pounds, 28 more than when he played his last college game.

In one and a half years with the Pacers, he scored 1,125 points for an 11.1 average. His best game was thirty-two points, fourteen rebounds, and eight assists against Denver. Not long after a seventeen-point outing, he was cut "due to my size and my salary. I didn't say anything. I just got dressed and left. It was just before Christmas."

It *was* confusing, to say the least, because he always got the job done on the court. He recalled a game against New Jersey: "With four and a half minutes left in the first half, I had fourteen points. I led both teams in scoring and didn't get to play in the second half. What bothered me [about getting cut] was that I knew I was good enough to play."

So, the former Hoosier became an Indianapolis-area account representative for Xerox, a job he did very successfully for thirty years. Jimmy had married his high school sweetheart, Nancy, in 1964, and they had four children: Jimmy, Tom, Tim, and Ginger. The boys played basketball for Kokomo High.

Tim died in 1997 at age twenty-five in a tragic automobile accident and Jimmy, truthfully, never has gotten over the loss. "Tim was the best," Jimmy says proudly. "He was six-seven and he could shoot. He was everybody's friend. Judges, lawyers—close to 700 people—came to his funeral. He was a special kid."

Still, the Splendid Splinter never could fully let go of shooting a basketball. He would accompany his boys each summer when they came north to play in the competitive Plymouth, Indiana summer basketball league. On occasion, he would have to fill in when the Kokomo team was a player short. They still speak in reverent tones about the way he buried threes even when he was around forty years old, playing against opponents half his age.

Dennis Kasey was a high school student when he first ran into Rayl at the Kokomo YMCA. That was the place where Jimmy would play former Purdue star Bruce Parkinson and "beat him to death" in H-O-R-S-E. "I caught glimpses of his greatness, even when he was older," Kasey said.

Well, Dennis and his brother, David, became huge Jimmy Rayl fans, often playing pickup games with him. Eventually, Dennis was hired as sports director at Indianapolis TV station WHMB. Ten years ago, he did a documentary, *Hoosier Hysteria*, which included some footage of Rayl shooting on his driveway court.

"Should I stop down when he misses?" the cameraman asked Kasey.

"He hit about thirty shots in a row," Kasey noted. "I said, 'Jimmy, you didn't shoot your patented hook shot.' Sure enough he made one from forty feet and my cameraman almost fainted."

In 1989, Rayl was inducted into the Indiana Basketball Hall of Fame. Even today, his fame remains. "It's surprising the number of letters I'll get," he said. "I get index cards from younger people to sign. I still get eight or ten a year. I always get a little enjoyment out of that."

He still attends a lot of high school and college games. At Kokomo's Memorial Gym, he can be found seated near the very top of the bleachers, where he wishes to be "as inconspicuous as possible."

Incredibly, the sixty-five-year-old legend now weighs 250 pounds. He suffered a stroke three years ago, which left him with a slight limp. Sadly, he has not shot a basketball "for the last three or four years. I have no interest in shooting anymore. What's the point?"

Please, say it ain't so, Jimmy!

OSCAR ROBERTSON:

Still the Greatest

Fifty-one years after he graduated with every conceivable honor from Indianapolis Crispus Attucks High School, Oscar Robertson still is the greatest all-around basketball player ever produced, not only in Indiana but in the entire world. No player—past or present—ever has matched his overall wizardry as a scorer, rebounder, and passer.

Nicknamed "The Big O," Robertson dominated basketball at every level—winning two state championships in high school, named National Player of the Year three times at the University of Cincinnati and setting an NBA record that never has been approached by averaging a triple-double over an entire season in the NBA.

The sixty-eight-year-old legend was named "Player of the Century" in 2000 by the National Association of Basketball Coaches. He had been enshrined in the Naismith Basketball Hall of Fame since 1979, the Indiana Basketball Hall of Fame since 1982, and the National High School Hall of Fame since 1983. The prestigious United States Basketball Writers Association awards the Oscar Robertson Trophy annually to its national player of the year.

Retired Purdue University assistant coach Bob King calls Robertson "as good of a player as I ever saw. He had the ability to know where everyone was on the floor at the same time. Whatever level he was at, he dominated. He did it so gracefully. He just flowed through everything. He made everybody else pale by comparison."

Former high school teammate John Gipson affirmed, "I'd take him over Michael Jordan. Jordan was a great offensive player, but … Nobody could touch Oscar. He was a perfectionist on the floor. He got everybody involved, plus he controlled the game. When you played with him, you just gave way to him."

Another teammate, Bill Hampton, called Oscar "a student of the game. When it was over, it wasn't over. He analyzed things and always has been competitive. There was no jealousy. Our team was like a Swiss watch. The ultimate goal was to win."

Hallie Bryant, who starred for the Harlem Globetrotters, played against the younger Robertson in pickup games. He recalled that Oscar "always was a person able to focus because he had a passion for the game. He always wanted to be the best and he did what he had to do. He was dedicated and believed in himself. He was self-disciplined, had courage and persistence."

Former Indianapolis Sacred Heart player Joe Wolfla, who had to guard Robertson in high school, said, "He was so superior. It was like having a symphony orchestra against a five-piece band. He was a man in motion—way, way above his time."

Oscar was born to Bailey and Mazell Robertson on Thanksgiving Day 1938, in Charlotte, Tennessee, one of three boys. Their farm had no running water or electricity. When he was four years old, his family moved to a poor section of Indianapolis—referred to as Frog Island because it often flooded—where his tiny world revolved totally around family, school, church, and sports.

In the beginning, all he did was shoot a ball of rags at a tree, which served as an imaginary basket. Later, playing with brothers Bailey Jr. and Henry, Oscar honed his game on a makeshift court, appropriately called the "Dust Bowl" because it was nothing but dirt (mud when it rained) and rocks surrounding a pole, backboard, and hoop planted in a vacant lot. It wouldn't take much imagination to visualize the dust constantly stirred up by young hoopsters going head to head from sunup until sundown. It's no wonder he became such an adept dribbler.

In addition, he played on an asphalt court at the nearby Lockfield Gardens housing project and at the Senate Avenue YMCA. Though he also played football and baseball in season, he realized early on that basketball was the "emperor" of them all. He worked at his game tirelessly, beginning to excel in all phases. Nobody, of course, ever heard of a "point guard" or "small forward" at that time.

Each summer, however, he would return to his Tennessee roots, where he had many relatives. Every day, he worked in the fields, picking tobacco and shucking corn. He also milked cows and stacked heavy bales of hay. The only thing he didn't like about those visits was the abundance of snakes, especially copperheads. He claimed that copperheads smelled like cucumbers, so he always knew when one was lurking nearby. These annual summer trips were instrumental in helping Oscar develop physical strength and a tremendous work ethic.

Mrs. Robertson began working for a wealthy white family. One Christmas Day, she brought home an item that the family had discarded, and Oscar had his first basketball at age eleven. His parents also divorced that year, but Oscar never learned about it until he was in high school, because nothing was said, and Bailey Sr. continued to live with his family.

Robertson began making his own mark by helping Public School 17 win the Indianapolis city championship in his eighth- and ninth-grade years. He had received ample inspiration one year earlier by watching his talented brother, Bailey, and future Harlem Globetrotters Hallie Bryant and Willie Gardner take Crispus Attucks—an all-black high school in an era still choked by segregation—to the coveted state finals. The Tigers lost to Evansville Reitz, 66-59, but a great tradition had been launched.

Playing against such talented, taller, older players in the off season forced Robertson to develop a unique—and very lethal—one-handed jump shot, because he tired of getting his shots blocked. The rugged competition also forced him to develop many fakes and other moves which served him quite well in future years.

Teammate John Gipson pointed out, "Even in eighth and ninth grade, you could tell he was at another level. He never played around. I wasn't concentrating one day, and his pass hit me right in the chest. I was embarrassed. He said, 'Hey, you gonna catch the ball?' He was serious all the time. We were playing with all older guys and one of them asked Oscar why he didn't take a shot. He said, 'Because you had a better shot.'"

At the end of his freshman year, Oscar was five-eight. By the time he tried out for the Attucks varsity as a sophomore, however, he had shot up six inches to six-two. Despite hand-me-down uniforms and no home games, he was prepared to take on all challengers.

First came a note of caution. Already a fancy ball handler, Oscar was told by Coach Ray Crowe before he ever played a varsity game that there would be "no dribbling between your legs or passing behind your back. We won't see any of that."

The Tigers opened against Fort Wayne North at Indianapolis Tech (they had no home gym). Oscar had to travel to the game by bus and survive a knife threat from a passenger. (Each player received fifty cents for the bus and one dollar for his meal.) Despite the obstacles, he came off the bench after three minutes had elapsed and finished with fifteen points.

He broke into the starting lineup in the second game and stayed there for three brilliant years. Though he averaged just twelve points as a sophomore, he clearly established himself as a clutch player. He also proved that nobody could outwork him. Ray Crowe had to turn off the lights to get him out of the gym.

Prior to a game against Indianapolis Tech, Oscar was one of several players who received threats on their lives, probably from gamblers.

In the rugged Indianapolis semi-state, Robertson swished the winning free throw to nip Columbus, 68-67. He then poured in twenty-two points (eleven in the first quarter), in a valiant effort against eventual state champion Milan, but the Tigers lost, 65-52. It was to be the worst loss in Coach Ray Crowe's brilliant seven-year career. The young Attucks crew finished with a 24-5 record, and great things were on the horizon.

Bobby Plump, who scored twenty-eight points for Milan, admitted, "We didn't know about Oscar at the time. Within the first four minutes of the game, we knew he was good," he laughed. "We didn't know he was going to turn out to be the greatest ever to play the game."

Though quite shy and reserved off the court, Robertson was the acknowledged leader of a veteran team during his junior year. The six-five Robertson teamed with senior Willie Merriweather at forward. "He was the epitome of a basketball player," Merriweather said. "He could see all and do all. If I didn't get the rebound, Oscar had it and I would take off down the court. He'd say the same about me.

"Against a zone, Mr. Crowe would set the offense so Oscar would come out on the floor. He would take long shots and break down the zone. Their team would be in disarray, and then we would start to run."

Merriweather recalled one practice session in which Oscar tried to beat a double-team by firing a behind-the-back pass. However, it caught center O'Dell Darnell by surprise, hit him in the back, and soared out of bounds. Coach Crowe warned Oscar to "say nothing," but he mumbled something at Darnell because their team lost, and the losers always had to run laps. Oscar, who hated to lose and seldom did, had to run five extra laps.

The high-flying Tigers were becoming a major attraction, and when they played city foe Shortridge at Butler Fieldhouse, they drew a huge crowd of 11,561.

Rolling unbeaten toward the state playoffs, the Tigers stumbled late in the season when they suffered a 58-57 loss at Connersville. It was loud and hot, causing someone to open a door. Then the floor—situated above a swimming pool—became slippery as condensation formed, neutralizing the Tigers' famed fast break. Oscar scored eighteen of his twenty-two points in the second half, but even he could not quite overcome the Spartans' red-hot 60 percent shooting from the field. However, it was to be his last loss as a high school performer.

The Attucks players were ashamed to attend school after the Connersville loss. Crowe let them know how unhappy he was by serving up a rugged five-hour practice, complete with a marathon number of laps to run. Message received loud and clear, they thumped most opponents the rest of the year.

Robertson scored 450 points during the regular season, breaking Hallie Bryant's Indianapolis city record.

Sad to say, the all-black school at times had to beat seven men, because the refereeing often went against the Tigers. They felt as if they had to start many games with a ten-point disadvantage. In fact, it seemed that most of the white world wanted the Tigers to fail.

Bob King, then an assistant coach at Shortridge High, volunteered to scout opponents for Attucks during regional and semi-state rounds. "Oscar paid a lot of attention to those scouting reports," King recalled. "He said, 'Coach, Bob, you even told us what color socks they were wearing.' I even got criticized by some people for scouting for them. I still credit Ray Crowe for averting some problems."

The semi-state produced a huge 71-70 victory over number-one-ranked Muncie Central. Oscar scored twenty-five points and made a crucial steal at the end. "He came out of nowhere to save the game," Willie Merriweather said. He was mobbed by fans after clinching the biggest win in Attucks history.

At the Final Four, the Tigers ousted New Albany, 79-67, before a crowd of 15,000 in the first round. They then raced past another all-black school, Gary Roosevelt, 97-74, to become the first all-black school—and the first Indianapolis school—to win an Indiana state basketball crown. Robertson scored thirty points in the championship game.

Smiles and tears flowed freely. The players got to ride a fire truck to Monument Circle in the middle of town, but were unable to stay there, and quickly were whisked away to Northwestern Park in the black section of Indianapolis. Even though a crowd of 25,000 enjoyed the bonfire that night, many were left with a sour taste in their mouths because city officials had feared—for no reason—some type of disturbance. The traditional parade never was held either.

Oscar left in the middle of the celebration, headed home, and went to bed early. He had seen the handwriting on the wall—very clearly.

Robertson led all other Indianapolis scorers as a junior with a 21.7 average as the state-champion Tigers posted a 31-1 record. They also were crowned mythical national champions by Art Johlfs's National Sports News Service, based in Minneapolis, Minnesota.

The six-five, 210-pound Robertson was the only returning starter for his senior year, but he was a man on a mission. The Tigers opened with an 81-41 blowout of Fort Wayne Central behind his thirty-one points. He later exploded for a city-record forty-five points during a 123-53 demolishing of Michigan City Elston.

Not too long afterward, however, Washington's Jerry Lawlis pumped in forty-eight points to one-up Robertson. The Tigers wanted their star to get his record back, so they set out against Sacred Heart to do just that. He scored twenty points in the first quarter, then he began being triple-teamed because his teammates wouldn't shoot. Still, he scored ten in both of the middle two periods before exploding for twenty-two in the final stanza. That gave him sixty-two points—still an Indianapolis city record. He shot twenty-three-for-sixty from the field, and sixteen-for-twenty-two from the free-throw line.

Throughout Oscar's final go-round, he was a huge drawing card. Record crowds turned out everywhere. The Attucks Tigers legitimately could have been tagged the "Junior Globetrotters."

But there was that usual downside, too. Joe Wolfla pointed out, "They came to town and ate on the bus. When the game was over, they had to get out of town. It was like being invited to dinner, but they wanted you to eat the salad and leave before the main course."

Robertson refused to let the Tigers lose, though, as they marched relentlessly through the state tournament for the second consecutive year. Playing before another packed house of 15,000 at the Final Four, they eliminated Terre Haute Gerstmeyer, 68-59, in the semifinals, even though Oscar fouled out for the only time in his prep career. They then routed Lafayette Jefferson, 79-57, in the state championship game as Oscar, who was guarded by four different players, erupted for a record thirty-nine points. Legendary Lafayette coach Marion Crawley called him the greatest player he ever had seen.

This time, Attucks players at least got to climb the Monument Circle steps and wave to the crowd before they again were whisked off to Northwestern Park for their post-championship celebration. Again, the celebration was joyous and peaceful.

The Tigers finished with a perfect 31-0 record and were Indiana's first-ever undefeated state champion. Stretching back to the previous season, they also set a state record with forty-five consecutive wins—a mark which stood for fifty years. In addition, they repeated as mythical national champions, although they had to share the honor with Jerry Lucas-led Middletown, Ohio.

Robertson averaged 26 points a game and set a city record with 805 points in a single season. His career total of 1,825 points also set a city record. Oscar was named to the first annual Scholastic Coach All-American team and later was named Indiana's Mr. Basketball.

Attucks's unparalleled basketball success also will long be remembered for hastening integration in a state once dominated by the Ku Klux Klan. Indiana's most beloved sport proved to be a very subtle weapon in helping to neutralize the color line.

Ironically, as other schools began accepting more blacks, Attucks's enrollment dwindled, and in 1986—with just 900 students—it was converted into a junior high. The good news for Attucks fans, however, is that in 2006, it was re-converted to a high school with a freshman class and plans to add a class each year until it reaches full capacity.

A top student, Robertson graduated in 1956, ranked number 16 in a class of 171 students.

He still had two orders of business to finish, however. One was leading the Indiana All-Stars in their annual summer series against Kentucky and number two was choosing a college.

The All-Star series proved quite interesting, because Kentucky was led by King Kelly Coleman, who had scored a staggering 4,263 points during his career at Wayland High, and averaged an eye-popping 46 points as a senior.

With a crowd of 14,500 looking on at Butler Fieldhouse, Robertson volunteered to guard the Kentucky legend. The result: Oscar scored thirty-four points, the King seventeen, and Indiana ran away with a 92-78 victory. It was even more decisive a week later in Kentucky, as Oscar set a game record with forty-one points and Indiana routed the Bluegrass boys, 102-77. Oscar rightfully received a standing ovation when he sat down for the night. The King, meanwhile, quietly abdicated his throne with one-for-nine shooting and a measly four points.

The college choice was much more complicated. Coach Crowe took Oscar to nearby Indiana University, but the long wait and unsatisfactory interview with Coach Branch McCracken struck the Hoosiers off his list. Michigan lost out when coaches forgot to pick Oscar up at the Detroit airport.

Enter Cincinnati coach George Smith, who wisely courted Robertson's mother and wound up with the biggest catch of his career. Smith knew he had struck pure gold when his varsity barely beat the freshmen, 87-83, before a crowd of 6,000. Despite being constantly double-teamed, Oscar amassed thirty-seven points, eighteen rebounds, and eight assists.

Just to show that his freshman records of 429 points in a season (33.6 average) and 47 in one game weren't flukes, Robertson exploded onto the scene as a sophomore. He poured in 984 points (35.1 average), grabbed 425 rebounds (15.2), and shot .571 from the field as the Bearcats posted a 25-3 record. He also led the nation in scoring and was the first sophomore to be named National Player of the Year.

In his first appearance at New York's famed Madison Square Garden, he set a Garden record for a collegiate player by pouring in fifty-six points against Seton Hall.

College basketball never had seen anything like Oscar Robertson, and he was just getting warmed up. The six-five, 210-pound forward was so intelligent, talented, and versatile that he was virtually unstoppable.

Robertson was Cincinnati's first black basketball player and—despite his greatness—was forced to stay in dorms when the rest of the team stayed in hotels on many road trips. This humiliating practice finally ended during his junior year.

As a junior, he again led the nation in scoring with 978 points (32.6), grabbed 489 rebounds (16.3), dished out 206 assists (6.9), and shot .509 from the field. The Bearcats compiled a 26-4 record and reached the Final Four where they finished third in the nation. Again he was named National Player of the Year.

He was leading scorer and MVP in the 1959 East-West Shrine Game at Kansas City and the leading scorer as the U.S.A. won the Pan-American Games that same summer.

In unprecedented fashion, Robertson led the nation in scoring and was named National Player of the Year for the third straight season as a senior. He amassed 1,011 points (33.7), 424 rebounds (14.1), and 219 assists (7.3) while shooting .526 from the field. He also exploded for a school-record sixty-two points against North Texas State. The Bearcats went 28-2, again reached the Final Four, but again had to settle for a third-place finish.

Robertson finished his unparalleled three-year career with 2,973 points (33.8), 1,338 rebounds (15.2), and 425 assists (7.1—none were kept his sophomore year). He shot .535 from the field and .780 from the free-throw line. The team record was 79-9. Oscar set fourteen NCAA records alone.

UC officials immediately retired his famous uniform number (12), and in 1994 they erected a nine-foot bronze statue of him, which resides majestically outside the east concourse at the Shoemaker Center.

Though the Big O did not win an NCAA championship, he very definitely set the table for a recruiting bonanza which produced immediate dividends with national titles in 1961 and 1962.

In the summer of 1960, Robertson and Jerry West were co-captains of the U.S. team, which went undefeated and won the gold medal at the Rome Olympics. Oscar averaged seventeen points on what still is ranked as one of America's greatest-ever teams.

It should have surprised no one when, after being drafted by the Cincinnati Royals, Robertson was the NBA's Rookie of the Year in 1961. Shifted from forward to guard, he led the league with 9.7 assists per game and placed third with a 30.5 scoring average. He also was the All-Star Game MVP after scoring twenty-three points and breaking Bob Cousy's record with fourteen assists.

Oscar's second-year NBA statistics still are the "Holy Grail" of basketball at any level. In 79 games, he averaged an eye-popping 30.8 points, 12.5 rebounds, and 11.4 assists. No one ever has matched this incredible triple-double. In fact, his first five years in the pros produced these remarkable averages: 30.4 points, 10.7 assists, and 10.0 rebounds.

The Hoosier great played ten years for the Royals and was named the NBA's MVP in 1964. He was traded to the Milwaukee Bucks in 1970 and teamed with Kareem Abdul-Jabbar to win the 1970-71 NBA championship with a 78-18 record, including a twenty-game winning streak. In the championship season, he averaged 19.4 points, 8.2 assists, and 5.7 rebounds. He spent four years with the Bucks before retiring in 1974.

During his 14-year NBA career, Robertson scored 26,710 points (25.7), handed out 9,887 assists (9.5), and grabbed 7,804 rebounds (7.5). His career assists, free-throws made (7,694), and triple-doubles

(181) all were NBA records. Even in 2007, Magic Johnson is a distant second with 138 triple-doubles. He scored 246 points (20.5) in 12 All-Star games, and earned three MVP awards.

Robertson not only was a battler on the court, but he also fought for the entire membership as president of the NBA Players Union. In 1970, he filed a lawsuit against the NBA, which produced a major decision in favor of the players six years later. It's called the Oscar Robertson Rule, and it forever changed the balance of power in professional sports, paving the way for unrestricted free agency.

That's one of many reasons why he has the right to be bitter that the NBA never offered him a position as coach or front-office executive. Or, indeed, it may be *the* reason he never has been embraced by his former employers.

Longtime friend Joe Wolfla says, "To me, he is the most misunderstood person. When we do interviews, he answers the question. It's not always what people want to hear, but he's no phony. We were doing an interview at Hinkle Fieldhouse one time and his answer was not what the guy wanted, so [Oscar] left. I said, 'Why don't you write down your questions and give us the answers.'"

Over the years, Robertson has built a number of successful businesses, been a humanitarian, social activist, television and radio commentator, and author. Obviously, he's been just as versatile off the court as he was on the court.

Oscar and Yvonne, whom he married in 1960, live in the Cincinnati area and have three daughters—Shana, Tia, and Mari. In 1997, he donated a kidney to Tia, who was suffering from lupus-related kidney failure. He had to lose a lot of weight to be fit, and entered the hospital under an assumed name. Somehow, the news got out, and he received a lot of unwanted publicity.

A deeply religious man, he eloquently summed up who Oscar Robertson is when he said quietly, "I'm no hero. I'm just a father."

GLENN ROBINSON:

Region's Best

The Region—basically Gary, Hammond, and East Chicago—has produced many great basketball players over the years, but none better than Glenn "Big Dog" Robinson. Though he was six-seven, over 200 pounds, and always played inside, Robinson had many guard skills and was a superb outside shooter. And, above all, he was "money" when the game was on the line.

Robinson shattered many records while leading Gary Roosevelt to the 1991 Indiana state championship, was named National Player of the Year as a junior at Purdue University, and then had a distinguished eleven-year professional career, climaxed by a reserve role for the NBA champion San Antonio Spurs.

Though he always was tall for his age, Robinson had miles to go before he reached stardom. Roosevelt coach Ron Heflin first spotted him at Norton Elementary School and admitted, "He couldn't play a bit. People would run him off the court and take his ball. What really sold me on him was that he had quickness for his size."

Robinson still was so lacking in confidence as a seventh grader that he refused to even try out for the team.

Possibly because of the way he had been treated growing up, Robinson eventually developed "a lot of toughness," Heflin noted.

"He's always been well-coordinated. He could run all day and not get tired. As freshmen, I ran them for forty-five minutes straight one day. Everybody else fell by the wayside, but he wouldn't give up. I said, 'We can teach him the rest,' and the rest is history."

Robinson, who lived one block from Roosevelt High, stood a shade under six-five as a freshman. "He was good enough for the varsity," Heflin conceded, "but I didn't want him to play varsity. We used him on the freshman and JV teams, and he had a fantastic year. By then, we knew he was the top talent in Gary."

As a sophomore, the six-five, 190-pound Robinson started at center for the Roosevelt varsity and averaged 16.9 points as the Panthers posted a 20-3 record. "He was thin but pretty strong," Heflin said. "He scored well and he always could rebound and block shots."

He was even more dominant as a junior, leading the 23-3 Panthers in ten categories. He averaged 21.5 points, 11.6 rebounds, and 4.0 blocks while shooting a sizzling .634 from the field.

"He easily could have averaged thirty points," Heflin pointed out, "but I believed in sharing the ball. He had so many good games—a lot of double-doubles. He'd get twenty-eight or twenty-nine points, and I'd take him out and sit him the last quarter. We pressed a lot and played up-tempo. I used a lot of players. To tell the truth, I didn't want him to have too much success too early."

Off the court, Robinson would spend a lot of time at Heflin's house. "He was always a very quiet, reserved person," Heflin related. "He was very serious-minded."

Entering his senior campaign, Robinson was a legitimate contender—along with six-nine Michigan standout Chris Webber—for National Player of the Year honors. "He never thought he was that good," Heflin revealed. "It kept him hungry and working hard."

Roosevelt did not have a lot of size, and Heflin needed to keep Robinson as close to the basket as possible. However, the big guy, who was now almost six-seven, "wanted to play out on the floor," Heflin said. "I'd let him shoot a lot of threes after practice. We'd play H-O-R-S-E for an hour or so. That kind of satisfied him. I won quite a few of them because I could shoot the ball. He was a fierce competitor and he'd get mad because he didn't like to lose."

Heflin had to admit that Robinson, who patterned his game after Scottie Pippen of the NBA champion Chicago Bulls, "was the best three-point shooter we had. In our last [regular-season] game of the year, I let him play outside. It was Senior Night. He scored twenty-six or twenty-eight points and hit a few threes. He handled the ball really well."

Robinson saved his best for last, because he truly dominated the state tournament as a senior. The Panthers trailed East Chicago by five or six points in the regional. "Glenn almost single-handedly turned that game around," Heflin praised. "East Chicago stole the ball and was going for a lay-up. Glenn passed everybody on the floor, stripped the ball from the dribbler, went right back, and laid it up. He could have been a heck of a track star. He ran the 400-meters in 52 seconds in gym and wasn't even trying.

"I said with about two or three minutes left, 'Nobody shoot the ball but Glenn the rest of the game,' because they couldn't stop him inside or outside." Despite being closely guarded, Robinson later drilled a long jumper to nip East Chicago, 81-80, in a double-overtime thriller. He took game honors with forty-one points.

The next week in the semi-state, Robinson eliminated Anderson Highland, 42-41, with a thirteen-foot jumper at the five-second mark. He had twenty points and fifteen rebounds on that occasion.

At the state finals in Indianapolis, Roosevelt rolled past surprise entry Whitko, 83-53, in the first round as Robinson scored twenty-three points and pulled down seventeen rebounds.

That set the stage for the dream match-up between Robinson and Alan Henderson of Indianapolis Brebeuf in the state championship game. They clearly were the leading candidates for Indiana's coveted Mr. Basketball honors, and this game easily could decide the winner.

Well, it wasn't even close. Glenn outscored his chief rival, 22-14, grabbed ten rebounds, and Roosevelt rolled to a lopsided 51-32 victory. "We knew all the time that Glenn was more advanced," Heflin affirmed.

The Panthers finished with a sparkling 30-1 record. The only loss was to Martinsville, 66-62, in the Hall of Fame Tournament. Robinson had fifteen points and thirteen rebounds in that game. "Had we won that game, we wouldn't have won the state," Heflin believes. "That really pulled us back into focus."

Robinson averaged career-highs of 25.6 points and 14.6 rebounds as a senior. He also averaged 3.8 blocks and shot .600 from the field. During his three-year career, he scored a school-record 1,710 points while pacing the Panthers to a sparkling 73-7 record. And he, indeed, was named Mr. Basketball.

He also made the prestigious McDonald's All-American team and scored twenty points to spark the West to a victory. Later he scored thirty-seven points and grabbed ten rebounds in an exhibition game against the Soviet Junior National Team.

"He's the best ball player I ever coached," Heflin says simply.

Longtime *Gary Post Tribune* sportswriter John Mutka calls Robinson "the best high school player I ever saw. He was a great offensive player."

Robinson had college scholarship offers from across the country, but Purdue had the inside track, because he had been attending the Purdue Basketball Camp since eighth grade. Coach Gene Keady recalled, "You could see that he was going to be a special player. He liked us and his high school coach liked us. If he didn't win a lot of awards [at the camp], we were pretty dumb," Keady laughed. "I thought he had Mr. Basketball potential as a sophomore."

Indiana and Nevada-Las Vegas pushed hard, but the Boilermakers ultimately won the bidding war.

Unfortunately, Robinson's grades and test scores were not high enough, forcing him to sit out his freshman year as a "Prop 48."

The academic problems had first cropped up during his sophomore year when his mother, Christine Bridgeman, briefly pulled him off the Roosevelt basketball team until his grades improved to her satisfaction.

"Glenn was a C-D student," Heflin said. "But he was much brighter. He could have been a B student had he worked at it. Glenn had a very high IQ. He's close to a Purdue degree. That was always my top priority for him to finish school."

Robinson paid the price, because he was unable to play basketball as a freshman and put on some unnecessary weight. "It was very hard on both of us," Keady admitted. "He could have made us a lot better. He had a good attitude and kept working at it."

The biggest positive from that idle season is that it gave the young freshman time to become a truly great shooter. With nothing else to do, he just shot and shot and shot. Purdue's opponents were going to pay the ultimate price for his frustrating rookie year.

Before the Gary great played his first varsity game, he already had been nicknamed "Big Dog" by a Purdue custodian. He liked it so much that he had the head of a snarling bulldog wearing a spiked collar tattooed on his chest. Later, campus bookstores began selling thousands of Big Dog T-shirts. Feeling exploited, he put a stop to it.

As a sophomore, Robinson stepped right into the starting lineup and had a great year. He averaged an impressive 24.1 points and 9.2 rebounds while shooting .676 from the field and .741 from the free-throw line. He produced thirteen double-doubles and scored less than ten points just once. The Boilermakers finished with an 18-10 record, and he was named second-team All-America.

Keady found out early that Robinson could be a huge defensive factor if he hounded the player who was going to inbound the ball. His long arms, quickness and thirty-four-inch vertical jump made him a formidable obstacle.

He also quickly discovered that his standout sophomore "was very good at taking the last shot to win the game. He never panicked. He and Troy Lewis were the greatest shooters I ever coached."

"My wife, Pat, did a lot of PR work for him," Keady revealed. "She advised him and told key media people how good of a player and kid that he was. She did a good job of selling him.

"For me, he was great to coach," Keady continued. "We did a lot of defensive drills, and all I would hear [when he went to the NBA] was that he couldn't play defense. He was our best practice player. He played hard and I really enjoyed him. I was hard on him. I told him, 'I'm going to be harder on you than anyone. If I'm soft on you, all the other kids will follow suit.' If he was going to make the NBA, he had to be tough. He never took it personally."

No matter what Keady dished out, Robinson took it like a man. Sometimes, of course, he deserved it. One day, Keady said his star "was goofing around in the dorm and was being kind of rude on the phone. I chewed him out in front of the team. I said, 'Why don't you go pro and quit being a jerk?' He took it well. Another time I stopped practice and chewed him out about rebounding. He got every rebound the rest of practice.

"He was an easy guy to coach. He was fun in the dressing room and could take teasing."

The summer before his junior year, Robinson averaged an impressive 28.4 points and 10.2 rebounds, to lead the Boilermakers on a European tour.

Classmate Cuonzo Martin, now a Purdue assistant coach, said there was no jealousy when Robinson got the headlines. "We had a lot of laid-back guys," he pointed out. "It was great to have him as a teammate. He was a good guy, fun to be around. The greatest compliment is that he didn't want the spotlight."

Robinson had an awesome junior year, which culminated in 1994 National Player of the Year honors, first-team All-America, and a big NBA contract. "Almost every game was a highlight game," Keady praised. "He was tremendous."

It started with MVP honors in the Great Alaska Shootout. In the Big Ten opener at Northwestern, the Big Dog drilled a ten-foot baseline jumper with eight seconds left, for a 68-67 win. The

Boilermakers set a school record by winning their first fourteen games. Later, Robinson stunned Michigan with a running jumper at 0:07 for a 95-94 victory.

In Purdue's final regular-season game, Robinson erupted for a career-high forty-nine points to help the Boilermakers clinch their nineteenth Big Ten crown with an 87-77 victory over Illinois.

Purdue finished third in the Associated Press national rankings and received a number-one seed in the NCAA tourney. Robinson left his mark during a Sweet 16 match-up by pouring in forty-four points to eliminate Kansas, 83-78, and send the Boilermakers to the Elite Eight. Fans held up "Beware of the Dog" signs, and Purdue cheerleaders "woofed" every time he scored. However, his career ended the following week with a thirteen-point output during a loss to Duke. Just one game short of the Final Four, the Boilermakers finished with a 29-5 record.

Robinson poured in a Purdue-record 1,030 points for a 30.3 average. He also grabbed 344 rebounds for a 10.1 average and shot .796 from the free-throw line. He was the first player in sixteen years to lead the Big Ten in scoring and rebounding.

During his two-year varsity career, he scored 1,706 points (27.5 average), grabbed 602 rebounds (9.7 average), shot .479 from the field and .773 from the free-throw line. He was held under ten points only once—a two-point effort as a sophomore during a 48-45 victory at Southwest Missouri State.

Another significant statistic is that Purdue sold out twenty-seven consecutive home games during Robinson's two-year career.

Looking back at Robinson's brilliant career, longtime Purdue assistant coach Bob King noted, "He had catlike agility, great body balance, and was a great leaper. He was a big guy who played like a six-one guard. As an all-around player, he was awfully hard to beat."

Asked about the loss of Robinson for his senior year, Keady replied, "I think it kept us from winning the national championship—or at least going to the Final Four. We won the Big Ten without him."

In the summer of 1994, the Milwaukee Bucks made Robinson the first overall pick in the NBA draft. Following an early holdout, he signed what then was an unprecedented ten-year, $68 million contract. He averaged 21.9 points and was named to the NBA's All-Rookie Team.

Robinson made the 1996 U.S. Olympic team, but was unable to play due to an injury.

He starred for the Bucks for eight seasons, and twice made the NBA All-Star team. He averaged at least twenty points seven times and finished number two in Bucks' career scoring. Never forgetting his roots, he donated fifty tickets to youth groups from Gary and Milwaukee for each Milwaukee home game.

During the 1998-99 season, Robinson paced the Bucks in scoring (18.4), while finishing second in free-throw percentage (.870) and rebounding (5.9). In 1999-2000 he averaged 20.9 points, second on the team.

He later played for Atlanta and Philadelphia before finishing his career as a reserve for the San Antonio Spurs, where he picked up an NBA championship ring in 2005. A late-season pickup, he averaged ten points in nine regular-season games, then averaged 3.8 points in thirteen playoff games.

During 11 NBA campaigns, the 225-pound Robinson averaged 20.7 points, 6.1 rebounds and 2.7 assists. He shot .459 from the field and .820 from the free-throw line. He scored 14,234 points and pulled down 4,189 rebounds. His career highs included forty-five points, seventeen rebounds (twice), and ten assists.

Ankle and knee injuries plagued Robinson during the latter part of his career and ultimately caused him to pull down the final curtain.

Robinson returns to Gary each summer to conduct the Glenn Robinson Basketball Champions of Fundamentals Camp. "He gets three hundred to five hundred kids for five days in July," Ron Heflin indicated. "All of them are inner-city kids and can't afford to pay, so he picks up the tab. He runs it really well."

What does the thirty-four-year-old Robinson do with the rest of his time? "His first love was not basketball—it was music," Heflin revealed. "He likes rap. Even now he can hook up any speaker. That's what he's doing now. He's working in a music studio in Atlanta. He's a tech guy behind the scenes."

Not wasting a moment, Glenn Robinson already has launched a second career, one that he undoubtedly would have started much earlier had he not been such a tall and talented "Big Dog" on the basketball court.

BILLY SHEPHERD:

Mighty Mite

A strong case can be made for Billy Shepherd to be ranked as the most gifted little guy (five-ten or under) in the history of Indiana high school basketball. The five-ten, 160-pound Carmel guard revived a dormant program in the late 1960s, and finished his brilliant four-year career with 2,465 points—including a seventy-point explosion—which still is number five in Indiana history. He averaged 26.5 points, dished out 356 assists, and shot .800 from the free-throw line.

"I've looked at the guys in the top ten over the years," the fifty-seven-year-old Shepherd noted. "It's unreal—Damon Bailey, Marion Pierce, all tremendous high school players. I can't believe that thirty-nine years later I'm still in the top five. If I'd had the three-point shot, I'd have scored another five hundred points for sure. But I may never have gotten inside the three-point line," he laughed.

Shepherd not only was a deadly shooter from faraway places that would make today's best three-point shooters blush, but he also was one of the quickest and best ball-handling guards ever to rule the Hoosier hardwood.

"I never looked at my size as a handicap," Shepherd emphasized. "The position I played, I was able to play my whole career. I overcame my size with quickness and brains. Passing was the best part of my game. There was no such thing as a point guard then. If you were a good basketball player, you were supposed to do all those things. When I was in junior high, I had a cousin, Max Perry, who taught me a few moves to get people off of me. I never came across anyone who was able to contain me and keep me from doing what I wanted to do."

Bill Shepherd, Sr. was coaching at Mitchell, Indiana, when Billy was born. He was just two years old when his dad took him to his first state tournament. Younger brother Dave came along two years later, and soon they were both totally involved in their father's basketball program.

"When I was four or five years old, we'd lead the team out on the floor," Dave recalled. "We'd stand in the center circle during warm-ups. We'd be in the locker room, at all the practices. It was something we grew up with, and it gave us a huge advantage."

When the Shepherd boys couldn't get into a gym, they'd make rims out of hangers, hook them to their closet door, and fire socks in place of a basketball. They often played after they were supposed to be asleep—until one or both got mad and made such a ruckus that a parent was alerted.

Even in cold weather, they would shovel off their driveway court and play outside. They'd wear gloves and caps, and when their apparel became too soaked, they'd come inside for a moment and don new clothes.

"We got along great," Dave continued. "We were always competitive. I looked up to him and had a lot of respect for his work ethic and knowledge of the game. His passing and shooting ability were unbelievable. The hours he spent playing versus [the hours put in by] other kids—it reflects. It was really all about working out and practice time. I remember beating him on a rare occasion. No question, it made me a better player and athlete competing against him all those years."

Bill Shepherd Sr. stressed that he "never had to push" his oldest son into the game. "He really studied the game. He looked at other players over the years. He got serious very early in grade school. He always was kind of small and didn't have a lot of weight, but he had a lot of knowledge."

Several life-changing things happened to Shepherd when he was in fourth grade. First of all, he moved to Carmel, because his dad was named head coach. Then he received a bad grade in citizenship—definitely a no-no for the son of a teacher. "I wasn't paying attention and smarted off," he admitted. "My mom [Edie] put the hammer down." The result was that young Shepherd never slacked off in the classroom again. It eventually paid off with a 3.8 scholastic average, which placed him number 8 in the 1968 class of 245 at Carmel High School.

Another thing happened while Billy was watching the state tournament from the upper deck at Butler Fieldhouse— he couldn't read the uniform numbers. Soon afterward, he began wearing glasses, then switched to contact lenses as a freshman.

He was good enough as a freshman to start for his father's varsity. Standing just five-seven or five-eight, Shepherd nevertheless left a gigantic impression during his second start against Indianapolis North Central. In the closing seconds, he raced down court and flipped a perfect behind-the-back pass to teammate Jack Edwards for a lay-up and an exciting 59-58 victory.

Shepherd averaged an excellent 14.4 points as a freshman, helping the Greyhounds post a 15-7 record in what he termed an "ice-breaking year." The biggest win was a 72-66 upset of number-one-ranked Tipton as Shepherd fired home twenty-four points. For the year, he shot .722 from the free-throw line and dished out 54 assists. It was a table-setting season for Carmel's first sectional championship in forty-one years.

That freshman year also was memorable for a prediction by *Noblesville Ledger* sportswriter Don Jellison—he said Shepherd, whom he dubbed "Billy the Kid," would be crowned Indiana's Mr. Basketball as a senior.

With his dad's coaching job potentially on the line, Shepherd greatly elevated his game as a sophomore. He averaged 26.0 points, shot .786 from the free-throw line, and handed out 85 assists, even though the Greyhounds slipped to an 11-13 record.

The losing record, however, quickly was forgotten when Carmel avenged three regular-season defeats to win the coveted sectional crown. The big one was Noblesville, which had ruled the roost in recent years and never had lost to a Bill Shepherd-coached team. Thus, it was only fitting that Billy Shepherd would drill a long shot from the top of the key to stun Noblesville, 58-56, and finish with thirty-one points in the championship game.

"To this day, that still is the biggest shot I ever hit," Shepherd declared. "It got me, Dad, and Carmel over the hump."

Entering his junior year, Shepherd was beginning to draw big crowds, even folks from out of town who wanted to get a close look at this little guy who was turning Indiana basketball upside down. He did not disappoint as he led the state with a 32.0 scoring average, shot .462 from the field, .841 from the free-throw line, and had 77 assists while leading the Greyhounds to an 18-6 record.

The Carmel star's most memorable game as a junior was spawned by what could have been a tragic accident. Billy and Dave delivered the *Indianapolis Star* each morning, and on this particular day, he fell into an eight-foot sewer excavation hole between two houses and badly sprained his right wrist.

Making matters even worse, the Greyhounds were to play number-one-ranked Fort Wayne South and its six-seven star, Willie Long, that very night. At first, Billy thought his wrist was broken, but wild horses couldn't keep him from playing in the big game. Necessity is the mother of invention, so he decided to shoot left-handed for the first time in a game. Though Carmel lost, it wasn't his fault, because he scored twenty-four points that night.

The next night, however, the pain caught up with him after scoring what was to be a career-low four points against Indianapolis

Broad Ripple. "I was hurting," he admitted. "Dad took me out in the middle of the second quarter. He could see I was in pain. They were on me and there was nothing I could do."

The gritty little guy missed only one game during his prep career and that was due to a sprained ankle as a senior.

At the end of that season, Shepherd was thrilled to make the *Indianapolis News* Junior All-State team with the likes of Bob Ford, who had sparked Evansville North to the state title that winter. "That inspired me to work hard in the summer," he confided. The biggest reason: maybe he, indeed, did have a shot at becoming Mr. Basketball.

Shepherd's senior year was his best, and it was greatly aided by the addition of younger brother Dave, who would have played varsity a year earlier as a freshman, except for a new rule passed by the local school board.

"We were really close," Billy said of his relationship with Dave. "We did a lot of things together. He was probably a little meaner than me—he had more of a football mentality. We could really read each other on the basketball court. He always complains that he had only three years, but I say that he took only twenty fewer shots than me."

Dave still likes to brag about the night (January 6, 1968) that he and Billy combined for a mind-boggling 86 points during a 117-69 rout of Brownsburg. That was the night Billy outscored the Bulldogs by himself as he exploded for a school-record seventy points—still number twelve in state history. "Had they had the three-point shot, he'd had a hundred," Dave insists. "I [later] scored sixty-six and I don't have the school record. That's what I've been facing all my life," he lamented.

At halftime, Billy had twenty-four points, but he really took off in the second half with forty-six big ones. "After it got to about forty-five or so, we just kind of let it go," he recalled. "I never scored in the fifties or sixties, but I had seventy. That basket looked awfully big that night. It was big headlines in the [*Indianapolis*] *Star*. Brownsburg was a good team and won its sectional that year."

The career night also landed Shepherd in *Sports Illustrated* magazine's prestigious "Faces in the Crowd" section. "That was huge, because very few Indiana athletes made it," he pointed out.

For the third straight year, Carmel won the sectional and posted an outstanding 21-3 record. For the second year in a row, Shepherd led the state in scoring (32.9). He also handed out 140 assists, and his school assist records stood until his son Scott broke them.

Shepherd will be remembered for his deep-freeze ball-handling wizardry, as well as his scoring and passing. "Our game plan was to try to build a lead, and if we were up in the last three minutes, we were going to sit on it," he related. "There were no five-second counts, making it tough on the defense. I probably was a low-80 percent free-throw shooter, but in the fourth quarter, it was more like 90 percent. I don't ever remember losing a game in my high school career when we had the lead in the last three minutes."

A little-known fact is that Shepherd won fifteen varsity letters at Carmel. He earned four each in basketball, baseball, and cross-country, and three in track.

The Carmel star was just as well-rounded off the court. Besides carrying a 3.8 scholastic average, he was Student Council president, a member of the Fellowship of Christian Athletes, and a member of the First Methodist Church of Carmel. "My spiritual life is very important," he stressed.

About the only thing left to cap his prep career was to make Don Jellison a prophet with honor, and be crowned Indiana's Mr. Basketball. "It really wasn't a goal," he revealed. "If I could just be an Indiana All-Star, that would be the greatest. I beat out Bob Ford. He won the state as a junior, and I figured he was the guy."

Billy got the call from game director Fred Corts, but it was April Fool's Day and he needed assurance. "Outside of my children being born, that was the greatest feeling anybody can have," he affirmed. "Talk about being in a fog for a few days," he laughed. "I always thanked my mom and dad that I wasn't born a year later. You know what that meant—George McGinnis [who dominated Mr. Basketball voting the following year]."

Two years later, younger brother Dave, who sparked Carmel to state runner-up honors, followed Billy as Mr. Basketball. Bill Shepherd Sr., a six-one center at Hope, had been an Indiana All-Star in 1945, and Billy's son Scott made the dream team in 1992. That placed the Shepherds in elite company with the Mounts of Lebanon as the only families to have three generations of Indiana All-Stars.

The only Shepherd to be on a state-championship basketball team, however, was the youngest brother, Steve, who got his coveted ring in 1977.

College was the next order of business, and Shepherd estimates that he received "over 200 offers. I could have gone anywhere in the country—UCLA, North Carolina, Purdue, Florida, Kentucky. I wanted to go where I would be able to play pro ball. The ABA had the three-point shot, and that would be a great fit. Indianapolis was an ABA city with the Pacers. Dad said it would be nice to go to a college where you were going to live, and I've been around Indianapolis all of my life."

By the way, Shepherd still has all those college letters, stuffed in a large suitcase and resting in his storage shed. He has framed two of them—one from North Carolina's Dean Smith and the other from Bobby Knight when he was coaching at West Point. Interestingly, they now rank one and two all-time in victories among NCAA Division I coaches.

He chose hometown Butler University for all of the above—plus the outside possibility that Bill Shepherd, Sr. might succeed legendary Butler coach Tony Hinkle, who was nearing retirement.

Robin Miller, who covered Butler for the *Indianapolis Star,* calls Shepherd "one of the last guys who had a wide-open basketball style that was fun to watch. There was a flair to his game that's missing today. People don't remember how quick he was getting his shots off against anybody, or how good of a ball handler he was, especially on the fast break. I remember him leading fast breaks and throwing these amazing passes. The ball would bounce off hands and hit some guys in the face. He had such great range. It's a shame there was no three-point line when he played."

Playing for Hinkle was special. "He had a calming influence on a lot of young people," Shepherd said. "My first four or five games as a sophomore, he'd take the final stat sheet and circle things in red that he didn't like. You could shoot eight-for-twenty-two, but if you made five turnovers ..."

Shepherd made his first mark as a Butler sophomore when he set a school record with fourteen assists against Evansville. "I had the ball all the time," he recalled. "I couldn't score, but I could find the open man. I got a thrill out of making that great pass."

Playing in Hinkle's last game is still fresh in Shepherd's memory. He estimates that a standing-room crowd of 17,000 crammed into Butler Fieldhouse—capacity 14,900—and that included many of his former players. "They were standing four and five deep around the top," he described. "They sold out at 5 PM for a game at 8 PM. It was pretty emotional, because all his former players were there. There was a telegram from the president. When it was over, it was kind of hard to recall what all had happened."

The game itself was a classic. The Bulldogs lost a wild 121-114 verdict to visiting Notre Dame. Shepherd scored thirty-nine points, but he was dwarfed by Irish stars Austin Carr and Collis Jones, who poured in fifty and forty points, respectively.

Hinkle's last team lost its final two games, to finish with a 15-11 record. Shepherd averaged a school-record 27.8 points—with a low of 21—and finished number 16 in the nation. His season-high was forty-two points against DePauw. He made 287 field goals, still a school record. He totaled 724 points, which ranks number 3 in school history. He also shot .750 from the free-throw line.

The next year, George Theofanis succeeded Hinkle as head coach, and Shepherd's dream of again playing for his father ended. His junior campaign was noteworthy for a college-high forty-nine-point effort at the University of Arizona. He dumfounded onlookers by sinking nineteen of thirty-two from the field, most of them between twenty-five and thirty-five feet. He also made eleven of twelve from the free-throw line and had nine assists. "I kind of got in a zone, and everything I threw up went in," he said. He also scored forty-three points against DePauw.

When the Bulldogs faced Earlham College, Shepherd tied his school record with fourteen assists. He handed out thirteen against Illinois. But he also continued to score in bunches, averaging twenty-four points. He made a school-record 171 free throws (still number 3) while shooting .770. He was named MVP, but the team record slipped badly to 10-16.

Shepherd's senior year was marred by a torn hamstring, which sidelined him for six games, and the Bulldogs were saddled with a 6-20 record. He shot a career-high .785 from the free-throw line, but his scoring average slipped to 19.3. Still, he earned MVP honors for the second straight year.

In three years, Shepherd scored a school-record 1,733 points, which since has slipped to number 5. His 26.3 average still is number 1 in Butler history. No other Butler player ever has averaged more than twenty points for his career. Butler has had seven All-Americans, none since Shepherd was honored by *Sport* magazine in the 1971-72 campaign.

To say Shepherd ended his college career in a blaze of glory would be an understatement, because he earned MVP honors in the NABC East-West All-Star Game by sparking the East to a 96-91 victory in overtime. He scored twelve points (6-of-12 shooting) and dished out eight assists. What really put him over the top, however, was grabbing a loose ball that was going out of bounds and throwing up an incredible fifty-foot hook shot that went through at the halftime buzzer.

One day, the Virginia Squires came to town to play the Pacers, and Shepherd decided to impress Coach Al Bianchi, because he badly wanted to play in the ABA with its inviting three-point shot.

He bought a new pair of shoes with two-inch heels to appear taller, but then he had to also buy a new pair of pants. At that point, he admitted, "It looked like I'd been in a flood," because his clothes were so big.

Nevertheless, he did get to shoot the "three" the very next year because he was indeed drafted in 1972 by the Virginia Squires and became a teammate of Julius "Dr. J." Erving. After ten games, however, he hurt his knee and was sidelined for six weeks. He appeared in just sixteen games, scoring twenty-seven points, and was cut the next season.

However, Shepherd was picked up by the San Diego Conquistadors and had visions of running up big assist numbers by feeding player-coach Wilt Chamberlain. Unfortunately Chamberlain was only allowed to coach, because he had jumped his contract with the Lakers, and the NBA slapped an injunction on him. Even as a coach, Chamberlain was a great drawing card and filled ABA arenas all over the country.

Shepherd started all 84 games, scored 507 points (6.0 average) and dished out 392 assists. His high games were sixteen points and thirteen assists. He also had an excellent four-to-one ratio in assists to turnovers.

One night, Memphis was whistled for three technical fouls, and Shepherd—assuming he would be chosen—jumped in to shoot the free throws. He missed all three—probably for the only time in his life—but he was saved further embarrassment when San Diego won the game. Later in the locker room, Chamberlain exclaimed, "Hey, from now on, I'll determine who shoots the free throws!" Shepherd quickly agreed, because he wasn't about to argue with the seven-foot-two giant.

Bumped from San Diego's starting lineup by a new coach, Shepherd wound up with the Memphis Sounds for his third and final pro campaign. He scored thirteen points in his first game, and later had a career high of twenty-nine. His high assist game was fourteen. As a part-time starter and key substitute, he appeared in sixty-nine games. He scored 434 points for a 6.3 average and set an ABA record by drilling 42 percent of his three-point shots.

The following year, the ABA started to crack, folding up several franchises, including Memphis. Shepherd, whose salary shrunk every year in the pros, was married and had his second child on the way by then, so he decided to join Converse as a sales representative.

Shepherd is just as proud of his children as he is of his own amazing career. Scott broke all of his assist records at Carmel and made the Indiana All-Star team. He was highly recruited and finally accepted a full scholarship to Florida State University.

His son Jeff, three years younger than Scott, is a fascinating story. Robin Miller watched him play at Carmel, and he used to tell Billy, "He never looks to shoot. He can't be your son!" But when he went to Huntington College, Jeff gained some confidence and blossomed into an awesome shooter. He scored 2,500 points and made 442 threes, which placed him number 4 among college players of all time at any level. He also made NAIA All-American.

In 1997, Billy joined his father in the Indiana Basketball Hall of Fame. "It was awesome because I'd been going to [Hall of Fame] banquets for years," he noted. "Dad had been installed. Those are things that have been so rewarding. I did things because I had a passion and love for the game. I'd have played if there were two people or 2,000 in the stands."

Shepherd, then in his late forties, was headed for a lunch date one day when he ran into Pacers star Reggie Miller. He ended up challenging the NBA star to a game of H-O-R-S-E for a crisp $100 bill. He was wearing penny loafers and a sweater. He had not even shot around for many months, but he wound up winning and still has the money in a picture frame at his house.

Shepherd had been coaching an AAU summer basketball team for three years when he unexpectedly was hired as head coach at perennial power Muncie Central. As editor of *Indiana High School Hoops*, he was checking out rumors that Muncie Central coach Bill Harrell was going to either resign or be fired. Harrell soon did resign. Shepherd was asked to apply, and he got the job just ten days before the season started in 2004.

He hired his son Scott as one of his assistant coaches, and they drove nearly an hour each way for practice and games. The Shepherds led the Bearcats to a sectional championship and a fine 20-4 record. "I was coaching like I was going to be there for a long time," he stressed. "But they opened the job up again, interviewed eight people, and it went to Matt Fine, who had been my assistant. I kind of served as a buffer for the year, and then they could do what they wanted to do. Muncie's a tough town. I called my dad and said, 'Now I know why coaching is such a tough job.' I wouldn't trade that year for anything."

Today Shepherd is a mortgage broker in Indiana and Florida, and writes a syndicated column for sports parents called "Ask Billy."

Looking back on his distinguished career, Shepherd says simply, "I was never satisfied. In my last game, I still was trying to get better. But of all the things I did, I still got more of a thrill out of watching my kids play."

SCOTT SKILES:

The Warrior

"He had great confidence and wouldn't back down to anybody. He always thought he was a little better than he was, and went out and proved it. I only coached two guys who could will a team to win—Magic [Johnson] and Scott Skiles." —Jud Heathcote, former Michigan State University basketball coach.

Because he carved out such a stellar career in high school, college, and the NBA—despite having limited physical tools—Scott Skiles has earned the right to be called the greatest overachiever in the history of Indiana high school basketball.

Skiles was a little pudgy (180), not very tall (six-one), didn't possess great quickness, and played for a small school (Plymouth). He also had a rather abrasive on-court personality, which helped to fire up opponents.

So, how was Skiles able to lead a small school to one of the greatest state championships in Indiana history, make All-America at Michigan State, and set a single-game assist record that still stands during a ten-year NBA career?

Scott Skiles was born with an abundance of all the great intangibles, qualities that only show up on the scoreboard. Nobody displayed greater intensity or a stronger will to win. "From the time

I was a small boy, that's the way I was when it came to sports," Skiles conceded. "If I was playing in a Little League baseball game that night, I was all business. I would have my hand in my glove [in the car]. If it started raining, I cried and would be almost inconsolable. If we lost, it burned inside me. I wasn't that competitive about everything outside of sports."

His father, Rick Skiles, molded the competitive edge as his Little League baseball coach. "Dad pushed me in the right direction," Scott said. "He was very competitive. He was way harder on me than on the other kids. He figured, 'I'll push him as far as I can.'

"That's one thing that is missing today in a lot of households," he continued. "At no time could I come home and make excuses about a coach or teammate. I'm thankful for that, because it made me look at myself first."

Physically, Scott Skiles could shoot with the best. He believes that made his first step appear a lot quicker because opponents had to play him skin-tight, making it easier to drive around his defender. He also was an excellent passer and possessed a very high basketball IQ. "I was probably stronger than most high school guards at that time," he added. "I did some weights. I had a lot of stamina. I played all the time and didn't get tired."

And then there was the toughness created by Plymouth coach Jack Edison's no-holds-barred practices. Skiles's running mate, Phil Wendel, described the practices as "brutal. There were no out-of-bounds lines. Sometimes we'd chase the ball into a hallway or run into the bleachers. I don't think anybody liked guarding [Skiles]. He was a strong kid, too."

"Guys always were diving all over the place," Skiles recalled. "At the time, it was just the way we did things. When I moved to college, I started to realize what it did to help me be physical and gain some toughness. You never pulled up. You played to the end of the possession. We were out there to get after each other. No matter how physical the other team was, it was going to be almost a relief [from practice sessions]."

What developed was a warrior mentality. Scott Skiles definitely was the kind of guy you wanted with you in your foxhole.

Skiles was born in LaPorte, but grew up in the town of Koontz Lake near Walkerton. His family moved to Plymouth when he was in sixth grade. He resisted the move at first, but it was made easier because he had been playing Little League baseball in Plymouth.

That was a double-edged sword, however, because the combative youngster already had a reputation. "We remembered an athlete that we all despised—in a good way," said future teammate Phil Wendel. "You get over that in a week or two. We ended up being part of the same goals. He was such an intense competitor. I'd much rather have him on my side."

When Skiles arrived in Plymouth, varsity coach Jack Edison admitted, "I had no idea how good he might be, because I couldn't measure his heart, desire, basketball savvy, will to win, and leadership capacity which made him the player he was."

However, the newcomer's impact was felt even in junior high, where his seventh- and eighth-grade teams lost only once each year. As a freshman, he was placed on the varsity JV squad. He did get into enough varsity games to score seventeen points. By then, Edison realized, "He had some real basketball sense about him and he was a tough kid."

As a sophomore, Skiles moved into a starting guard role on the varsity. He immediately began to show leadership ability and was high scorer with a 19.4 average. He also pulled down eighty-three rebounds as the Pilgrims posted a 16-7 record.

Skiles became really dominant as a junior, although he missed four games due to illness. He averaged 27.9 points, 7.2 rebounds, and 5.0 assists while shooting .590 from the field and .810 from the free-throw line. Plymouth won fourteen games and lost seven, but still was without a sectional title during the Skiles era.

The fiery guard had several offensive explosions as a junior. The most dramatic effort was the night he set a LaPorte gym record with thirty-seven points during a 72-60 victory, even though he was suffering from mononucleosis and had a 103-degree fever. "I felt pretty bad," he understated. "For some reason, I ended up having a good game. I had nothing to lose, so I just let it rip. To be honest, I don't remember much."

During a 94-56 rout of visiting Elkhart Concord, Skiles poured in fifty-three points, which was believed to be a school record. "The last few minutes of the game, he'd been on fire," Coach Edison recalled. "I checked with the scorer's bench and someone said it was a record, so I took him out. The next day, I found out it was a gym record, but not a school record. I saw him in the training room and told him I was sorry. He said, 'I could care less.'

"Two weeks later at Penn [Mishawaka], he was hitting from well beyond where the three-point line would be. With five or six minutes left, he had forty-eight points. I kept him in after all the rest of the starters were out. He had a two-on-one and threw a bounce pass to someone else. With two minutes left, he needed one more basket. I called him over and said, 'Hey, you know why you are still out there! Now shoot the ball!' He scored with one and a half minutes left [for a record 56], and I took him out that very second."

But Skiles's impact on the game always went far beyond scoring points. "He was a catalyst for everything—a lightning rod," Edison described. "There was something inside him. You'd think he couldn't rise any higher, but he was a big-game player. All the way through college, opposing fans got on him."

Teammate Phil Wendel added, "He was such a competitor that everywhere we went, opposing teams would get on him so much. He kind of had a swagger to him. I think he fed off of it. He was just really confident."

Known to fight fire with fire and do his share of trash talking, Skiles explained, "I wasn't afraid to play physically. It was partly my mannerisms. I got heckled unmercifully in college. I never blamed people. I knew my style was conducive to it. I never really got thrown off of my game."

That spring Skiles, a shortstop who led Plymouth in hitting, put his name in the national high school baseball record book by slamming four consecutive home runs during a doubleheader against LaVille. The record lasted for several years. He noted, "I loved baseball, but the pace [slowness] really bothered me."

Skiles's senior year was so incredible that it would make Cinderella blush. He left an indelible mark on his teammates during the second game against Elkhart Memorial. Senior substitute Pete Rockaway, who never had played varsity ball previously, bravely drew a charging foul with one second left and needed to make two free throw to force an overtime.

"Pete was just shaking," Wendel related. "Nobody in the gym thought he could hit those free throws. Scott was a very loyal person and he told him, 'No matter what happens, you made the play.' He always could say the right thing at the right time. Pete hit two and we won in overtime."

Wendel admitted that the Plymouth players' relationship with Skiles "was kind of a love-hate situation. He was so good, but hard to play with. He played at a higher level than anybody. He made you such a better player."

South Bend LaSalle, loaded with quick, talented players, was the Pilgrims' major competition in the northern part of the state, and they faced off in three memorable games that year. Coach George Griffith said, "I didn't think [Skiles] was a Michigan State University point guard as a junior. As a senior, he obviously was a big-timer."

Plymouth won the first meeting, 73-57, in the South Bend Holiday Tournament as Skiles scored twenty-two points. In the last game of the regular season, Plymouth still was undefeated and ranked number one in the state when they tangled again. This time, LaSalle staged a 64-62 upset, despite Skiles's twenty-one points. "We got in his face," Griffith said. "We talked to him and got him really mad. He missed the last shot and that was about the last, last shot he ever missed," the LaSalle coach laughed.

Their third meeting came at the Fort Wayne semi-state after Plymouth had won its first sectional and regional in five years. Griffith, who later won a state title at Richmond, admitted he was praying for Marion to beat Plymouth in the afternoon round. However, the Pilgrims overcame an eight-point deficit in the fourth quarter and eked out a 56-55 victory in overtime. Skiles sparkled with nineteen points, ten assists, and seven rebounds.

"He was such a competitor," Griffith praised. "There was nothing he couldn't climb. At the end of the third quarter [against LaSalle], I know he just said, 'That's enough!' He's probably the fiercest competitor I ever coached against."

Skiles dominated with thirty points and seven rebounds as Plymouth caged the Lions, 77-71.

On to the coveted Final Four. The Pilgrims first encountered Indianapolis Cathedral with five Division I players, including towering six-ten Kenny Barlow and smooth six-three Scott Hicks, who both later starred for Notre Dame. Plymouth's tallest starter was six-two. Skiles pumped in thirty points as the Pilgrims squeezed past Cathedral, 62-59.

The state championship game against quick, powerful Gary Roosevelt still ranks as one of the greatest Hoosier classics. Skiles rightfully joined Milan's Bobby Plump among Indiana's basketball immortals when he drilled a twenty-two-foot jumper at the buzzer to knot the score at sixty and force the first of two overtimes. The underdog Pilgrims eventually posted a heart-stopping 75-74 victory. He scored twenty-five of his game-high thirty-nine points after the third quarter. He finished with thirteen of twenty-five from the field and thirteen of seventeen from the free-throw line.

Before Skiles made his legendary shot, he knew in the huddle—with only four seconds left—that it would be do or die. If he missed, the dream would go up in smoke. "We knew on our way to the huddle what we were going to run," Skiles said. "We had worked on it two or three times a week and never had run it in a game. I said,

'Just give me the ball. I'll make it.' It was so mechanical," he added mater-of-factly. "We had learned all the way through high school to prepare, prepare, prepare."

Was there any doubt who was going to take the final shot? "There wasn't even a question," Phil Wendel affirmed.

"If you miss, you want to miss with a guy like him," Coach Edison said of Skiles. "We made three very good passes. When I saw the ball in the air, I felt real good. It caught a little left of the rim. People claim it had a little curve."

Reflecting back, Skiles says, "Honestly, I felt that every ounce of effort since I was a little kid culminated in making something happen. What if I had missed the shot? Would I have learned anything less? We had such a great team. Phil and I got a lot of credit, but everybody played their roles."

In 1982 Plymouth was a town of 10,000 with 894 students in grades 9-12. It was the smallest school to win Indiana's greatest prize since Milan in 1954.

Skiles wound up scoring a school-record 850 points and leading the entire state with a 29.2 scoring average as the Pilgrims completed a brilliant 28-1 campaign. He also led the team in rebounding with a 7.1 average, and his 164 assists were only one behind team-leader Wendel. He shot a superb .530 from the field and .850 from the free-throw line.

His career record of 1,788 points stood for 23 years until it was topped in 2005 by Kyle Benge with 1,979. Skiles also finished with 366 rebounds and 337 assists.

Plymouth Summer Basketball League director Ida Chipman summed up the Pilgrims' fairy-tale season this way: "It seemed like every team we played had more physical talent. We had a bunch of role players and one great player. That combination just wore teams down."

Chipman watched Skiles play for eight years. She observed, "He was just so darn good that he could beat you anywhere on the court. He had great anticipation on defense. He could read passes. He was so strong that he could carry you right to the basket. I know his determination and confidence level. Nothing that Scott does amazes me. I can't picture him failing at anything."

The next step was to choose a college. "After we won the state, my phone rang off the hook," Skiles said. "I told them all I didn't have any interest. A couple said I would start [as a freshman]. That wasn't the way to recruit me. I didn't have my hand out and I didn't want money."

The summer before his junior year, he had attended the Purdue camp and played well, despite being slowed by a football thigh pad on his leg from a baseball injury. The next summer, he revealed, "I was two or three weeks from mentally saying I was going to Purdue. Then I got a letter from Jay Williams [assistant Purdue coach] telling me to feel free to choose another college. I was hurt by it and shifted my thinking."

Bob King had been retired after seventeen years as a Purdue assistant coach, but he still tried to talk the Boilermakers into signing Skiles. "We needed somebody tough like him," King said. "He was one of those guys you weren't sure that you wanted him on your team, but you sure didn't want to play against him. He was mean and had an indomitable will to win. He was tough on defense, solid on offense—a winner. He ended up going to Michigan State, and that was the best move they made in a long time."

Michigan State coach Jud Heathcote watched Skiles play in the Fort Wayne semi-state his senior year. "He was really smart," Heathcote noticed immediately. "He was as good with his left as with his right hand. What he did was take charge. He ran the ball club with confidence and knowledge. He was an extension of a coach on the floor, like Magic Johnson. His knowledge of the game and basketball skills overcame his lack of athletic ability. Gyms are full of guys who can run and jump out of the gym, but can't play basketball. Here was the reverse."

Four games into his freshman year at MSU, Skiles became a fixture in the starting lineup. He was named Big Ten Conference

Freshman of the Year after averaging 12.5 points, 4.9 assists, and shooting .493 from the field and .831 from the free-throw line. He and Sam Vincent shared team MVP honors.

Skiles also enhanced his reputation as the "Human Floor Burn" by diving for every loose ball and playing with overall reckless abandon. His intensity was just as great in practice, which greatly endeared him to the Spartans' coaching staff.

During his sophomore year, Skiles raised his scoring average to 14.5, though his assist average slipped slightly to 4.6. He shot .480 from the field and .832 from the free-throw line.

Skiles' scoring average again rose as a junior, reaching 17.7. His assists (5.8) and field-goal percentage (.505) also improved. However, his free-throw percentage slipped to .790. At the post-season banquet, he received the Spartans' Sportsmanship Award.

That spring, Heathcote called Skiles into his office in order to give him a list of ten things to work on during the summer. He also stressed, "Don't goof off in classes. I want you to get your degree, because somewhere you are going to be a coach."

Looking somewhat forlorn, Skiles replied, "Coach, how about pro ball?"

Heathcote answered, "I don't think with your athletic ability and size you are going to be a success in the NBA."

"Give me that list!" Skiles exclaimed, and off he went to prove himself for the umpteenth time.

"I knew where he was going with it," Skiles acknowledged. "I knew the odds were against me. The gist of Jud's conversation was 'Don't put all your eggs in one basket.'

"Every summer, Tuesday and Thursday at 8 PM, we played. Magic was there. The Pistons would come with Isaiah [Thomas]. Right from the very beginning, I knew I could hold my own with those guys. After one year, I went back to Plymouth and I was markedly better. I didn't see a ceiling on it."

Making sure he wasn't doing a disservice to his young star, Heathcote asked Magic one day during a pickup game early in the summer if Skiles had a shot at the NBA. The Magicman gave the expected reply: "Coach, no he can't make it. He's not big enough, fast enough, or athletic enough."

At the end of the summer, however, Magic ran past his old coach during another pickup game and exclaimed, "Hey, Coach, Scott CAN play now!"

Heathcote confessed, "I never had a kid raise his level so much in one summer."

The scrappy Plymouth product soared into his senior year on top of the world. He averaged a career-high 27.4 points—second in the nation—6.5 assists, 4.4 rebounds, .554 from the field, and .900 from the free-throw line. His single-game highs included forty-five points, twelve assists, and nine rebounds. He scored more than forty points three times, and reached thirty or more on nine occasions. It's no wonder he was named National Player of the Year by *Basketball Times* and made five other All-American teams.

Skiles had one three-game span during which he averaged a dominating 40.3 points, 5.7 assists, and shot a blistering .768 (53-of-69) from the field and .882 from the free-throw line. Thirty-one of his baskets during that stretch were from NBA three-point range.

The Spartan great was so unstoppable as a senior that he fouled out seven players and drew four fouls on eight others. He had such great stamina that he played the full forty minutes in thirteen games.

During his four-year career, he set school records with 2,145 points (18.2 average), 645 assists (5.5 average), 175 steals, and a .850 free-throw percentage. His one-season records included 850 points, 54 steals, and a .900 free-throw percentage. The Spartans compiled a 75-43 record (23-8 as a senior) in the Scott Skiles era.

Adding to Skiles's legend is a conversation he had one night following a blowout of archrival Michigan. The Wolverines' Antoine "Judge" Joubert told him, "We'll get you at Chrysler Arena." Always supremely confident, Skiles shot back, "Not unless you lose some weight, fat boy!"

Skiles's MSU days also were well-known for an alcohol-related stop and a brush with drugs. "I did some things I shouldn't have been doing," he readily confessed. "I got caught and I paid for it. It took me awhile, but in hindsight, I'm glad it happened. My main regret was the effect it had on my family and school. I'm thankful I didn't hurt anybody. Whatever I did, I did to myself. An experience like that was good before I made money [in the NBA]."

In the 1986 NBA draft, Skiles was taken in the first round by the Milwaukee Bucks, but only as the number twenty-two pick. "He was just livid [that he didn't go higher]," coach Heathcote said.

Skiles was chomping at the bit to prove himself at the highest level. However, he suffered a herniated disc during training camp and was limited to thirteen games during his rookie year. Still, he called it "a great year for me" because he was surrounded by talented veteran players, and soaked up a lot of knowledge while riding the bench.

Doctors recommended that he have back surgery, but he opted to implement a strict flex and conditioning program, which he used throughout his professional career.

That next summer, he was traded to the Indiana Pacers. "They were a mess," he said. "I saw both sides during my first two years." He stayed with the Pacers for two years. The second year, he averaged close to twenty minutes per game and started close to a dozen times.

One night—through no fault of his own—Skiles and the great Michael Jordan became linked forever in a famous six-foot poster. Jordan made one of his patented dunks and Scott was watching from below.

"You could only see one-half of my body, one-half of my head and 'les' on my uniform," Skiles said of the giant poster that sprung from the "Kodak moment." "I was just under the basket. Literally, I didn't even move. He had his hand in the rim."

Adding insult to (near) injury, Skiles was sent a poster of the embarrassing event and had to sign it for a Pacers' fan.

His salvation came the third year, when he and former MSU teammate Sam Vincent were among those taken by the Orlando

Magic in the expansion draft. Jud Heathcote admitted, "I actually cried," because he knew his former players would be battling for the same starting position.

The first year, Skiles averaged 7.7 points and 4.8 assists. He served as the sixth man early before taking over at midseason as the starting point guard.

He made national headlines on December 30, 1990, when he dished out an NBA-record thirty assists as the Magic crushed the visiting Denver Nuggets, 155-116, before a capacity crowd of 15,077. The record, which still stands today, puts him ahead of such superstars as Oscar Robertson, Magic Johnson, Bob Cousy, and John Stockton.

Modestly, Skiles explained, "It was the style that Denver played at that time. They let it fly. The pace of the game was conducive to getting up and down the floor. My teammates deserve a lot of credit [they made 57 percent of their shots]. All kinds of records were set that night. My high before then had been twenty assists."

Skiles averaged a career-best 17.2 points and 8.4 assists that year, and was named the NBA's Most Improved Player.

In 1992, he left a mark of another kind—he took on teammate Shaquille O'Neal during a tension-filled practice session. Shaq and teammate Larry Krystkowiak kept getting into squabbles and had to be separated. The irritated Skiles jumped in and said, "Why don't you guys just shut up and fight?"

Suddenly the seven-foot-one, 300-pound center threw a haymaker punch at the 185-pound Skiles, who adeptly ducked. "It was either react or walk away," the combative Skiles said. Since he didn't believe in turning the other cheek, he "wrapped my arms around his legs. He was hanging on to my neck, and we fell into the bleachers. I had a stiff neck for six weeks.

"People still talk about it. I joke that I was the only guy who ever beat him up. He is one of my all-time favorite teammates."

In five years with Orlando, Skiles averaged 12.9 points and 7.2 assists. He dished out a franchise-record 2,776 assists.

Skiles later played one year with Washington, and then just two months with Philadelphia before he officially retired from the NBA. During his ten-year career, he played in 600 games and started 371, while averaging 11.1 points and 6.5 assists. He also shot a sizzling .889 from the free-throw line—still number four in NBA history.

"I'm proud of playing as long as I did," Skiles said with the satisfaction of someone who reached the top of every mountain and finally won over every critic.

In 1996, he decided to play for PAOK in Thessaloniki, Greece, explaining, "It was an awful lot of money, virtually tax-free. If I got worked up, the coach [Michel Gomez] would take me out of the game. He would say, 'You must calm down.' I told him, 'You don't understand. That's my game. When it gets crazy out there, I still can keep a cool head.'"

Then Skiles, who has had knee and wrist surgery, hurt his shoulder. "I knew that was the end of my career," he conceded. "I could have had surgery, and rehab was possible. I did get tired of being hurt, even aches and pains."

So he again announced his retirement, this time permanently. All the aches and pains prompted him to borrow a quote from another NBA veteran, Dick VanArsdale, who affirmed, "Getting old ain't for sissies."

Preparing to fly home in two days, Skiles boxed up all his belongings for UPS. This retirement lasted a mere twelve hours, however, because his coach was fired and officials gave him the head job. The team had been in turmoil, but he turned the season around well enough to finish with a winning record.

"As a kid, I already had decided I wanted to coach," Skiles said as he looked back on his basketball life. "I just inherently knew. Once I got to this league [NBA] as a player, I knew this was where I wanted to start. Greece was a great experience for me. They were floundering around, and I ended up righting the ship. There would be smoke in the building and riot police standing around. If you can keep your head in that environment ..."

The following year, Skiles got his wish when he was named assistant coach of the Phoenix Suns. He became the youngest head coach (age thirty-five) in the NBA when Danny Ainge resigned in December of 1999. He then coached the Suns to a 116-79 record in three years and made the playoffs twice, ousting defending NBA champion San Antonio in 2000.

Jud Heathcote and Jack Edison were not at all surprised that their former protégé could coach at the highest level. Heathcote noted, "He was one of the few kids I encouraged to go into coaching. He had a passion and knowledge for coaching."

Edison acknowledged, "I knew he could coach. I didn't know what his preference would be. He had a camp at Donaldson, and I helped him run it for a couple years. I remember a really humid day. It was break time, but he was helping a little kid, an eight-year-old boy, with a dribbling drill. He was not gifted, but Scott was working with him like he was a member of his national championship team. He pulled him over—sweat running all over him. I could tell then that this guy was a teacher. He had a passion for it. He worked his head off on kids who were unskilled.

"Those kids had more fun with him. They hardly had time to get a drink. They were just hanging on him, hacking him, and he was hitting eighteen-footers. At the same time, he can be firm and have high expectations. He has sent needy kids to camp and never tried to get any publicity. He does things so quietly. He gives things back to our community and is really generous."

No matter how talented a coach is, however, he can expect to be fired. It happened in Phoenix, leading Scott to spend the next year and a half totally outside of basketball. "It was the first time in my life, I hadn't had basketball," he pointed out. "I had a great time. I learned I could be happy without basketball."

The father of two sons and a daughter had plenty of time for his favorite hobby—books. "I'm a huge reader," he pointed out. "I read almost anything I can get my hands on. I also have followed the financial market for the last fifteen years."

But his lifetime love of the game flamed anew when the Chicago Bulls came calling in 2003. General manager John Paxson said he did not believe the perceived image of Skiles as a hot-headed coach who would spin out of control and expect his players to be clones of himself on the court.

"He hasn't changed from high school 'til now," Paxson affirmed. "He had a kind of strut and confidence. You didn't get the feeling that his team was going to lose. He wouldn't let them. He was always out there to win. That has carried over to his professional life as a coach.

"He's a very good coach. He knows the game. He's still old school. He believes in holding players accountable in terms of playing and work ethic. He's feisty. He'll wear his emotions on his sleeves at times, but he keeps his cool during games. He's had one ejection in four years."

Skiles explained why the perception is far from reality. "Part of that stems from the way I played," he believes. "My style was kind of reckless. That [image] stays with some people. If you're smart at all, you have to realize that screaming at people every day is not going to get it done. I don't expect anyone to be like me, but there is nothing wrong to expect them to do their best at all times—at the very minimum."

In December of 2006, Skiles was able to set his coaching duties aside long enough to attend the twenty-fifth reunion of Plymouth's 1982 state championship basketball team. "Just walking into the gym and looking around, you see all the faces, and every face was a memory," he said of the nostalgic evening.

During his first three years in Chicago, Skiles led the Bulls to a 107-123 record and two playoff berths. As he heads down the stretch in 2007, he continues to tutor the Bulls in unselfish play and stifling defense. That defense has held opponents to the lowest field-goal percentage (barely over 42 percent) in the NBA for the past two years. During the 2004-05 campaign, the Bulls set a franchise record by holding opponents under 100 points in 26 consecutive games.

Skiles has had a multitude of thrills during his career, but he can't say which one is tops. "It's hard to answer, because I'm still in it," he says honestly. "You only start thinking about that stuff when you're done. I never got to play in the [NBA] finals."

The forty-three-year-old warrior hinted that the greatest thrill of his basketball career still lies ahead. An educated guess is that he hopes someday to put an NBA championship ring on his finger. Then—and only then—can he point to his greatest thrill.

HOMER STONEBRAKER:

First Hoosier Great

Homer Stonebraker was Indiana's first authentic high school basketball superstar, leading tiny Wingate to state championships in 1913 and 1914. He later starred for nearby Wabash College and made All-America three times. Abe Saperstein, owner of the famed Harlem Globetrotters, once called him the greatest all-around center he ever had seen, and his face graced the cover of the popular *Collier's* magazine.

His prodigious high school feats projected him as the Paul Bunyan of his era. For example, he once scored the incredible total of eighty points in a single game—still number five in state history—as Wingate crushed Hillsboro, 108-8. His point total included thirty-six baskets and eight free throws. Even future Hoosier greats who followed on his heels, such as Fuzzy Vandivier, Johnny Wooden, and Stretch Murphy, never approached that prolific total.

Attesting to his fame, Crawfordsville historian Bob Whalen said, "I suppose there have been more articles written on Stoney than on any other Montgomery County great."

The six-three, 180-pound Stonebraker built his strength—and added to his legend—by running four miles to school each day. During the winter, he would carry a shovel with him to clear the snowdrifts along the way.

Though he didn't play as a freshman, Stonebraker quickly became a dominant performer as a sophomore, leading Wingate to ten straight victories following an opening loss in the 1911-12 season. Because of the low ceilings in most gyms, he learned to shoot a low-trajectory shot with a lot of backspin. On the occasions that he set up low, he also had great moves around the basket.

In reality, it was a miracle that Wingate even was able to field a team. After all, the high school had just twelve boys, and seven of them were on the basketball squad. Making matters considerably more difficult, Wingate had no gym. The team had to practice outside or travel six miles to New Richmond by either horse and buggy or Model T Ford. As the team became successful, it became known far and wide as the "Gymless Wonders."

Stoney's junior campaign—only the third year the state tournament was held—established his superiority on the basketball court. Even though the defense often picked him up at half court because of his great shooting range, Stonebraker sparked Wingate to five victories in two days at Bloomington to capture the 1913 state championship.

The powerful center was at his absolute best in the final two games. He scored seven points in a 23-14 semifinal victory over Lafayette Jefferson. He tallied nine points in the championship game, a marathon five-overtime, 15-14 victory against South Bend Central. The first four two-minute overtimes were scoreless before forward Forest Crane got the winning basket. It still is the longest state-title game in Hoosier history.

The 1914 state title was even more hard-earned because Wingate had to beat seven teams in two days. Stonebraker, who served as team captain, was one of four Wingate starters who played every single minute of all seven games in a true iron-man performance. He again dominated by scoring eight points in a 14-8 semifinal victory against Lebanon, then exploding for eighteen in a 36-8 championship rout of Anderson.

However, Stonebraker really showed his greatest toughness earlier in the tournament, when he scored all of Wingate's points in their closest game, a 17-14 victory over Clinton.

During Stonebraker's three-year varsity career, Wingate compiled an outstanding record of fifty victories against just ten defeats.

In the fall of 1914, Stonebraker received a grant to attend nearby Wabash College in Crawfordsville. He not only played basketball, but also football. During his career, Wabash won fifty-one games and lost just fifteen, even though it had a different coach every year. Wabash posted a 17-4 record during his sophomore year and a 19-2 mark when he was a junior. He received honorable mention All-America honors as a junior as Wabash defeated the likes of Purdue, Illinois, Indiana, Notre Dame, and the semipro Indianapolis Emroes.

Following graduation in 1918, Stonebraker joined the U.S. Army and reached the rank of sergeant while seeing duty in France during World War I. After his discharge, he began playing professional basketball, and entered the high school coaching field.

During his ten-year professional career, Stonebraker played for the Fort Wayne Hoosiers and Chicago Bruins. He helped start the Fort Wayne team, which, in turn, led to the formation of the American Basketball League. He was considered the finest outside shooter in the game, and was believed to have made close to 50 percent of his shots. In addition, he was surprisingly quick for his size.

In his heyday, he was the biggest drawing card in the American Basketball League. Discussing his almost mythic presence, author Tom Gould once wrote, "The way he brushed his hair, walked into the circle, or moved his eyes told where he would tip the center jump."

Since pro ball, at that time in its infancy, was basically a weekend affair, Stonebraker also took up high school coaching. His first team at Hartford City compiled a 15-13 record in the 1918-19 season. The next year, his record jumped to 27-5, which included a berth in the Final Four. Unfortunately, his season ended with a loss to Lafayette, which then bowed to Franklin in the 1920 title game. His most memorable game was a 164-6 rout of Roll.

The next season, Stonebraker moved to Logansport, where his first team posted a 16-14 record, losing to Walton in the sectional. The next year, his team improved greatly to 21-7, but also was eliminated in the sectional. He completed his four-year coaching career with a 79-39 record.

Following his retirement from coaching, Stonebraker was elected sheriff of Cass County and served two terms. Then he moved to Indianapolis and worked for Allison, a division of General Motors, for thirty-one years.

On January 10, 1973, Wabash College held a "Homer Stonebraker Night," honoring its former star at halftime of a basketball game against DePauw. Stonebraker told the gathering, "This is home to me and the finest and the sweetest days of my life were spent at Wabash College and [it was] one of the greatest experiences of my life."

He told the audience that victories over perennial conference champion Illinois and Emroe Sporting Goods of Indianapolis were his two biggest wins as a collegian. Emroe, which was dominated by former college stars, had won 136 consecutive games. The ballyhooed contest drew a packed house of 3,500 to Tomlinson Hall in Indianapolis. A man on the fire escape had a megaphone and described every play to fans who filled the streets below.

When the Indiana Basketball Hall of Fame was established in 1962, Stonebraker was one of the charter members. He was joined by the likes of John Wooden, Piggy Lambert, Griz Wagner, and Fuzzy Vandivier.

Stonebraker died at age eighty-two on December 9, 1977. Though the tiny school he made famous has twice been swallowed by consolidations, its memory has been preserved by a billboard which greets visitors. It proudly proclaims: "Welcome to Wingate, State Basketball Champions, 1913, 1914."

FUZZY VANDIVIER:

Ball-Handler Deluxe

Robert "Fuzzy" Vandivier got his first taste of basketball when he was around six years old. His brother, Riehl, four years older, was preparing to take part in a pickup game on a Saturday morning at the south school building in Franklin when Fuzzy began bugging him to tag along.

Ten boys were scheduled to play. Each had to fork over ten cents to the school janitor to let them in the gym for one hour.

Fuzzy's niece, Ann Turner, tells it this way: "Grandma made Dad [Riehl] take Uncle Fuzzy. He told me, 'He jerked my hand and took me with him.' One kid didn't show up, so Dad (already greatly irritated) had to put in an extra dime. After the game, Uncle Fuzzy said that he ran all the way home. He was so excited. He told Grandma that all he wanted for Christmas was a basketball. Grandma didn't know anything about basketball.

"When Uncle Fuzzy opened his present, he got a FOOTBALL! He learned how to dribble the football and shoot with it."

No wonder Fuzzy Vandivier still is considered one of the greatest ball handlers in Hoosier prep basketball history!

A year or two earlier, Vandivier had received his famous nickname, which stuck throughout the rest of his life. There was an old man named Vest (called "Fuzzy" by the townspeople), who used to roam the streets of Franklin. He was considered a slow learner, wore shabby clothes, had long, stringy hair, and always needed a haircut.

Vandivier wasn't old enough to play in neighborhood "scrub" games, so he was assigned the task of chasing any ball which eluded the catcher. This job was called "pigtail backup." Well, one day Vandivier—sporting a dirty face and hands and badly needing a haircut of his own—took off after a loose ball and the catcher observed, "You look exactly like Fuzzy." Thus was born a tag that never left him.

Of course, there was one exception. "He was called that by everybody else, but his mother [Isabel]," Turner pointed out. "She always called him Robert."

Fuzzy's father, Ara, was a prominent mortician, and as the boys grew older, they shot at a hoop placed on top of the old barn where they housed the company's hearse. They also spent even more hours shooting baskets in the loft of a carriage barn owned by the parents of Roger Branigin, who later was elected governor of Indiana.

Displaying speed, excellent outside shooting, and pinpoint passing ability, Vandivier started on the 18-2 Franklin High varsity as a freshman. That team reached the state finals at Purdue University before being nipped in the first round, 18-16, by Crawfordsville. Playing in shoebox-sized gymnasiums, he was forced to develop great footwork and his excellent ball handling just got better and better.

During Vandivier's first three years of high school, his home games all were played at Franklin College, because the high school gym was too small to support the sold-out crowds, which averaged about 2,000 fans. They finally got a new gym for their senior year—after they had won two state titles. During the rapid construction of the gym, a strong wind collapsed a brick wall and killed one of the workmen.

This was the era of the center jump, which lasted until 1937. There was no three-seconds rule, so players could camp out in the lane. The players were much, much smaller. The gyms often had low ceilings, forcing players—who all shot two-handed—to shoot mostly line drives instead of today's high-arching shots. Obviously their shooting percentages were nothing to brag about.

Guards, basically, stayed in the half court to play defense, while forwards dominated the offense. The game was much slower-paced and methodical. A player was allowed just four fouls, and there were no bonus free throws. Until 1923, when a player was fouled, anyone could shoot his free throw. A player could return only once after being taken out of a game. The clock only stopped for timeouts, and no player could talk to his coach during a timeout. Trips of any distance had to be made by train and were very tiresome.

This is the real shocker, however: When a player was called for traveling or double dribble, he was charged with a technical foul, and the opponent got to shoot a free throw. Pity today's players—especially in the NBA—if that rule still was in the books.

During his sophomore year, Vandivier became the leader as Franklin won the first of three consecutive state championships—a record that stood for sixty-five years and has been matched just twice. He also was named All-State each year.

The veteran Franklin quintet compiled a 29-1 record in that first state-title campaign and routed Lafayette, 31-13, in the finale as Vandivier poured in seventeen points for game honors. He also starred in the 14-12 semifinal win over Anderson, forcing an overtime with a free throw, then scoring the only basket on a long shot in the extra session. He was high in that game, too, with ten points. Fuzzy's sixty-four points in the state tourney trailed only the sixty-six scored by his teammate, Paul White. Franklin outscored its opponents that year by a dominating average of 37.7-14.5.

Franklin's only loss that year was at Martinsville, 24-18, on Christmas Eve. The gym capacity of 2,000 was reached early, and an estimated 1,000 were turned away—including close to 150 angry Franklin fans who had actually purchased tickets.

Fans who couldn't get into Franklin road games would jam the local opera house, located above the fire station, where they would intently watch a makeshift lighted scoreboard which provided play-by-play from a description received by telephone. Basketball obviously was the town's chief form of entertainment at that time.

The lone returning starter in his junior year, the six-foot, 170-pounder moved from forward to center, was named captain, and led the Grizzly Cubs with 488 points during a 30-3 campaign. He also was high in the state tourney with forty-four points, scoring thirteen in the 35-22 title-game victory over Anderson. Several times during the championship game—which drew a record 10,000 fans—Vandivier's teammates were able to get easy lay-ups because the defense concentrated so heavily on him.

During Vandivier's senior year, Franklin suffered an early 18-17 loss to archrival Martinsville, leaving future Hall of Fame coach Ernest "Griz" Wagner with the uneasy feeling that his veteran players weren't devoted enough to the game. So he banned them from dating—even walking their girlfriends home—for the remainder of the season. Vandivier once said that Wagner was the kind of coach who "would make you want to die for him," so the players eagerly gave 100 percent from then on.

Vandivier went out in a blaze of glory as a senior. He led Franklin to a 30-4 record, including a 26-15 victory over Terre Haute Garfield in the state-championship game, which drew still another record crowd of 12,000. He again paced all other state-tourney scorers with forty-seven points, and was unanimous first-team All-State.

The Franklin community celebrated with a civic dinner, which drew 3,500 people, a Johnson County record at the time.

The Franklin High yearbook waxed poetic, calling Fuzzy "one of the most popular boys in school, a wonderful captain that none can fool."

Indiana basketball historian Herb Schowmeyer attested to Vandivier's ball-handling wizardry when he commented, "He could do everything. They couldn't take the ball away from him. He ran the ball team all four years."

Another legendary Hoosier superstar, John Wooden, came along later, but he was quick to point out, "He was, more or less, my idol. I had heard so much about him. He was a great all-around player, and would have been great in any era. I got to know him, and he was a wonderful person."

The famed "Wonder Five" tag was not put on Vandivier and his four teammates until they enrolled one block down the street in the fall of 1922 at Franklin College, again to play for Griz Wagner. They earned the tag their freshman year by outscoring their opponents by a wide 34.7 to 19.3 margin while posting a perfect 17-0 record. Included was a very unusual 32-31 overtime victory against the professional Indianapolis Omars.

The young collegians left Tomlinson Hall through an alley and entered their Indianapolis hotel, believing they had won the game, 29-28. But as they undressed—Burl Friddle already was in the bathtub—they received a message that an opposing player, future Butler University coaching legend Tony Hinkle, had been fouled. Putting their cold, sweaty clothes back on, they returned to the hall, where Hinkle tied the game with a free throw. However, in the five-minute overtime, Vandivier scored a free throw and basket to give Franklin a hard-earned 32-31 victory. Hinkle later said the player accused of fouling was nowhere near him at the time.

As sophomores, they compiled a 19-1 record. Including games from their final year of high school, they won forty-eight in a row until a loss to Butler. As juniors, it was 15-3, and as seniors, it was 12-6. Vandivier, a two-time captain, sparked the Wonder Five to many victories over the likes of Notre Dame, Indiana, Purdue, and even a professional team, the Indianapolis Omars.

The versatile Vandivier also played two years of football and one of baseball in college.

On March 23, 1924, Fuzzy was named to the prestigious Chicago Tribune All-Western team. Sportswriter Fred Young wrote, "Franklin's scintillating player was given a forward position on the first team ... In Vandivier, Coach Wagner of Franklin has the sweetest piece of basketball timber in the United States today. He can do everything that a basketball player should be able to do and do it a bit better than anyone else. A wonderful floor man, a power on defense, he is also an exceptionally accurate shot at the basket and is always good for his share of the points."

The Butler University Collegiate newspaper proclaimed, "The Lord must have made Vandivier and then turned around and made basketball."

The last year and a half of Vandivier's career was plagued by injuries and illness. During his junior year, he was sidelined for several weeks because he fell and severely bruised several ribs while helping to put out a fire in the attic of the Phi Delta Theta house. The summer before his senior year, he was struck by a spinal infection, which affected the feeling in one leg. He chose to assist Wagner and coach the freshman team before being cleared to play in January. However, he never again reached great heights as a player. He finished his career with 1,540 points.

So Vandivier turned to coaching and took over at his alma mater, Franklin High, where he won fourteen sectional and three regional championships in eighteen years (1926-44). His 1939 team reached the state-championship game, where it bowed to Frankfort, 35-22. The Grizzly Cubs' star, future Major League baseball player George Crowe, was named Indiana's first Mr. Basketball. Many years later, Crowe served as one the pallbearers at his coach's funeral.

Over the years, Vandivier turned down Michigan State University and several other tempting offers to coach at the college level. "He said his backyard was as green as any grass he wanted," Ann Turner said.

After Vandivier retired from coaching, he served as athletic director for another eighteen years. Interestingly, he always attended the basketball games, but couldn't watch them because he would get "too nervous." He retired from teaching in 1968 after forty-two years at his alma mater.

Ann Turner enjoyed having her uncle as a history teacher. "He was very humble," she recalled. "He was always fair [in class]. It was always the team. It was never him. Nobody every bragged very much in our family."

However, Turner quickly found out that her uncle was strict about players' curfews. She and her cousin, his daughter Ginnie, faced several situations where their boyfriends were caught and paid the price. She noted that, "The boy I was going with [Lefty Turner, whom she later married] had to take a few extra laps once in a while."

On one occasion, three boys went flying out the back door at the Vandivier house as the coach unexpectedly came home early from a college game. Poor old Lefty Turner, however, was the only one who fell and didn't make it over the backyard fence. "All three had to run laps," Turner related. "Nothing was ever said, but they knew why."

Another time, Vandivier had instructed his players to go directly home following a loss, but some of them went to Turner's house. They dropped their duffel bags inside the front door and were dancing in the basement when the suspicious coach showed up. He never saw them, but he did see their duffel bags, which were inscribed with their uniform numbers. Again, many extra laps were run the next day, with no explanation needed.

Despite the run-ins, Turner stressed, "He loved them all. He showed no partiality. He was as genuine and honest as could be."

Sam Alford, later a fine Indiana prep coach in his own right, recalled teaching alongside Vandivier at Franklin High fresh out of college. "What a great guy!" Alford exclaimed. "He was such a big help, me being a first-year teacher. He was very humble. It was neat for me, because I'd just sit and listen [to his stories]."

The Franklin star's greatness first was recognized by legendary Butler University coach Tony Hinkle, who named him to his all-time Indiana Dream Team. Hinkle said that he had studied the movements of Vandivier's hands, head, and feet very closely—including the way he ran the middle of a fast break in such a devastating way—and incorporated many things he did into his own coaching style.

In 1962, Vandivier and his coach, Griz Wagner, were among charter members inducted into the Indiana Basketball Hall of Fame. Thirteen years later, he made the coveted Naismith Memorial Basketball Hall of Fame in Springfield, Massachusetts. On the latter occasion, Tony Hinkle proudly introduced the Franklin legend at the induction ceremonies.

Forever humble, Vandivier said, "I never did think I was that good and they haven't convinced me yet. I always felt overrated. There were other guys on that team, too."

In 1966, the Franklin gymnasium was named in Vandivier's honor, and at the same time, the baseball field was named in George Crowe's honor.

Franklin sportswriter Cliff Melvin, who visited Vandivier in 1975, recalled, "I realized even at that time that I was shaking hands and chatting informally with one of the true greats in sports, a gent who could stand up against and be recognized alongside the Jack Dempseys, the Babe Ruths, the Lou Gehrigs, the Wilbur Shaws, and the Johnny Woodens. I was meeting what had been termed in many other cases, a true living legend."

Vandivier continued to get requests for autographs and pictures, and never failed to reply. His philosophy was: "If they take the time and effort to write to me, the least I can do is acknowledge it."

The Franklin legend died at age seventy-nine on July 31, 1983. Three years later, he was named to the National High School Sports Hall of Fame, then based in Kansas City, Missouri—along with such other greats as Johnny Bench, Rick Mount, Jerry Lucas, and Arnold Palmer. His daughter, Ginnie, did not want to make the trip. Her cousin's husband, Lefty Turner, jumped at it, however, and had a ball accepting the award on her behalf. It undoubtedly made up for all those extra laps coach Vandivier made him run in high school.

JOHN WOODEN:

Indiana's Greatest Legend

There are legends; then there is John Wooden, who—if anyone—deserves to be listed at the very top of the numerous greats whose lives were shaped by Indiana high school basketball. He had superb careers at Martinsville High School and Purdue University before becoming the most successful coach in college history at UCLA.

At the prep level, he led Martinsville to one state championship (1927) and a pair of runner-up finishes while being named All-State each year. At Purdue he was a three-time All-American and was named National Player of the Year while sparking the Boilermakers to a mythical national team title as a senior in 1932. All he did at UCLA was post a 620-147 record from 1948-75, with an incredible four undefeated seasons and ten national championships—seven in a row from 1966-73. Six times he was chosen National Coach of the Year.

When Wooden was named to the Helms Athletic Foundation all-time team in 1943, he was called "probably the greatest all-around guard of them all. Brilliant on defense and an exceptional shot."

He was the first person enshrined in the Naismith Hall of Fame as both a player (1961) and coach (1973). He was a charter member (1962) of the Indiana Basketball Hall of Fame, where visitors may listen to his specially-taped inspirational three-minute locker-room talk. There are numerous national awards given each year in his name. He has written two books and co-authored several others. A gym and street are named after him in his hometown. In Southern California, where he has lived since 1948, a high school, post office, and street carry his name.

"I kind of agree with [television broadcaster] Dick Enberg," said Morgan Wootten, a fellow Naismith Hall of Fame member who has worked with Wooden for many years on behalf of the McDonald's All-American high school basketball game. "He always says that he knows God doesn't make any perfect people, but He came awfully close in this case. He is a fantastic person. When you've been around him, you feel like you have been to the mountain. I've never met a more impressive person."

Born October 14, 1910, Wooden grew up on a farm outside of Martinsville. His first basketball was a combination of old socks and rags, sewed together by his mother, Roxie Anna. His father, Joshua, nailed a tomato basket to the hayloft, but he was unable to dribble the ball, of course. When his parents could afford it, they later bought him a rubber ball.

One of his first playmates was Branch McCracken, who lived on a nearby farm. McCracken, who later starred at Monrovia High School and Indiana University, is best known for coaching Indiana University to a pair of NCAA basketball titles. Both came before Wooden captured his initial championship at UCLA.

As he attended elementary and junior high, Wooden became captivated by Hoosier Hysteria. After all, Martinsville High School had a huge basketball palace that seated 5,200 people— about 400 more than lived in the town. It was believed to be the largest of its kind in the world at that time. Still, the gym was packed for every game, and tickets were pure gold. Interest in basketball was so intense that homeroom teachers were responsible for figuring out a way to purchase season tickets for students who had no money.

Wooden once told *Indianapolis Star* sportswriter Bob Williams, "In those days, you couldn't grow up in Indiana and not have a basketball touch you in some way."

As a freshman, Wooden also was greatly touched by a Martinsville girl—one year younger than he—named Nellie Riley. "I thought that she was very cute and attractive," he said. "That summer, I was working on our farm and a car drove up. She got out and motioned for me to come over, but I wouldn't do it." So Nellie and her two friends had just wasted a sixteen-mile round trip!

Starting his sophomore year that fall, Wooden was confronted in the hallway by Nellie Riley and her best friend, Mary Schnaiter. "Why didn't you come over?" she asked.

"I was perspiring and dirty—you'd have made fun of me," the ultra-shy Wooden replied.

They, of course, were destined to begin dating. She played cornet in the band, and throughout their high school days, they would acknowledge each other before every game. This was a ritual they repeated during a marriage that would last fifty-three years. Their daughter, Nancy, described it like this: "He rubbed his feet on the floor, turned around and winked at her. My mother then made a circle with her thumb and forefinger. They were sweethearts for sixty years."

Perhaps spurred by his relationship with Nellie—the only girl he ever dated, and the love of his life—Wooden helped the Artesians reach the 1926 state championship game, where they suffered a 30-23 loss to Marion and its six-foot-seven giant, Charles "Stretch" Murphy. The state tournament schedule in that era dictated that an eventual champion play four games in barely more than twenty-four hours, with three being held on the final day.

That year also was memorable because it was the initial time that Wooden faced his boyhood idol, Fuzzy Vandivier, who was a first-year coach at his alma mater, Franklin High. After watching Wooden, Vandivier was quoted as saying, "He was so good, he almost made me wish I'd never gone into coaching."

As a junior, Wooden took the Artesians one step further as they defeated Muncie Central 26-23, to win their second state championship. (The first had been in 1924.) The five-ten, 175-pound guard was high scorer with ten points. Interest for the final state-tourney game to be played at the Indianapolis Cowbarn had been so high that scalpers were getting an unheard-of $2.50 for a ticket.

Wooden's senior year, 1928, was the first time the finals were played at Butler Fieldhouse, and a crowd of nearly 15,000 showed up. Unfortunately, he suffered his greatest disappointment as a player, because Martinsville dropped a 13-12 heartbreaker to Muncie Central in the state-title game on a spectacular shot by six-foot-five Charlie Secrist. Martinsville was leading 12-11 and holding the ball when the Bearcats called an over-the-limit timeout and were assessed a technical foul. Wooden, the team captain, shot the free throw, but missed after going three-for-three up to that point.

On the following center jump, Secrist tipped the ball to himself, but found no one he could pass to due to the Artesians' airtight defense. So, shooting the style of the day—two hands, underhanded—he launched what Wooden called the highest-arched shot he ever saw from beyond half court. It appeared to reach the gym rafters and then "went through clean as a whistle," Wooden lamented. "We still had a last shot, but it spun out."

Secrist revealed after the game that he was hoping to get the rebound and put it back in when the ball swished perfectly through the net.

Wooden climaxed his final campaign by being named All-State for the third consecutive year.

In the spring of 1928, Wooden entertained thoughts of attending West Point or the Naval Academy, but that would have been a total commitment for the next six years. Nellie threatened to join a convent. "She wouldn't have done that," he insisted. However, he did elect instead to attend nearby Purdue in the fall, and was extremely happy to have old Marion tormentor Stretch Murphy on his side this time. Having played his high school ball for a legendary coach, Glenn Curtis, he was fortunate to hook up with another legendary coach, Ward "Piggy" Lambert, at Purdue.

Wooden became an immediate favorite of the Purdue fans because he played the game with reckless abandon. Diving for loose balls and going all-out on every play, he picked up nicknames such as the "Human Floorburn" and the "Indiana Rubber Man." Wooden said the monikers were accurate "because of my aggressiveness. I went down on the floor a lot."

As a youngster, longtime Purdue assistant coach Bob King watched Wooden play during his college years. "The thing I remember the most," King recalled, "is that he was so fast. He ran into the stands and they threw him [gently] right back on the floor."

During Wooden's career, the Boilermakers won Big Ten Conference titles in 1930 and 1932. They were named mythical national champions in 1932 when they posted a near-perfect 17-1 record. He served as captain during his junior and senior years. He was a three-time Helms Athletic Foundation All-American and 1932 Player of the Year as a senior. During his three-year career, the Boilermakers compiled a 42-8 record.

In addition to his outstanding defensive play, he set a school record by averaging 12.2 points as a senior. He also set a Purdue record by twice scoring twenty-one points in a single game. His 475 career points (9.9 average) were second only to Stretch Murphy, and he broke the Big Ten single-season record held by Indiana's Branch McCracken. He excelled in the classroom, too, winning the coveted Big Ten Medal for proficiency in scholarship and athletics.

Wooden was ninety-six years old when this book was written, and he said emphatically that the Big Ten Medal was his proudest achievement, "because I earned it myself. All my other honors have been because of my players. Grades were always very important to me. I had many Academic All-Americans and most of my players graduated."

Shortly after graduation from Purdue in 1932, John married Nellie after a seven-year courtship, and they celebrated by attending a Mills Brothers concert at the Circle Theater in Indianapolis. He then took a job as an English teacher, athletic director, and head coach of football, basketball, and baseball at Dayton, (Kentucky) High School. His first year in basketball produced his only losing record (6-11) in what was to be an illustrious forty-year career.

After two years at Dayton, Wooden moved to Central High in South Bend, Indiana, where he coached basketball and baseball, and served as athletic director. He also worked part-time as an editor for a local book publisher. His most memorable game over nine seasons was against Gary Froebel in the 1941 Hammond regional. Central led the entire game until David Minor drilled a half-court shot at the buzzer for a stunning 37-36 upset victory. He calls it as disappointing of a loss as he ever had in coaching.

Occasionally, Wooden would serve as a speaker at athletic banquets. This item appeared in a 1946 edition of the *Elkhart Truth*: "Elkhart school officials announced today that John Wooden, English teacher and coach at South Bend Central High School, would be the principal speaker at their recognition dinner, although they had hoped to get a prominent person."

During the first seven years of his high school coaching career, Wooden played—though mostly on weekends—what then was the highest level of professional basketball. Playing for three different teams over 46 games, he scored 453 points for a 9.8 average. He left an indelible mark by sinking an incredible 134 consecutive free throws while playing for the Indianapolis Kautskys.

"When I made my hundredth in a row," Wooden related, "[team owner] Frank Kautsky stopped the game and gave me a $100 bill. I facetiously said I'd have it for only a moment because my wife would grab it. He paid us after each game, and when we'd have a good game, he'd put a few extra dollars in our envelope."

In 1942, Wooden joined the U.S. Navy and emerged four years later as a lieutenant. A ruptured appendix kept him from his first assignment aboard the USS *Franklin*. Freddie Stalcup, a friend and football quarterback during his Purdue days, took Wooden's place, and was killed during a kamikaze attack in the Pacific.

Wooden had accepted Jesus Christ as his Lord and Savior at age seventeen, and had relied heavily on his Christian faith over the years. If the navy incident wasn't proof enough that he had a guardian angel, then he must have been convinced following a summer basketball appearance in North Carolina. He was scheduled to fly home on Saturday, but was asked to speak at chapel on Sunday, so he changed his ticket. The plane he would have been on Saturday crashed.

After being discharged from the navy in 1946, Wooden returned briefly to South Bend Central. His high school coaching record has been listed as 218-42 over 11 years, but he says it is not accurate. He never kept track, but he is sure JV games must have been included with the varsity record.

In 1947, Wooden was named athletic director and head coach of basketball at Indiana State University in Terre Haute, where he compiled a two-year record of 44-15. This period was marked by his staunch stand against segregation, because he was raised to be "color blind." His first team was invited to the NAIA tournament, but he refused to go because of policies against African Americans. The second year, he did accept an invitation, since his convictions had forced some of the policies to be changed. Indiana State reserve guard Clarence Walker became the first of his race to play in the NAIA tournament.

Wooden admits he "got some nasty letters," but he continued to fight against segregation.

After two years at Indiana State, he was primed to take the head job at the University of Minnesota until fate—or was it that guardian angel?—again intervened. He was supposed to get a call at a certain time, but a snowstorm stifled the phone lines and UCLA called in the meantime. Indiana's Branch McCracken, already a big name, had just turned UCLA down. Believing Minnesota had rejected him, Wooden took the UCLA job.

"I never looked back," Wooden emphasized. "The second year at UCLA, I was offered the Purdue job. It was twice the money and more. I would have loved it, but they reminded me that I had insisted on a three-year contract."

The Woodens had a daughter, Nancy, and a son, Jimmy. Seven grandchildren and thirteen great-grandchildren have followed. Most have grown up and live near him in Southern California.

Nancy, who graduated from University High School in Los Angeles, followed her father's coaching career closely. "Because he was my dad, I had a lot of respect for him," she said. "I thought it was really great to have a coach for a dad. My brother and I loved to go to the games. He never cussed. He did not bring it home. You could never tell by his demeanor whether he won or lost."

Money was not plentiful in the Wooden household, so every penny counted. Nancy recalls the day that her father prepared for a picnic at the park by squeezing oranges—one at a time—into a big pitcher to make orangeade. "He knocked over the pitcher," she said. "Then he mopped up the floor with a towel and squeezed the juice back into the pitcher. He said it was no problem because Mom was a meticulous house cleaner. He said it was the best orangeade he ever had."

Nellie, indeed, was a meticulous house cleaner. Nancy added, "Her whole life was about her husband and children. She also entertained Daddy's players."

It took John Wooden fifteen years at UCLA to capture his first NCAA championship, as his undersized Bruins defeated Duke, 98-83, in Kansas City., Missouri, in 1964. When asked why it took so long, he fired back, "I'm a slow learner."

The morning after the championship game, Wooden was waiting for a taxicab outside of his hotel, when a pigeon dropped an unwanted greeting on top of his head. "I think the Lord was giving me a message," he said with his usual sly wit. With or without the pigeon droppings, the humble coach never was going to get a "big head."

His first two titles actually came under quite adverse conditions, because the Bruins did not even have a true home court. They had to practice in a gym each day, surrounded by wrestling and gymnastics teams. Before each practice, he had to help the managers sweep the gym floor. During his first seventeen years on the West Coast, he had to use eight different "home" courts. Entrance requirements at UCLA also were generally tougher than most other schools in the West Coast Conference.

For his final ten years, however, Wooden was given a sparkling palace, Pauley Pavilion. "It was such a blessing when we got that," he said. "Alcindor [Lew Alcindor, now Kareem Abdul-Jabbar] never would have come if we hadn't gotten Pauley. It helped recruiting so much." He responded by happily carving out an incredible 149-2 record on his new home court.

On January 20, 1968, UCLA and Houston tangled at the Houston Astrodome in the first-ever nationally-televised, regular-season college basketball game. Houston and its star, Elvin Hayes, nipped the Bruins, 71-69, before a monstrous record crowd of 52,693, plus a record TV audience that included 150 stations in 49 states. The six-foot-eight Hayes dominated with thirty-nine points—including the two deciding free throws—and fifteen rebounds. Number two had beaten number one, and television had found a new vehicle to showcase.

Wooden admits that he was against the game at first because "I thought they were trying to make a spectacle of it. J.D. Morgan [UCLA athletic director] thought it would be very good." Afterward, Wooden agreed with his boss, even though the lights shining on each basket made it difficult for most of the shooters.

As the championships began piling up, the Bruins won an incredible eighty-eight consecutive games, which still stands as the NCAA record. It ended with a 71-70 loss at Notre Dame on a jump shot from the deep right corner by Dwight "Iceman" Clay, with twenty-nine seconds remaining. During the post-game press conference, a writer told Coach Wooden he thought it was good that the streak ended, because it probably hadn't been healthy for college basketball.

Wooden disagreed whole-heartedly and still does today. "I think it was good for basketball," he affirmed. "Other teams should have tried to build up and knock off the streak. Tiger Woods is good for golf."

The UCLA coach accepted the defeat graciously because he recalled the Bruins' previous game at Notre Dame during which they won their sixty-first in a row (82-63) to break the NCAA record set by the Bill Russell-led University of San Francisco.

His unprecedented success caused writers to begin calling him the "Wizard of Westwood." Today, the humble retired coach admits, "I hated it and didn't like it at all."

John Wooden was, above all, a superb teacher, whether working with English students in high school or using the basketball court to impart valuable lessons throughout his coaching career. "His favorite thing was practicing," Nancy Wooden said. "He thought his players were so well-taught that they could play without him and he could sit up in the stands."

For twenty–seven years at UCLA, Wooden would carry his rolled-up program and wink at Nellie in the stands. "Everybody thought that [program] was for good luck," Nancy said. "But he had notes on it: like which [opposing] players were poor free-throw shooters."

Nellie continued to get her share of the limelight, though she did everything she could to shun it. "She didn't like to be interviewed," Nancy revealed. "Once an interview ran past [the allotted] time. She said 'Thank you, but we have to leave.' He followed us onto an elevator and asked, 'What's the most memorable thing you have received from basketball?'"

Nellie Wooden then left the writer absolutely speechless when she replied, "Colitis."

On another occasion, she was having dinner with actor Walter Matthau. Speaking about being interviewed, she asked, "How do you stand it?"

He replied, "Just mumble a lot."

Wooden retired from UCLA in 1975 after winning his tenth NCAA crown in twelve years. His last contract paid him a meager $32,500 and he received another $8,000 for post-game radio appearances. Ten years later—March 21, 1985—Nellie died, taking a huge hunk of his heart with her.

Twice Wooden has been named "coach of the twentieth century" by prominent national organizations. In 2003, he received the highest civilian honor in America—the Presidential Medal of Freedom, at the White House. In 2006, he was one of five charter members enshrined in the new National Collegiate Basketball Hall of Fame in Kansas City, Missouri.

He lives in an Encino, California condominium, and is visited by a steady stream of relatives and friends. His telephone rings constantly. He loves reading and writing poetry. His fifteen-step Pyramid of Success still is copied and used religiously by coaches throughout the country.

Many of his former UCLA players are among his greatest admirers. Sven Nater, for instance, has written numerous poems and songs for him, and Bill Walton calls constantly. As a UCLA student, Walton once balked at shaving off his facial hair. Wooden told him he could do as he wished, "but we'll miss you, Bill." The hair came off immediately, of course. Walton, now a TV broadcaster, spent twenty-two minutes to introduce his old coach before his most recent hall of fame induction.

Wooden can only partially explain how he has lived to such a ripe old age. "I've practiced moderation all my life," he said. "I never drank alcohol and only smoked very lightly [before 1950]. I have a relative peace with myself. My faith gives me tranquility."

If Indiana officials ever carve out a Mount Rushmore for their basketball greats, John Wooden's face undoubtedly will be the one at the very top.

ABOUT THE AUTHOR

Dave Krider has covered high school basketball for forty-five years, including eighteen with *USA Today*, and he currently works for *Sports Illustrated*. He is a member of the National High School Hall of Fame and the U.S. Basketball Writers Hall of Fame. He also has been either sponsor or co-sponsor of the LaPorte, Indiana, High School Fellowship of Christian Athletes for thirty-two years.

Printed in the United States
78893LV00003B/1-108